small steel craft

By the same author

Sea Saint
Log of the *Maken*
Building the *St Mary*
Dinghy Cruising
Outboard Boats and Engines
Ian Nicolson's Guide to Boat Buying
Designers Notebook
Surveying Small Craft
Boat Data Book
Cold Moulded Wood Boatbuilding
Marinize Your Boat
Build Your Own Boat
Yacht Designer's Sketchbook

Ian Nicolson
FRINA

small steel craft

Design, construction and maintenance

Second edition

INTERNATIONAL MARINE PUBLISHING COMPANY
CAMDEN, MAINE

© 1971, 1983 by Ian Nicolson
Library of Congress Catalog Card Number
82-084779
International Standard Book Number
0-87742-170-6
Printed and bound in Great Britain

Published in Great Britain by
Granada Publishing in Adlard Coles Limited
First American edition 1983

Published by
International Marine Publishing Company
21 Elm Street, Camden, Maine 04843
(207) 236-4342

Printed in Great Britain.

To my daughter Beth
in thanks for crewing in our yachts

contents

list of illustrations

photographs

this varied art

Building ships is every bit as much an art as a science. With very little practice it is possible to pick out one designer's work, or discern who built a particular boat. As a result there is a vast difference in detail between two ships of the same size built for the same job.

This makes the study of small steel craft interesting, but it also makes it a very wide subject. It means that there are very few firm fixed rules which can be laid down about steel building of small craft. If a flippancy can be excused, it is not even true to say that all ships should be sharp in front and blunt at the back. In Holland so many craft have the same degree of bluntness at each end!

One result of this situation is that no book on steel shipbuilding which concerns small craft can be precise on each subject. There are as many exceptions as there are conformities. General precepts can be laid down for many assemblies, but it is almost always wrong to state that there is only one way to do something. It is often possible to do a job in six different ways, each entirely satisfactory, each with subtle advantages, each worth considering.

Introduction to the Second Edition

There was a cheerful story going round the shore-side pubs and clubs about a blustery afternoon when a fishing fleet was coming back into harbour. Last in was a boat which had obviously had a successful trip, as she was deep-laden with a heavy catch. Most of the fleet were wood-built boats, with a few of fibreglass, but this tail-ender was steel.

As she slowed to come alongside the quay, which was already packed five deep with the earlier boats, the wind piped even harder, blowing straight on shore. The steel boat swung round parallel to the quay, slowed, went astern and it looked as if the skipper had made a good job of coming alongside. But at the last moment a more vicious squall than all the previous ones came blasting in from seaward. The steel boat lurched and crashed into the already moored craft . . . there was a noisy rending of wood and fibreglass . . . crews of the other boats ran, shouting and brandishing fenders.

When his boat was secure, the skipper of the steel boat ambled aft to survey the damage. He ran his hand along the gunwale murmuring 'Nothing but a wee bit of scratched paint'.

Behind him the mate burst into laughter: 'For six months, every time we meet these other skippers in the pub, we've been trying to convince them that steel is better than wood or glass. I reckon the last ten seconds has made more impression than anything we've said in the previous six months'.

This just about sums up steel boat-building. While good boat-building wood gets scarce, and the people who can work it are fewer each year, steel continues to be cheap, reliable and is now fabricated by more people across the world than ever before. Fibreglass has its problems, with osmosis, rapidly rising costs, and a lack of ruggedness which gets worse each year as builders try to make boats lighter to save on expensive resins and glass cloth.

Since this book was first written the advantages of steel have been proved so often that it is not surprising that small steel craft are quietly increasing in numbers and popularity. The beauty of steel is that it is well known, it is developed, and now with modern paint techniques hulls can be guaranteed rust-free for ten years.

Ian Nicolson
November 1982

background of this book

Personal background

Almost all my early training in naval architecture was concerned with yachts. It was just after the 1939–45 war ended, and one of the fascinating conundrums was the few steel yachts that were about or being built.

There was a shortage of wood: fibreglass was not yet being used, aluminium was expensive. Gradually it became obvious that there was virtually one reason only for the absence of steel yachts: ignorant prejudice.

The Dutch built them, the Americans imported them, but most of the rest of the world was not interested. Wood became less scarce so there was no strong incentive to explore new fields of small ship construction in Britain, though of course there was always a little group of yards turning out small steel commercial craft.

On the yachting front, which continued to be my main interest, aluminium virtually died. Fibreglass began to appear, but still it was held that steel yachts were too heavy. It was said that they corroded while you watched them, and were hard to maintain. These rumours evidently never reached Holland because the Dutch went on building in steel as they have done since the material became available decades ago. Before that they built in iron.

Then steel yachts started to win races. They were not all Dutch built, nor were they all large, as so many experts said they would have to be if they were to be competitive. Several experienced and successful British designers, particularly Robert Clark, brought out cruiser-racers in steel which had the winning touch. As these boats amassed prizes, the rumours began to die.

Over the years I noticed how commercial

small steel craft were regularly built in such a way that the frames could be counted from outboard, due to the unfairness of the plating. It offended me then, and still does. I began to realise more and more that the Dutch lead in the art of fair plating, using their various techniques. It takes practice and persistence to learn this trade.

When the Churchill Trust offered travelling scholarships to the shipbuilding industry, I applied for one. The committee liked the ideas I put before them at my interview, and backed me up in every way. I toured Holland, and the Dutch were so helpful that no thanks would be adequate. They showed me with justified pride the way they work and the results it produces. If this book has merits, they come from the Dutch builders of small craft, as well as the British builders and designers who have also shown me their work and loaned their plans for illustrations.

This book is a token of my thanks to the committee, the executive and the subscribers to the Churchill Trust.

Scope of this book

In many ways there is little difference between the building of big and small steel ships. Both are fully welded. Both are often, but not always, put together in the traditional sequence — backbone, frames and beams, plating, decking, superstructure, deck fittings, and so on. Then again steel small craft in plenty of ways are like their cousins built of wood or fibreglass. For these reasons this book does not contain treatises on subjects like launching, stability or powering.

It does contain descriptions of the special features of small steel ships and boats. It concerns designing, building and maintaining these craft. It shows the differences between small *steel* ships and those built of other materials, and between big steel ships and small ones. For instance big ships seldon have their masts removed, small ones sometimes have theirs out yearly. Big ships have breasthook plates at every deck and sometimes extra ones as well. Small ships often have none. And if they do have them they might well be flanged upwards to form stowage shelves, which would be unthinkable in a big ship. The big ship designer would probably assume that no water would ever lodge on a breasthook plate. A competent small ship designer puts a drain-hole in the breasthook plate to prevent it holding water, because he knows that small craft live nearer the surface.

Building big ships tends to be merely a job for those who do it, whereas boatbuilding is a vocation for many of the people involved. A hard-bitten successful small craft builder, totally unprompted, once said to me: 'Boat-building is 80 per cent good fun.' I cannot imagine a *shipbuilder* saying that.

Big ships are weak, small ones tough

When building in steel different criteria apply according to the size of ship. Small ships have to be built with steel scantlings which are mostly too strong. This is because steel corrodes and due allowance must be made for this rusting. If this problem could be ignored, then small steel craft would be much lighter in very many cases. Small ships seldom suffer from lack of longitudinal strength, or indeed strength in any plane or location. In fact they are nearly always strong enough to go aground (on a sandy bottom) with impunity, so that it is not unusual for craft like barges to be deliberately grounded a dozen times every month.

Big ships are entirely different, because they are normally relatively weak in a longitudinal direction. Their scantlings are calculated to be just strong enough to withstand the bending stresses caused by straddling the most awkward wave or trough, with due allowance for factors of safety. If a big ship grounds it is often a serious business. If she grounds at high water and dries out even partially the consequences are usually very expensive, possibly disastrous.

Steel craft are like other ships…mostly

Considering that steel ships float in the same medium, and do the same sort of jobs as other craft, there are an astonishing number of controversies about them. For instance builders in wood like to insist that a steel ship cannot be as light as a timber one below a length of 60 feet. This blinks the fact that some light, strong steel boats of 45 feet have been made.

Hull smoothness, especially the finish of the topsides, is another argument that waxes and wanes. Mostly it waxes, especially at boat shows. Steel antagonists insist that metal hulls are either unfair or heavily coated with filler compositions which will fall off in a day or two. These people forget to mention that wood boats show their seams when the sun beats hotly down. They ignore the troubles which fibreglass is heir to, such as cracks round repairs made on aged hulls, or dullness on the surface after a few years, or gel coat chipping.

The truth is, as honest designers, builders and surveyors will admit in private, every material has its advantages and its faults. No one sensibly claims that steel is the perfect material for every boat. It has its place in the spectrum and sometimes it is much the best material for a particular job.

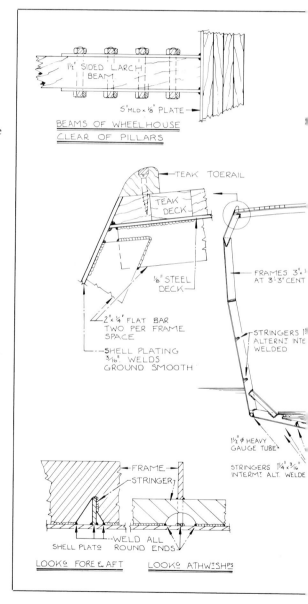

Background of this book

Fig. 1 Midship construction section (right) and aft section of a 45 ft twin diesel motor cruiser designed by A. Mylne and Co. of Royal Terrace, Glasgow. Enlarged details show this to be an easily built yacht with longitudinal framing.

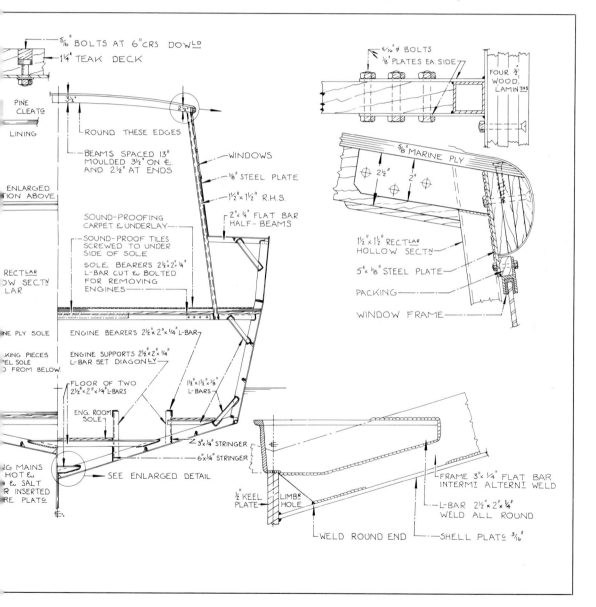

the virtues and vices of steel

Steel's bad reputation

It has to be admitted that steel has a bad reputation in some areas. There is some logic behind this: it is not just that blind prejudice which afflicts most seamen, professional and amateur. The adverse talk about steel has come from two sources: it is relatively easy to build a boat in steel once welding techniques have been mastered. Basic welding skill can be picked up quickly enough, so that all sorts of people have had a go at building in steel. Too often the result was a mess because the design was poor, the material badly prepared, the procedures wrong and the finish rushed.

Just as important, all over Holland, and to a lesser extent in the adjacent countries, there are miles of canals and lakes. These waters are sheltered and shallow, and the worst any boat has to withstand is the wash from barges, or thumping into bridge piers. For this region a mobile houseboat is entirely satisfactory. Such boats are much in demand, and many of them have to be built inexpensively to meet the market. This type of craft is unsatisfactory at sea or even on a rough tidal river, but in their native waters, which are so shallow, they are fine. It is unfair to condemn the whole field of steel boat design and construction just because these rather simple, plainly finished boats are seen in such numbers.

Total watertightness

A welded steel hull does not leak at all. It will stand up to surprisingly severe punishment, and still not let in water. As proof of this there are whole fleets of charter yachts without a single bilge pump among them.

For anyone doing serious cruising in a yacht, this absence of leaks is a blessing indeed.

The virtues and vices of steel

Fig. 2 Royal National Life-boat *Grace Paterson Ritchie* LOA 70 ft 0 in, LWL 64 ft 0 in, Breadth moulded 17 ft 6 in, Depth moulded 9 ft $5\frac{7}{8}$ in. British lifeboats have traditionally been built of wood. Comparatively recently the RNLI changed to steel when it ordered 70 ft boats to replace the smaller craft previously in service. Yarrows built this boat, using all-welded steel with an aluminium alloy superstructure.

The transverse watertight bulkheads are of $\frac{1}{8}$ in

plating above the tank top and the main shell is of $\frac{1}{4}$ in. The stem is also of $\frac{1}{4}$ in plate with $\frac{1}{4}$ in webs flanged $1\frac{1}{2}$ in. The bilge keel shell connection is 4 in $\times$ $\frac{1}{4}$ in flat bar with a 6 in $\times$ 0.35 in one-sided bulb plate; it extends from frame 9 to frame 30.

The aluminium alloy plating of the superstructure is $\frac{3}{16}$ in thick with stiffeners of 2 in $\times$ 2 in $\times$ $\frac{3}{16}$ in angle-bar, while the flying bridge is of $\frac{1}{8}$ in plating stiffened by $1\frac{1}{2}$ in $\times$ $1\frac{1}{2}$ in $\times$ $\frac{3}{16}$ in angle.

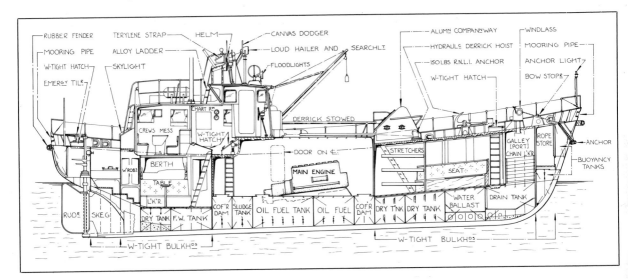

Comfort is dependent above all on internal dryness. To get the best of the situation experienced yachtsmen insist on a boat which is all-welded steel throughout, including the deck, cabin top coamings and cabin top deck. In this they are wise because a laid, or even a ply deck on steel beams is sometimes just a little less than perfectly tight.

For commercial craft this watertightness is important since cargoes must be kept perfectly dry, radio rooms must not suffer from leaks, crews cannot work well if their cabins have overhead drips, and maintenance increases apace if water gets in anywhere.

A designer trying to achieve a totally dry ship will have to concentrate on every point of ingress. Hinged hatches must be built to clamp tightly shut on rubber seals. Sliding hatches must have covers over their forward ends, double baffles at the sides where the slides are, as well as some form of seal at the aft end. The anchor

chain-pipe needs a proper cover, not just a polythene bag lashed over the open end. A threaded end with a screw-on cover is effective. However, the most important defence against water getting into the main part of the ship is to have the chain-pipe leading into the chain locker, which is cut off from the rest of the interior by a watertight collision bulkhead.

The high local strength of steel small craft

Compared with big ships, small steel craft are relatively enormously strong. The designer of a big ship takes trouble to have stiffening in local areas all over the ship. At bollards, by propeller brackets, at scupper openings, at every hatch, there are dozens of doublers, extra plates, knees and bars. In small craft, especially those under about 50 feet, it is rare to fit doublers or extra plates simply because the ship's structure is

Fig. 3 The mid-section of the Yarrow-built RNLI 70 ft Life-boat *Grace Paterson Ritchie*. Construction is halfway between big ship practice and small craft steel building methods. The deck edge treatment makes an interesting comparison with the photograph of the Dutch lifeboat on page 22. Buoyancy is kept well up, so that if flooding occurs the ship will have no tendency to turn over. In addition the buoyancy tanks prevent flooding in the event of the topsides being pierced.

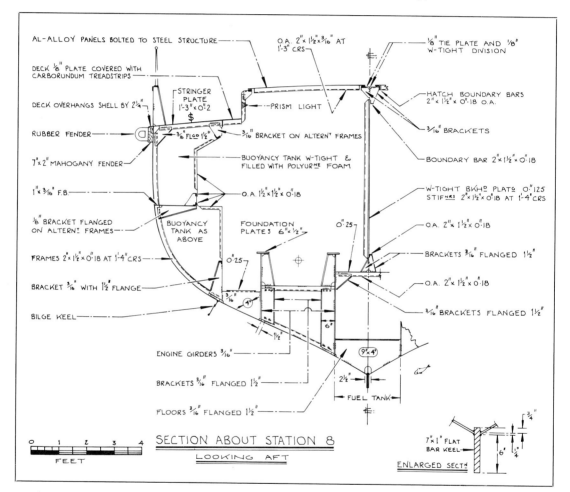

amply strong. The scantlings are selected more for adequacy after several years of corrosion rather than for the stresses likely to be met.

A good example of this occurred when a 40 foot ocean cruising ketch built to our design was damaged. She was just being completed, and to move her from her berth, which was

well inland, she had to be loaded on to a lorry. She was raised several feet to allow the lorry to back under, when a support failed and the yacht came crashing down. The keel must have been 5 feet off the ground at the time, and as she was deep-drafted, the deck must have been another 9 feet higher at least. She fell sideways and the deck crashed down onto a heavy old-fashioned machine tool with a massive framework. The machine tool was wrecked, but the yacht was not badly damaged. Her dent was no more than 5 feet long and though it occurred across a frame and stringers, it was all repaired in well under a week's work.

This high degree of strength is appreciated when additions have to be made. Extra winches or hatches are fitted nonchalantly on craft of the size under discussion, and even when considering 70-footers it is only where items like powerful trawl winches are concerned that heavier local plates are needed. Of course there are exceptions to this principle, as in so many facets of ship and boatbuilding. But often the thicker plate is fitted because there will be a higher incidence of corrosion as well as higher stresses.

An example of the ample strength of a small steel boat's deck is seen in the way pairs of vertical tubes are sometimes welded to the deck, to form bollards. A 40 foot yacht may have two 3 inch diameter tubes 6 inches high welded to form a main mooring bollard. Admittedly there will be a linking bar across the top, but no additional stiffening to the main deck, apart from an ordinary beam, which in any event should pass beneath a mooring bollard.

Compared with aluminium alloys

Steel is $1\frac{1}{2}$ times as strong, but 3 times as heavy as aluminium alloys. This is the favourite theme of light alloy salesmen. Later they admit aluminium costs 10 times and sometimes 15 times as much. What they forget to mention is the extreme difficulty of actually buying small quantities of aluminium of the right specification for small shipbuilding. Though the material is

advertised, the companies which market marine quality aluminium alloys are only interested in selling big tonnages of each size of extrusion and plate.

Steel, mild steel such as is used for most small ships and boats, is sold extensively through stockholders who are to be found in any classified telephone directory. Anyone planning a boat or small ship of light alloy should first get a definite quotation, then an irrevocable promise of delivery in writing, before making any serious plans.

Aluminium alloys are easier to cut than steel. It is not unusual for a band-saw, designed for wood, to be used for cutting a light alloy after a special blade has been fitted. Filing is far easier, in fact many aspects or working are simpler because it is much softer, but it is more difficult to weld. As more and more yards go over to MIG welding techniques, the difficulty of welding is reduced, but skill is still needed.

Aluminium alloy ships last wonderfully well. Corrosion is often negligible, though where it does occur it can be fast and serious. It is important in a steel ship to avoid introducing other metals except where they cannot be avoided. Precautions must be taken so that electrolytic action cannot be set up (see page 152). But in an alloy ship the precautions must be three times as stringent, as the results are more serious because they occur so much more quickly and extensively.

Limited building space

Steel is a versatile material. For instance it is possible to build under a shed only one-third the length of the completed craft. In a few big shipyards this technique is the basis of all their building. The stern is first made and erected,

This 'search and rescue' lifeboat, built of steel to
the best Dutch tradition, is magnificently seaworthy.
The rolled deck edges give strength and ease of
maintenance, but are mainly shaped like this to
reduce the risk of damage when alongside another
ship in rough weather. The all-round rubber fender
is neat yet strictly practical and long lasting. Guard
rails are set inboard, to avoid damage and fouling
when alongside. To withstand the worst seas the
wheelhouse is fully rounded, broad at the base but
tapered and with quite small windows.

then the next section is put on, and the stern is
slid out of the end of the shed. It will normally
be covered with a tarpaulin after being given
two coats of primer. Each succeeding section is
welded on and more of the ship is eased out of
the shed. The difficulty with this method is to
get fairness, and a good deal of time will have
to be spent making sure that the keel is
precisely straight, the sheer sweeps sweetly,
and so on.

Where the building shed lacks height the
cabin tops and wheelhouse may be made as
units and added after the ship is out in the
open. Because there will often be no lifting
facilities outside the shed, it may be necessary
to make the cabin tops and just tack them or
bolt them together during the initial assembly.
They are then taken apart for carrying outside
and putting up on deck in relatively small, light
components.

Lengthening steel ships

A special advantage of steel craft is that they

can be easily lengthened. In Holland batches of fishing boats were found to be uneconomic because they were too small except for herring fishing, which had declined. Many of them were lengthened and converted to profitable fishing.

On the Dutch waterways there are thousands of barges. It is possible to stand at lock sides and watch 800 barges pass every day. This volume of traffic is not confined to one waterway. Many of these barges have been lengthened by having a section welded in the parallel middle body. There is one yard which specialises in doing the job in ten days, including the cutting athwartships, inserting the prefabricated new section, pulling the three sections together, welding up, repainting and relaunching. This elapsed time of ten days applies to a barge of around 100 feet overall!

Naturally this sort of operation depends on the hull form. On curvaceous craft it is likely to be hard, if not bordering on the impossible. However I know of one steel boat which has been lengthened at the bow, and the next year at the stern. I have seen a steel tug receive an entire outer shell to give her more beam and stability, and it is not unusual for big motor yachts to be given extensive face-lifts to modernize them.

This sort of work needs very careful planning and design work. It is often a more difficult design feat than creating an entirely new ship.

Winter and ice conditions

Steel is the ideal material for small craft which have to cope with ice afloat. It is worth remembering that very large areas of the world which are populated by small craft suffer from ice. The south coast of England is erroneously considered ice-free. In practice, places like Poole harbour and rivers like the Hamble have ice floes at least one winter in ten. These sheets of ice are generally very thin, but this makes them all the more dangerous, as they cut through hulls less tough than steel. Wood hulls can be chiselled away in the course of a weekend because the ice attacks on a narrow front. It slices away as the tide and wind carry the ice against the ship, till a tiny slit at the waterline goes right through. The ship then gradually sinks. The damage is done silently, often at night, and surreptitiously so that it is not noticed till too late.

Ice conditions occur all over northern Europe, in the northern part of the United States, naturally all over Canada, and so on. Places which have remained free from ice for long periods sometimes get afflicted seriously during the course of one winter. The Essex rivers are a good case. All this adds up to a strong argument in favour of steel hulls. Not only fishing boats and commercial craft have to be able to withstand ice. The trend is towards marinas for yachts, with boats staying in their special berths afloat all winter. In such conditions a yacht will not receive careful daily attention during the winter. And even if she does, the ice may strike during the course of a long, dark cold night. A steel hull can take it, some other materials fail.

When discussing ice conditions, two separate situations have to be borne in mind: the majority of small craft need nothing more than a conventional steel hull to be able to cope with occasional thin ice sheets, such as are found in harbours in Britain during many winters. These thin sheets are light, easily broken and will not stress a normal hull. But there is a second type of situation, more likely to be found in Canada, in the northern Baltic and in places where massive ice builds up every winter. For these areas a hull has to have structural strength far above the normal, to cope with the great pressures of the ice against the shell.

Lloyd's rules have a special section for ships which have to operate in ice conditions. However these rules do not cover small craft such as we are considering. In this situation, as in comparable circumstances, the designer puts forward his suggested scantlings, and Lloyd's will comment, alter and approve—judging each case on its merits.

The bow and forward plating need strengthening most, though the whole hull will need to be made more rugged than usual. Frame spacing is reduced, though seldom below 12 inches, to give added strength, also hull-plate thicknesses go up. In this connection it is worth remembering that the ice will scour the plating at the waterline, taking off paint. It also takes off the build-up of rust, polishing the metal; so that corrosion is especially fast in an area which is already vulnerable due to excess of moisture and oxygen together.

Craft which have to operate in areas of severe icing may well be polyurethane foamed inside. Ideally this foaming should be so thorough that in the event of the shell being pierced, the ship will still float even though flooded. However, this is likely to require foam which will take up too much internal space. The alternative is to foam in as much as possible at the bow, and as a secondary measure along the waterline and as thickly as possible elsewhere. Then in the event of a plate being started the ingress of water is likely to be checked by the foam.

Among ice floes the ship's propeller is likely to suck chunks of ice towards itself. This results in damage to the appendages, so that the

rudders, A-brackets, shafts and so on should all be massive. It is usual to use nylon-bladed propellers made by such firms as Hundestadt of Denmark because they stand up to ice best.

For operating in ice, various special features are recommended. There should be an observation platform as high as possible, ideally in a crow's nest. This gives the lookout a good view for finding a way through floes. Because of the added dangers for small craft in ice conditions it is customary to use red or orange paint all over the outside of the hull to make sighting easier.

To keep open canals and rivers during the winter, some form of icebreaker is needed. The authorities will seldom want to spend money on a special boat for this job because it would be idle for too many months each year. The usual arrangement is to have one of the waterways service craft specially built or adapted for ice-breaking. A favoured design has a scow bow, raked at 30° to the horizontal and reinforced on the outside with angle-bars which are welded with their flanges on the bow plating, that is 'heel welded'. Their protruding flanges cut the ice as the bow rides over it.

One of the attractions of steel craft is the ease with which they can be altered. Stiffening for ice conditions presents few problems. In the past river and canal authorities have modified existing boats to deal with icing up, sometimes doing the work after the onset of icing. I have seen one highly effective icebreaker made from a scow-shaped dumb lighter mobilized with a 'Harbourmaster' propulsion unit. This is a large size outboard, driving a fully reversible propeller which can be turned through 360° and also be lifted out of the water. If the propeller gets damaged it is quickly angled up, the propeller changed, and the drive unit rotated down into the water again. These 'Harbour-master' units are diesel driven and rest on deck, where they are wonderfully accessible, if perhaps a little exposed to the elements.

Costing

It is extremely hard to get true accounts of boat costs. The indications are that above 50 feet steel hulls are the cheapest, and steel superstructures too. Below this size much depends on the type of boat. Wood has become very expensive almost everywhere in the world, particularly in the countries with a tradition of good boat-building. Fibreglass is often the cheapest if a standard unexceptional boat is wanted. But steel can be the cheapest material right down to small launch size if the builder is skilled, determined to take trouble over the planning, and the work goes forward quickly with no delays due to materials and equipment being unavailable.

For heavy duty work steel is almost always the cheapest if not in first cost, then certainly over a short number of years. Fibreglass costs go up every time the cost of fuel goes up, whereas steel reacts more slowly to increasing energy expenses.

Particularly when a simply 'short-life' boat is wanted, steel tends to be cheaper. If a fine finish is needed then a steel hull needs grinding off and trimming, and this takes time and some skill, which adds up to money. So for ferry boats, barges, and work launches steel wins almost every time. They are given thick scantlings to deal with corrosion, and they are often the cheapest first cost, over the short, medium and long term.

Another confusing aspect concerns the comparative costs of a hull and superstructure.

On a 43 foot ketch with centre cockpit and stern cabin the yard manager reckoned that the ratio of hull cost to superstructure cost was 60 : 40 per cent. This was an approximation, not based on carefully summed hours, but it is likely to be close to the truth. It shows how the quite small cabin tops, because of their complexity, need a lot more time per ton of steel worked.

This is strongly confirmed by an owner/builder who came to our firm for plans. His first boat was 40 feet long with a doghouse and long cabin top. When construction was well advanced, but before the cabin top was made, he asked us to alter the plans to eliminate the doghouse. He was certain its construction would involve a lot of extra work. His next boat was specified as much larger but flush decked. In order to avoid the need for a cabin top she was increased in length during the earliest planning stages from 50 feet to 55 feet. The extra length was essential if the boat was not to look ghastly, but the owner was happy to accept this in order to avoid the long, tedious job of making the cabin top. He went further, and ordered the access hatch and mini-wheel-house in teak, even though he was building the boat with his own hands, on a limited budget. This was his experience dictating the specification.

It all boils down to the fact that when costing, it may pay to have a wood or light alloy cabin top or wheelhouse made by a specialist. If wood is the choice, then teak is much the best, taking a five-year view. In the past mahogany has been used very often, but it blackens so easily, and once this has occurred it never looks good again. It is more expensive to maintain, so that the fact that teak costs five times the price of mahogany is soon unimportant.

Repair costs

The problem here is to compare like with like. At one yard, which does both steel and wood work, two boats were repaired within a few weeks of each other. Both had suffered collision damage, so that in each case it was a nasty bow rupture that needed attention. The wood boat was a moulded ply 26-footer, the steel boat a 30-footer, but the smaller wood boat cost four times as much to put right. Material costs had little bearing in this case, as labour accounted for most of the bill.

Naturally much depends on the location of the damage, the skill and equipment available, not to mention the ingenuity and determination of the management and craftsmen concerned. In the case mentioned above the yard did both wood and steel building and repairs, but their heart was in steel, which is likely to have influenced the costs.

Another yard, which specializes in small commercial craft, regularly builds small tugs and such like. It builds to a hard-chine form, because its clients live in remote areas where labour for repair work is unskilled. This yard can turn out attractive round bilge hulls quickly and well, but it deliberately goes for the less efficient hard chine because of this need to make repairs easy.

Where a repair is below the waterline, and finish is not important, steel clearly seems to be the cheapest. The work is started as soon as the boat is clear of the water, which does not always apply to rival materials. The repair is often completed within minutes, if the area is small, and relaunching need not be delayed. This is in contrast to wood and is far better than fibreglass, where repairs require a controlled temperature shed and time allowed for curing.

Fig. 3a *Salmo* is a 30-foot miniature landing barge, designed by A. Mylne and Co. of Royal Terrace, Glasgow. She can carry a heavily loaded Land Rover, and has a ramp forward so that a vehicle is easily driven aboard. This is an ideal example of steel building because a boat of this sort has to ground often, and the material stands up to harsh beaches better than any other.

There is ample space all round the engine, which is linked to the single propeller by way of a Vee-drive. Because this craft was designed for use at a fish farm where there are nets special care has been taken with guards round the stern gear. Twin skegs mean that the skipper can put this boat ashore with the propeller still turning. The skegs double as bottom stringers. Other features are the extra large fuel tanks, so that little time is taken up each month refuelling.

Fig. 3b A section in way of the fuel tank of the 30-foot work-boat *Salmo* shows how tanks are built in, to save steel and fitting time. The longitudinal stringers pass through the tank, so to be sure there are no leaks 'patch plates' are fitted at each stringer. These plates are welded all round.

The tank ends and inboard side contribute to the deck strength. To simplify fitting and ensure oil-tightness the inboard plate of the tank is kept clear of stringers. On larger craft the tank side might well be designed to line up with the stringer, and that section of the stringer in way of the tank inboard plate omitted.

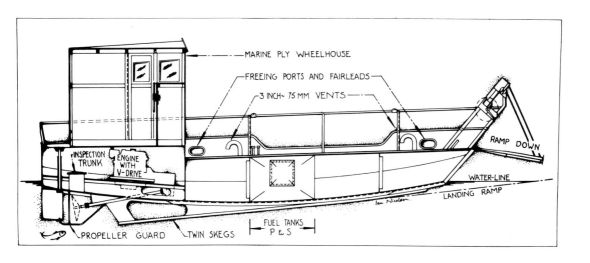

MARINE PLY WHEELHOUSE

FREEING PORTS AND FAIRLEADS

3 INCH~ 75 MM VENTS

RAMP DOWN

INSPECTION TRUNK

ENGINE WITH V-DRIVE

WATER-LINE

LANDING RAMP

Ian Nicolson

PROPELLER GUARD   TWIN SKEGS   FUEL TANKS P & S

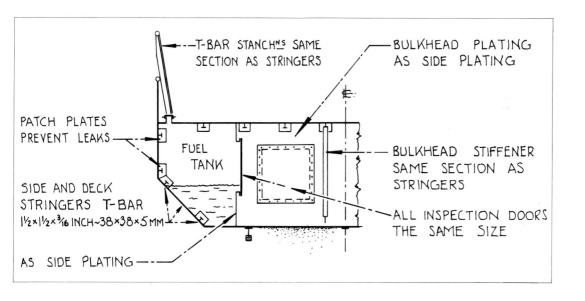

T-BAR STANCHⁿˢ SAME SECTION AS STRINGERS

BULKHEAD PLATING AS SIDE PLATING

PATCH PLATES PREVENT LEAKS

FUEL TANK

BULKHEAD STIFFENER SAME SECTION AS STRINGERS

SIDE AND DECK STRINGERS T-BAR 1½×1½×3⁄16 INCH~38×38×5 MM

ALL INSPECTION DOORS THE SAME SIZE

AS SIDE PLATING

special craft

Using steel's assets

Certain types of small ships and boats seem to ask to be built in steel. Where the need is for great strength, or where the demand is for a quickly built cheap ship, steel is unrivalled. If, in addition, weight is not a consideration, and if a short life is expected, then steel is definitely the material to select. This is not to say that steel ships are always heavy, or that they all corrode away in ten years. There are dozens of light, fast, successful steel vessels in every category.

There are also plenty of steel ships still going strong even though they were built thirty, forty, fifty years ago. Steel ships can both outlast and outrun different materials; but steel does have certain outstanding assets which only a foolish designer, builder or owner disregards.

Ocean cruisers

It is a mistake to think that only very few of these yachts are built. Long-range sailing is becoming popular, partly as a result of the publicity it has received in the popular newspapers, and on television. Such races as the Single-handed Transatlantic, with all its attendant ballyhoo, make everyone conscious of this branch of yachting. Twenty-five years ago long-distance cruising was little known. Now ports like Las Palmas and the Panama canal see a steady stream of far-ranging yachts passing through. In my own design office there are times when we seem to spend more time on this type of yacht than any other.

An ocean cruising yacht, whether sail or power driven, needs to be able to stand up to total capsize several times in one voyage. Records show that in a hurricane it is not

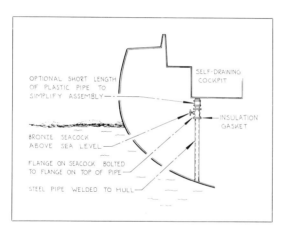

OPTIONAL SHORT LENGTH OF PLASTIC PIPE TO SIMPLIFY ASSEMBLY

SELF-DRAINING COCKPIT

INSULATION GASKET

BRONZE SEACOCK ABOVE SEA LEVEL

FLANGE ON SEACOCK BOLTED TO FLANGE ON TOP OF PIPE

STEEL PIPE WELDED TO HULL

Fig. 4 This sketch shows one technique for cutting down corrosion problems. It also shows how many ocean cruising yachts are fitted with an extra safety feature. The bronze seacock is located above sea level and is insulated from the steel connecting pipe by a fibre washer.
Even if the seacock does corrode it can be repaired without hauling the boat out of the water. On some ocean cruisers and similar stoutly built craft it is the practice to have all inlets and outlets made of welded steel pipe carried right up above the waterline, apart from such connections as the engine cooling water pipe which must be fully immersed at all times. Even here the connection is a steel pipe welded to the hull with a flange and seacock well inboard.

The stern of a steel police launch. One advantage of steel is the ease with which the structure can be made to 'change direction' suddenly. To get this recess into the curved transom of a ship built in another material would be expensive, and it could be weak or leaky within a few years. The recessed Schottel propeller unit is similar to the pivoting unit on page 176. The transom external stiffening is interesting, but the pimples on the deck will not be very effective as a non-slip agent. However that aft bollard should prove efficient in any emergency. The thick rubber continuous fender is typical of this sort of ship, but the flat bar upstanding toe rail looks harsh and a trifle unfinished.

unknown for a yacht to be totally inverted three times in the course of the storm. This calls for strength in excess of that normally built into yachts. There are plenty of examples of wooden cabin tops failing under this sort of treatment.

When living aboard, the first requirement is a dry cabin. A cramped one, a hot one, an ill-planned one are all far, far better than a leaky one! Also, if the cabin can be kept dry it will be warm in cold weather. With a totally welded all-steel vessel, having a steel deck and cabin top, there is little chance of leaks except at the hatches. A pioneer ocean cruising yacht, the *Tai-Mo-Shan*, was built with submarine type steel hatches because her crew realised the importance of leak-proofing the hatches, though she was otherwise a wooden yacht. So even in the hatches a steel yacht appears to have the edge.

It is easy to make the cockpit fully watertight in welded steel, though some owners might not like its apparent harshness. This slight coarseness is easily overcome with gratings.

Chainplates are welded without difficulty onto the hull, and here a steel yacht scores over a fibreglass one. A series of surveys of g.r.p. yachts will show that this is at present one of their weaknesses, so far as total watertightness and renewability are concerned. Other strong points like mooring bollards, mast steps, and rudder hangings are all fitted immovably and very strongly without any difficulty. Some owners have these fittings first galvanised, then welded on. On wood yachts it is often the fastenings which fail, not the fittings, and this is impossible with correct welding. It is also easy to weld in additional local strength in way of highly stressed fittings.

Ocean cruisers need large tanks for water.

Fuel tanks sometimes need to be very capacious, though the majority of long-range cruisers do the minimum mileage under power. However they all need ample fuel for cooking, and as this is often paraffin, which is much used for lighting too, here again ample tank capacity is essential. Naturally, power yachts used for distant voyaging must have massive tankage, and here the advantage of steel is very strong.

Tanks will be built in, using the skin of the ship as boundaries. The floors will form other boundaries, so in practice possibly only a top has to be added to make the tank. Hollow steel keels are particularly good for tanks, since the weight of the contents is concentrated low down: also the width is small, so that the free surface is limited. It is not exaggerating to say that a steel yacht can probably have 20 per cent more tankage than the equivalent wood yacht. The advantage over a g.r.p. yacht will be smaller, probably much smaller.

Wherever the tanks are located, they must be separated by more than one bulkhead so that leakage is not too serious. If there is no coffer-dam between fuel and water tanks, a leak could pollute the water and make the fuel unusable too. All tanks need very good access for cleaning, much better than the modest hand-hole which is considered adequate on the majority of quantity-produced yachts.

A conscientious ocean cruising crew will work on the maintenance of their yacht every time they make harbour. They should not have trouble keeping pace with the work on a steel yacht, though there may be more of it than on a wooden boat. If the craft is carefully built and coated with a large number of layers of paint when new, say seven, there will be a thick overall skin which will absorb a lot of wear and scratching.

Twenty years ago it could be argued that repairs to a steel yacht would be difficult in remote places. This is no longer the case. If anything, repair work in steel is more universally available than facilities for other materials. Certainly g.r.p. repairs are impossible over vast tracts of the world. Wood repairing skills are still widely spread over the earth, though the standards of craftsmanship are not always as good as owners wish. In traditional yachting centres wood repairs are getting more expensive, and the number of men available to do this type of work is not always sufficient for the amount of work available.

A disadvantage of steel is the difficulty of getting a compass to work well. This problem is not insuperable, but it does call for planning and certain techniques must be followed. The compass is best set fairly high, perhaps over the main hatch. Here it will need special protection, which might take the form of a light alloy hoop over the top. Big ship practice might be followed in that the neighbouring structure may be of non-magnetic material. This is an argument in favour of a wood cabin top — or at least a ply cabin top decking — with perhaps beams near the compass of wood or light alloy.

Insulation is important, more so than in a wood boat. However it need not be complex or expensive. Polyurethane foam is probably best, but I have seen some very simple techniques used. On one steel offshore cruiser the owner used coconut matting in harbour and in fine weather to keep the sun off the deck. In bad weather the decks were kept wet and cool, so the matting was put away. This idea is rather rustic, but it does point the way.

A wood sheathing on steel deck need not be expensive. On this type of yacht the wood need not extend all over, not into the scuppers or right forward or aft, for instance. Alternatively a ply deck on steel beams might be the best, according to individual circumstances.

The two qualities which make steel so favourable for ocean cruising are the low cost (both new and second hand) and also the massive strength of steel. The history of ocean cruising is full of instances of yachts being heavily battered by big seas, and there are also plenty of cases of grounding. In these two circumstances steel stands the punishment better than rival materials.

Tugs

By tradition these craft are built of steel. They can use a lot of weight for inertia. In addition they are normally of heavy displacement to get good propeller immersion. To be sure, it is not impossible to design a light displacement tug, but for the most part a large displacement is desirable. This means that the high specific gravity of steel is a positive advantage.

Tugs live a very rough life, constantly bumped and nudged. In a Liverpool dock I have actually seen tug skippers deliberately playing bumper-cars, shoving and elbowing neighbouring tugs with robust good humour accompanied by brisk flurries of dirty diesel smoke from the funnels, as if the tugs themselves were guffawing at the fun. I did not appreciate the horseplay as I was locking through in a rather more delicate wooden yacht, and one accidental jostle from the tugs would have squeezed and sunk us.

Tugs built of wood tend to leak after a few years' hard work. To build tugs in fibreglass would necessitate heavy construction of high, and therefore costly, standards, for the hulls to stand up to the rigours of the job without crazing and worse.

Small workboats

In Britain there is quite a selection of series-built small work boats. They range from about 16 feet upwards, and are for the most part of fibreglass. They naturally vary in strength, finish, cost, versatility and every other quality, because they are the products of several different firms.

As a general rule it is fair to say that their builders have to sell a substantial proportion of these boats to week-end fishermen, yachtsmen, boatyard owners and similar people. This type of owner may well neglect his boat, sometimes run aground and otherwise treat it unkindly, but they are seldom truly harsh in their treatment.

Commercial users, on the other hand, expect their boats to lie alongside rough quay walls, rolling and thumping as tugs pass at full speed, chafing and grinding the stonework when the wind blows onshore. Under these conditions the relatively lightly built standard g.r.p. boats cannot take the bitter harsh usage. These fibreglass boats are for the most part designed down to a price, so that they must be relatively light, especially as their buyers so often press for the maximum possible speed. This is not to denigrate the g.r.p. work boat. Its growing popularity over the last few years shows that it fulfils its purpose in life. That purpose seldom coincides with the toughest usage, and this is where steel work boats score.

For hauling aboard fishing gear, especially trawls, steel hulls are hard to beat. For mooring work, for salvage or the carrying of building materials and similar abrasive cargoes, for beaching and bumping, steel is ideal for the job.

Over the years I have been able to observe

Found in large numbers all over Holland, these double-chined pram-ended work boats are remarkably cheap, long lasting and good load carriers. This one has frames at about 1 ft 8 in centres but plenty are built without frames. Steel is used throughout apart from the wood thwarts.

two roughly comparable types of small open work boat: the Scots inland loch fishing boat, and the Dutch pram bowed rowing boat. The Scottish boat is normally built of clincher larch, with bent timbers, a pointed stem and a transom stern. The Dutch boat is of double chine construction, usually of 3 mm steel but sometimes of 2 mm material with an overall length of about 16 feet. It may have frames, but often does not. It has wood thwarts, but is otherwise all steel.

The Scottish boat is easier to row, and has a pleasanter feel. The Dutch boat is a better load carrier, costs about half the price of its rival, and stands up to rough usage. It lasts as long if not longer, under comparable conditions of neglect. While this comparison is not entirely fair, it does show the advantages of steel. Some of the desirable attributes of a steel hull of this type are shown in the illustration page 36. The absence of buoyancy tanks is a regrettable

feature of the Dutch boats. The Scottish
dinghies seldom have buoyancy either, but at
least they will float when filled — though they
do not make ideal life-rafts.

Fishing boats

Fishing boats in Britain up to about 70 feet, and
sometimes up to 90 feet, have been built of
wood. In Holland fishing boats down to the
smallest size have for years been built of steel.
At the moment the British trend is towards
steel fishing boats down to 40 feet, and maybe
less.

Fishing boats lead a rough life. They are
driven hard at sea, so that craft which have
seemed strongly built in steel have developed
hollows between the frames forward. But this is
only unsightly; it does not mean that leaking or
worse follows. Wood boats tend to leak after
six or seven years. This is hardly surprising
since fishing boats have a tough life in harbour.
I have a photo of eleven fishing boats moored
abreast in Oban. The squeezing on the inside
boat, under some conditions of wind and sea,
must amount to many tons.

The various items of fishing gear, the gallows,
lead blocks, masts, light brackets and so on are
all easily fitted by welding, and ample local
stiffening can be put in quickly.

There has been plenty of feeling against
steel craft for fishing because the men who work
the small inshore boats of around 50 feet and
less are generally strong traditionalists. They
own all or part of the boat, whereas larger
fishing boats are owned by companies which
employ skippers and crews who have less
feeling for the ships they sail aboard. The
situation over the last few years appears to be
that the bias against small steel fishing boats is

fading, not least because this type of craft has
been a commercial success.

The speed at which repairs and alterations
can be done is popular with the owners who do
not want their boats out of commission for more
than a day or two. Another facet which helps is
the ease with which a watertight deck can be
fitted, on a lobster boat for instance, at whatever height is convenient. On a wood boat it is
awkward to work in a fully watertight deck
just above the waterline, where the boat has a
lot of shape. It is also expensive to caulk and
pay and maintain the seams round each frame
of a wood boat.

Ferries

The majority of ferries need to be inexpensive,
reliable pieces of industrial machinery. They
shunt back and forth, all day, all year, all
decade, docking sometimes ten, sometimes
forty times each day. To take this they need
strength, and they are an ideal example of
where steel should be used for construction.

Ferries often have to be repaired in the open
— 'on site' — in all weathers. Repairs must not
take longer than the overnight slack period, or
whatever time is allotted. A rain squall or
heavy wind, or both, which would make
fibreglass repairing impossible, have to be taken
as part of the game.

Ferries lie alongside quays, or beach on ramps,
while other ferries and craft foam past at their
best speed. This means that the ferry rolls and
thumps the quay as if determined to hammer it
down. Steel takes this type of punishment,
though naturally it needs some fendering to
help it through the worst. Other materials
stand up less efficiently and less economically.

There is a world-wide demand for faster

Fig. 5 A cross-river ferry which grounds at each end of its run must be built as light as possible to minimise the draft. If this is not done she will touch bottom too far offshore so that the ramp will not extend to dry land.

These sections show the construction of a 70 ft twin tunnel double-ended river ferry designed by A. Henderson. The scantlings are riveted so that if she was built today, when all-welded construction is almost universal, she would be lighter. A feature is the very strong beams to carry loaded lorries.

The bilge plating which extends round to the flat bottom, as well as the bottom plating, both suffer during grounding and so are of heavier plating than the topsides or the tunnel.

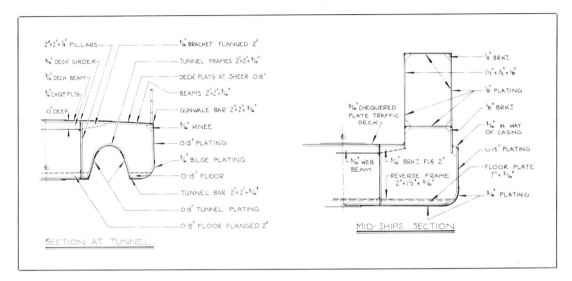

transport, and here steel, being heavy, seems to be at a disadvantage. However what matters on a ferry is the 'land-to-land' time, not the speed through the water. Therefore the designer needs to concentrate on the loading and un-loading facilities, to achieve the true journey speed. A glaring example of this is seen on the Clyde where at the height of the summer it may take as long to unload as the time spent actually under way.

Ferries need ample watertight subdivision. In passenger ferries this requirement is obvious. Vehicle ferries also need plenty of watertight bulkheads because they have loading problems which often result in low freeboard at one point or another.

If they load at one end, when the doors are open there is not much height between water and deck level. If they side load, there is either a lift, or a turntable, or some such restriction on freeboard, so here again the only way to provide

the requisite margin of safety is to subdivide fully.

Vessels for working off beaches

There have always been boats used off open beaches, all round the world's coasts. When transport by land and sea was slow, fish could not be sent far, so every cove had its few fishermen, who supplied the needs of the country immediately inland. The coming of refrigeration and sophisticated transport made the movement of fish over long distances easy, so beach boats became less often seen. Around Britain, for instance, fishing boats operating from open beaches are now quite rare. However the amphibious operations during the 1939–45 war, and various subsequent sea-borne military adventures, have awakened a strong new interest in craft which can operate without harbours. A typical area where this

This transom view shows one aspect of the versatility of steel. A semi-tunnel stern has been built, making this a shallow draft craft, yet one very economically built.

A boat like this is expected to take the ground so she has been given strong half-round coping along the bottom, just inboard of the chine. On the port side low down the exhaust outlet has been welded to the outside of the transom. It takes the form of a length of slightly curved steel tube which is intended to throw the exhaust gases well clear so that they will not disfigure the immaculate transom.

Fig. 6 This sketch shows design features of a small steel open boat. She is suitable for an outboard engine or for rowing. The details also apply to small open inboard launches.

The seats at each end form large buoyancy tanks which will not only support the boat but also the entire crew. Each tank has a Henderson hatch so that the space inside can be used for dry stowage. The top of each tank is sloped down towards the end so that rainwater, as well as much of the spray

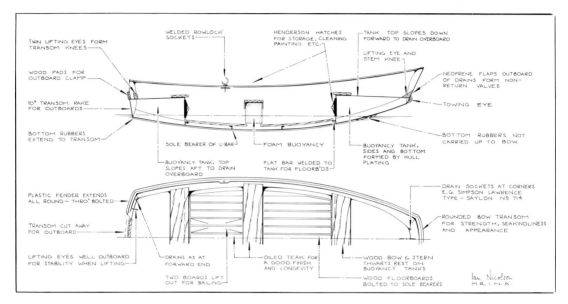

interest is growing is in the Western Isles of Scotland.

For this type of work, steel has much to recommend. It takes the ground well, and wears well. It can be dented deeply without actually puncturing, and it is easy to make the bilge into an egg-box pattern of watertight compartments. If one of these is punctured the damage is local and the boat can often go on working for days before repairs are essential.

Various forms of ferry, commercial and military landing craft and a variety of barges have been built of steel, often with bow doors, for work where there are no harbours. The bottoms of these boats need careful design. If they are damaged, it is not so easy to effect repairs quickly if up-hand welding is required extensively. Putting in a new bottom plate from below with limited facilities is normally far easier if the boat can be laid on its side, or

that comes aboard, will automatically drain overboard. This saves frequent bailing and is a boon when the boat is lying on moorings.

The tanks and centre thwart provide adequate stiffening in conjunction with the sole bearers and the bottom rubbers for a boat up to about 20 ft. The wood trim on the tank tops makes the boat more comfortable for anybody sitting here but an alternative would be a glued material like Trakmark which will often require less maintenance.

There are twin lifting eyes at the aft end so that when the boat is being picked up by davits or a crane she will have no tendency to roll over even if there is a lot of water on board.

This type of boat is particularly suitable where conditions are bad and where any boat gets hard usage. In canals and commercial rivers, small boats tend to be buffeted by bigger ships, used by passengers with metal shod boots and generally treated more like a piece of industrial equipment than a boat.

Fig. 7 No frame bending. By using deep plate floors it is possible to avoid the need for frame bending. This technique cannot be used for every hull form, and sometimes it only applies over the middle part of the ship.

The method of passing the stringers through the deep floor is interesting. This shape of cut-out makes it easy to weld all round the stringers where they meet the floor plate. Also, water trapped outboard of the stringers will all drain to the lowest point, whereas if the cut-away had been on the inboard side of the stringer there would be puddles at every stringer-to-floor intersection.

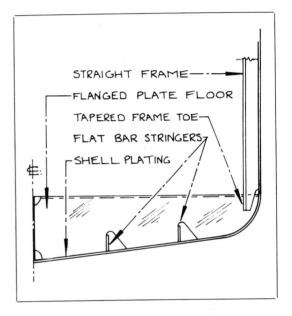

STRAIGHT FRAME

FLANGED PLATE FLOOR

TAPERED FRAME TOE

FLAT BAR STRINGERS

SHELL PLATING

better still turned right over to allow down-hand work. For this reason, among others, it is advisable to take some trouble to protect the bottom. One technique is to put in the bottom framing in the form of flat bars, toe-welded from bow to stern, spaced fairly closely and as deep as the draft requirements will allow. To these bars, wood rubbing strakes are bolted. The wood must stand down below the steel, and be a tough timber such as elm or iroko. The wood rubbers are made easy to renew, because this will often be essential. For instance, the bolts should be put in an easy driving fit, and heavily greased.

Loading ramps

Many types of beaching boats have bow ramps. Ferries, landing craft and so-called floating bridges (which are really double-ended ferries) have these ramps. Some are like drawbridges which just lift a little, to clear modest waves on well-sheltered rivers. Other are doors which fold right up to seal the bow.

The design of this ramp or door calls for a lot of care. They often have to stand high local loadings, and the people who use them regularly ignore warnings about maximum loads. The farmer turned boatman is notorious for abusing his vessels. He puts over-laden lorries onto quite small boats, often not realising the importance of tons-per-square-inch transmitted through the narrow tread of a tyre onto a small area of deck. As a result, when designing a ramp the factor of safety must be high.

However, the ramp must not be heavy because it will be impossible to lift without very powerful winches, possibly power-operated. Just as important, the ramp is right forward, where the vessel may have limited

reserve buoyancy, so here again weight is undesirable. Finally, a massive weight loaded on the extreme bow is likely to raise stress problems in the hull structure.

All in all, a case can be made for using aluminium alloy for a ramp, even though this material is so costly compared with steel. To get a strong section, it is worth investigating the possibility of designing the ramp in the form of a U. The sides will give the ramp a good depth and so a usefully large moment of inertia. Just as important, the up-standing sides prevent vehicles from driving off accidentally. The lively-minded designer will already have seen another important possibility: by keeping the ramp narrow (but not forgetting the safe high sides) the width of vehicle which may be loaded is limited. In this way a designer can prevent horny-handed yokels from overloading.

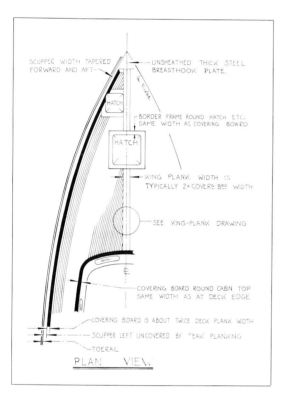

In the figure:
SCUPPER WIDTH TAPERED FORWARD AND AFT

UNSHEATHED THICK STEEL BREASTHOOK PLATE.

HATCH

BORDER FRAME ROUND HATCH ETC. SAME WIDTH AS COVERING BOARD

HATCH

KING PLANK WIDTH IS TYPICALLY 2× COVER'S B'RD WIDTH

SEE KING-PLANK DRAWING

COVERING BOARD ROUND CABIN TOP SAME WIDTH AS AT DECK EDGE

COVERING BOARD IS ABOUT TWICE DECK PLANK WIDTH

SCUPPER LEFT UNCOVERED BY TEAK PLANKING

TOERAIL

PLAN VIEW.

Fig. 8a Nothing beautifies a boat more than a teak deck. If the work is done in a cheap way, the planks are laid parallel with the centre line, but this sketch shows the correct and by far the most attractive layout. First, the covering board is put down, and it may be tapered at the forward end, as the scupper may be as well. Then each plank is swept round following the deck edge and nibbed into the king plank (see separate sketch on page 50). There must be a covering board round the cabin top, and border frames like covering boards round each hatch. For a good appearance it is essential that the covering boards and borders are substantially wider than the deck planks.

Straight-framed ships

Building time and money are saved if a ship is built with frames which have no bends in them. This type of shape, known as hard-chined, has long been favoured for high speed planing boats, but it is being used more and more for slow or moderate speed craft. In practice these ships which are not intended to plane usually have two or more 'knuckles' each side and are sometimes referred to as multi-chine craft. There is a useful paper about them in the 1964 *Transactions of the Royal Institute of Naval Architects*, though most of the information relates to freighters and large ships.

One conclusion of this paper is that provided the chines or knuckles are set in the true lines of the water flow round the hull, then there may actually be a *reduction* in resistance as compared with round-bilged, bent-framed ships. However there are plenty of instances when the resistance is higher. One trouble here is that only tank testing before building can show how the flow lines run. The cost of tank testing a small craft may be more than the expense saved when changing from bent to straight frames. In other words, when building a small craft one has to be careful not to lose more on the roundabouts than is saved on the swings. Where several craft are being built to the same set of lines the cost of tank testing will be spread over, so a real saving is likely.

The extra resistance, where it exists, stems largely from what is sometimes called 'edge effect'. This is the vortices of water where the flow is spoiled when it crosses a chine obliquely. In some localities the water will be pouring down round the hull, especially forward. Else-where it will be welling up, mainly towards the stern. This edge effect can be reduced by having a 'soft chine', that is a knuckle which is rounded at the edge. The usual way to achieve this is to have a large round section bar along the chine. Sometimes, though less often, the chine bar is a pipe.

It is possible to build ships with round bilges yet with few or no bent frames. The frames run straight from the sheer to the tops of the floors, and the outer sides of the floors are cut to a curvature to support the bilge plating (see illustration on page 37). The limitation of this technique is that the rise of the turn of bilge towards the bow and stern must be accompanied by a deepening of the floors. Even if the floors are cut in steps athwartships, there is likely to be a serious interference with the internal space of the craft. It amounts to this: straight frames throughout with a round bilge are possible on certain types of small ship; on many others the technique may be used over certain lengths, which cuts down the cost of frame bending. The idea is particularly attractive to a builder who has to contract out his frame bending.

Weight estimating

Working out the *precise* weight of a small ship at an early stage in the design is seldom possible or necessary. What is achievable and needed is a reasonably close approximation, and this takes a practical draughtsman about a day unless the craft is very special. It does not make much difference whether the ship is 40 or 60 feet, she tends to have about the same number of fittings and so the accuracy and time consumed do not vary much within the range we are considering.

There are quite a few short cuts to finding the sum of the weights. The first is to put down all the items in the same order each time, carefully

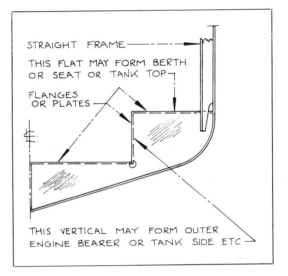

Fig. 8 Deep floors and straight frames. A development of the straight frame and round bilge idea is shown here. The floors would have to be very deep, and therefore heavy and expensive, because there is a steepish rise of floor. Where the ship's bottom is well veed it often makes sense to shape the floors something like this, using the outer part for one of several purposes. There may be fuel tanks, or it may be a base for a generator or berths set on the raised part. The lower part may support inner engine bearers, with the outer bearers stiffened by the vertical edge of the floor.

There are limitations here. For instance the bottom of the vertical must not approach the shell too closely or there will be a serious weakness at this point. As there is likely to be a line of floors with their vertical edges all the same distance off the centreline, it could be dangerous to run the vertical side too low.

Though only one step is shown, there may be more, with a fuel tank right outboard, then engine bearers, then a deep walk-way between the engines.

arranging the columns of figures. This will
show up common denominators such as the
fact that certain types of bar are (or should be)
used over and over again. Once the weight of a
foot of this bar has been looked up in the tables
it can be entered time and again in the columns.

In the same way, all the figures are put down
first, then all the multiplications of length ×
width × weight per sq. ft or sq. metre, and so on,
done in sequence. It is a mistake to measure the
total length of frames, work out their total
weight, note that down, then start assembling the
data of the next item on the list. This procedure
is both slower and more likely to let mistakes slip
in.

For the shell weight: measure the girth at
(say) five stations (i.e. every other displacement
section), add these five together and divide by
five to give the mean girth. Multiply this by the
overall length to give the overall area, and hence
the weight. An additional similar calculation
may be needed for thicker plating at the garboard, where this is applicable.

For the athwartships frames use the same five
girths and get their mean in the same way. Then
multiply by the number of frames to give the
total length. In every case remember that old
source of trouble: ships have two sides but
only half of each girth is measured on the
plans, so at some point there must be a doubling
of the figures to include both sides!

A similar technique is used for the beams,
bulwark stanchions and so on. Where windows
and ports are let into steel topsides and deckhouses it is generally accurate to assume that
the steel displaced by the window weighs the
same as the window. This means windows and
ports can be forgotten and no correction is
needed. It is true that glass only weighs about
170 lbs per cubic foot, against about 490 lbs

for steel, but there are the window frames and
fastenings to add, and these compensate. As well
as this, where the plating is light the window
and port surrounds will be relatively thin, but
at high stress areas both the plating and the
window frames will be more massive.

It is not a bad principle to add about 100
pounds for every 25 feet of length for small
fastenings and little items like hinges, odd
screws, locking nuts and washers. Allow another
100 pounds for every 25 feet of length for
bilgewater, etc. when assessing final weights.
Other useful figures are 50 pounds weight per
man of the crew for personal effects, together
with 150 pounds per person for the weight of
a fully clothed adult.

When adding the various items of equipment,
it is just common sense to 'round upwards' all
the weights given in leaflets and catalogues. If
a winch weight is listed as 177 pounds then it
will probably be more accurate to enter it as
180 pounds, and in some cases even as 200
pounds. This 'rounding up' allows for fastenings,
and the fact that manufacturers inevitably
advertise the lowest possible weight. It also
helps to compensate for the extras no owner can
resist. In addition all sorts of items are listed
without the sump oil they need, or without the
portable cover, or instruction manuals or tools.
It is never wrong to 'round upwards' to give a
simpler figure.

In spite of this continual addition plenty of
designers add a contingency figure to their final
total. It is my suspicion that the more experienced the designer, the more he will add in at
the end. By the same token, the more
numerous actual owners are, the more should
be added. For an individual owner, probably
allowing an extra 3 per cent is not far off.
If it is a yacht that is being built, and the

owner is married, then add say 5 per cent. If the vessel is for a company with a board of ten directors, as well as marine supervisors, better add 6 per cent. And so on. If building for a navy add 12 per cent plus another large unspecified percentage, because the ship will still be overloaded before she is complete. No navy can ever call a halt to the creeping paralysis of added weight.

A useful check to ensure that no weights have been forgotten is to run through a ship chandler's catalogue, such as those put out by Simpson Lawrence or South Western Marine Factors. Going through these page by page will throw up minor items which will all add up. These catalogues have the virtue that almost everything is listed with its weight.

Saving weight and money

There is no denying that steel is a heavy material, so to keep down a ship's displacement the designer must eliminate as much steel as possible. This does not just mean cutting lightening holes wherever possible. A better approach is to eliminate steel items entirely. A steel bulwark is not always necessary; if some form of toe rail is needed it can be of wood. An owner may decide on a steel hull yacht because of its strength and watertightness, but there is no reason to have anything more than the hull of steel. The rudder can be of wood, and the centreboard too, though surely the centreboard case would be of welded steel?

Concentrated thought is needed if weight-saving is to be a success. For instance it may seem clever to design the water tank so that one of its sides is the transom, another the ship's bottom, a third the ship's side, and the fourth is the rudder carrying plate. In fact a greater

saving might be achieved by carrying all the fresh water in four or six plastic containers. This might be cheaper, too.

An effective way to reduce weight is to make components do two jobs. The self-draining cockpit can be both drained and supported by the pipes which lead from it. Ventilators can double as dinghy chocks, gravity tanks as wheelhouse seats, a mast as an exhaust pipe, and so on.

It is fairly easy to save weight up to a certain point. Then suddenly it becomes much more difficult and expensive. Does one scallop away the athwartships flange of all the L-bar frames or machine off the excess metal from the sea-cock flanges?

A great deal of weight-saving is bound up with costs. Light alloy deck structures and spars certainly save weight but are likely to be twice as expensive. On the other hand the bonus sometimes goes both ways. For instance flexible plastic cowl vents are likely to be both lighter and cheaper than steel cowls. In this connection it is fairly safe to say that wherever a stock mass-produced article is available it is cheaper, and tends to be lighter because the makers pare their material to save money.

As the range of standard equipment spreads it becomes more obvious that special 'one-off' items built in a yard for a boat cost more than the mass-produced item. However anything made in large numbers needs to be advertised, held in stock, labelled, packed, posted, maybe wholesaled and retailed. All this costs money so that the designer and shipyard manager have to study the cost of every item. This study needs redoing every year, as market forces change the prices.

One corollary of this is that ordering equipment is an art. Clever buyers order first those items of equipment which the yard *cannot* make. Anything which the yard can fabricate if the bought-in items fail to arrive in time is ordered as late as possible. This avoids having to pay for equipment which lies in the store for weeks before it is needed.

In theory each piece of gear should arrive in the yard the day before it is needed. In practice this does not work because suppliers and transport cannot be trusted. An echosounder must be ordered well in advance because the builder cannot make it himself. Incidentally, in Britain this sort of equipment should be ordered before the London Boat Show, which is always the first week in January. After the show so many manufacturers spend the next six months trying to catch up with orders.

In contrast a helmsman's seat need not be ordered till quite late, unless it is a very special model. It is something that most competent all-round builders can make, and in any case some of the best versions are made from modified office seats which are easily obtainable.

Weight reduction by lowering freeboard

Where weight matters more than other considerations, a useful saving is gained by cutting the freeboard to a minimum. A 36-footer plated with 5 pound steel (approximately $\frac{1}{8}$ inch thick) will be more than 200 pounds lighter if the freeboard is cut by 6 inches. This calculation remembers that the topsides are curved, and therefore longer than the overall length of the vessel. In addition 6 inches chopped off the freeboard is a reduction on both port and starboard sides. Then again there is not only the weight of the topsides plating, but also the tops of the frames.

Naturally there are limitations to weight-saving in this way. If freeboard is cut too much then waves will come aboard. On inland waters there are serious waves from passing craft even if the wind never seriously stirs things up. Then again there is the problem of headroom. If the freeboard is cut then the cabin sides must be made higher to compensate. They will probably be lighter than the side plating, so there will be some reduction, but not so much.

But in certain instances the reduction can be dramatic. On a fast fishing boat preliminary plan the freeboard was cut so that in rough weather waves washed over amidships when at rest. This was acceptable because the boat was intended for skin-divers who were interested in getting out to their distant hunting grounds off the West Coast of Scotland. Speed was essential, and once under way, going hard, the seas would seldom come aboard. Low freeboard is a positive asset for skin-divers as it makes it easier to get over the side and back aboard. All round stanchions and triple lifelines give security to the crew when under way. To keep the gear aboard safely high wooden coamings were specified to form open-topped deck boxes. These have nylon nets stretched over, secured by thumb cleats all round. As the nets are so stretchy, it is easy to get access to gear or make everything secure quickly.

On this sort of offshore fast power boat all engine hatches have in any case to be watertight, with special high vents to let air in to the machinery. The whole of the low part of the boat is as watertight as a submarine, so that 2 or 12 inches of water swilling about over the deck makes little difference.

This particular craft is a rare speciality, but the general principle can be applied to quite a wide cross-section of power boats. The aft few feet, which contain the steering gear and occasionally equipment like Calor cylinders, can often be cut away to a minimum freeboard level. Instances of this are the various naval and RAF craft, such as those used for torpedo recovery, air-sea rescue and so on. The saving is not only in topsides weight but also in transom weight.

Sometimes the technique needs adapting. For instance on a fast power craft intended mainly for sheltered waters, where there is an aft cockpit, the closure of this cockpit may be by stanchions and wires or rails, perhaps with a Terylene dodger, instead of by a solid plated transom or bulwark. The idea is seen at its logical conclusion in racing planing sailing dinghies. This is a field where every weight-saving idea always gets driven to the ultimate, so that other fields of design have a useful full-scale research programme constantly advanced for everyone's benefit.

Diminishing weight by using soft materials

Here is an approach which saves not only weight, but also money. It does so at the expense of comfort sometimes, and also tends to increase maintenance costs. It helps towards stability by reducing top weight, but it has limitations. For instance on a fishing boat the crew will not thank the designer who gives them less than total protection against the worst the weather can do. In short, this ploy must be used with discretion, and mainly on craft used in protected or semi-sheltered waters.

The essence of the scheme is that instead of using steel plating (or wood for that matter) for the aft end of the wheelhouse, a Terylene, PVC or canvas curtain is substituted. Weight-saving is dramatic, because the curtain will be

of the order of one-fiftieth of the steel weight. It is sometimes possible to make the sides as well as the aft end of the wheelhouse of a cloth. For craft used in the tropics, the cabin coamings may also be lightened in this way, since the 'curtains' will only be lowered when it rains, or maybe at night.

Even the forward end of some wheelhouses or steering positions can be fitted up with dodgers instead of the conventional windscreen. This is especially popular in the tropics where it is pleasant to feel the breeze, caused by the speed of the craft, playing on the face.

In every case these curtains should have the maximum possible area of Perspex windowing. As a basic rule the windows should be made up in fairly small segments, probably not over 18 inches in any dimension. There will be vertical and horizontal strips of Terylene between the windows, which will allow for bending and folding. Without these the Perspex tends to get cracked when folding up the curtains, or when the curtain is under severe stress due to the weather or someone falling against it.

Though Terylene is mentioned for the curtains there are a variety of similar materials, some better, some cheaper. Plasticised nylon is a typical example, and straight heavy gauge polythene another. The latter is very cheap, and of course it is fully translucent, but it does not last long. The 1500 gauge type is used for tarpaulins. It is perfect for keeping out the weather for the minimum cost, but it tends to crack if subject to exposure and rough weather for a year.

It is usual to get a sailmaker or tent or tarpaulin maker to make and fit these cloth dodgers. Each will have his own favourite brand of material, varying from straight proofed canvas — through Birkmyers' cloth, proofed Terylene, Terylene and cotton mixture, or PVC proofed nylon — to the latest product of the textile mills. As in so many branches of shipbuilding (which is after all an assembly industry as much as a construction one) it pays to find a reliable firm, get their advice and follow their recommendations. Get this in writing and tell them in advance that if the dodgers give trouble they will be called in to put the matter right without charge. It is good policy to put the sub-contractors on their mettle, so that they share some of the burden of responsibility which rests so heavily on the shipbuilder.

Generally speaking these dodgers and curtains should be secured by turn-buttons or similar quick release clips. This makes it easy to take them right off when the weather is good. Sometimes it is better to bolt top, bottom or one side at about 4 inch intervals. The edges which are opened must be secured with Prestadot or similar patent fastenings. These should be bought when construction commences and tested in sea water for the months available before launching, as so many versions are incapable of withstanding high corrosion conditions. Plastics are best here, but they are not tough and need to be spaced close together. As a rough guide a 4 inch separation looks too close, but is about right for plastic fasteners and not too far apart for metal ones.

Each dodger or curtain should be fitted with ties, like reef points. These should be along the permanently secured edge, so that the curtain can be rolled right up and tied firmly out of the way. In some cases it will be useful to have a second row of ties at half height.

The implication up to now has been that the wheelhouse or steering position or cockpit cover has been a permanent erection with soft sides and back, and just occasionally with a dodger in front instead of the windscreen. But it is possible to go the whole hog and have the entire cover of Terylene. This is seen on some naval launches where there are folding hoods, sometimes called pram hoods. They are supported by metal hoops and the whole contraption folds flat in good weather, or when the boat is being stored, transported or lifted aboard the parent ship.

Whatever form the dodger or canopy or curtain takes, it must be made as strong as possible. In most materials, certainly in Terylenes and canvases, there are wide ranges of cloth weights. The thickest is occasionally just too stiff and awkward to handle, but as a basic precept go for the second heaviest. All the seams should be triple folded, and as the stitching is one of the first things to go, have this in three or even five runs along every seam. Just occasionally a backward or unscrupulous firm will use plain cotton thread for a Terylene or nylon canopy, so that the cotton rots quite soon, ruining an otherwise usable cover.

Good doubling at every corner and ample padding where the cover touches or rests on a stanchion, deck edge or coaming are needed. Along the outside grab-ropes or strips of webbing or some similar strapping, well sewn at intervals, are required for the crew to hold when walking forward.

Economy when ordering and stocking

It is expensive to order small quantities of steel. The cost comes down in useful jumps according to the tonnage bought, so the aim is to build every vessel in one yard from the minimum number of different plate thicknesses. The same applies to bars and extrusions. Where a ship is being built under rules which call for heavier frames forward and in way of the engine, it is not uncommon for the same heavier frames to be used throughout. This puts up the total weight of steel built into the ship, and steel is bought by the ton. But it is cheaper to buy all the frames in the heavier size nevertheless.

For the same reason, when talking to a yard manager about building economically, he will say, 'Let's use $\frac{3}{16}$ inch plate throughout', knowing that it would be usual to go for lighter plating for the wheelhouse sides, for minor brackets and so on. But by sticking to one thickness the cost of the steel will be reduced, and there will be no waste of time while the men on the job check the plans then check that the steel they select is right for the job. In addition off-cuts from major components will do for small parts like brackets. Naturally this attitude is no good when building to a minimum weight, as one must do for a very light draft freighter or a racing yacht. But then it is accepted that these boats cost more per ton than other types.

Shipyards, which naturally live in expectation of a steady flow of ships, sometimes keep their steel in two different stores. One is the main stock which they try to limit to three, or better still two sections. The other is a general stock which is often attached to the engineering shop, as opposed to the plating shop. The general stock will have rods and bars, tubes, odd sections, many off-cuts; it will be a bit of a rag-bag. If the drawing office are any good they will check this store before designing anything special, so that where possible the plan will incorporate sections already in stock.

The main stock will not be the same in each yard. One which specialises in small naval craft keeps two sizes of T-section, whereas another which builds dredgers favours two sizes of bulb angle. A small yard will probably have either two sizes of flat bar or two of angle-bar. The designers working in these yards will know these sizes, know what they can ask of them and gain a great familiarity with their use. A saving all round will accrue, and the sections will be bought in real tonnage, already shot-blasted and primed, so that what is left over from one ship will do for another. If a mistake is made and the order to the mill is too big or too small it will not matter very much, since shortfalls can be made up from what was left over from the previous ship. The excess will do for the next one.

Minimum wastage

When ordering steel, the aim will be to buy the least for the job. On plates it is usual to order them 1 inch over-length and $\frac{1}{2}$ inch extra on the width. However, for some jobs they can be ordered exactly to size. For instance for a hatch coaming or casing, where the precise height to the nearest $\frac{1}{4}$ inch seldom matters, the steel can be ordered the exact size off the drawing. A good average is a 5 per cent wastage of steel, which may sound high till it is remembered that this includes the off-cuts when lightening holes are cut out, the circle of steel left when a port is let in, and similar unavoidable waste. It is usual to sell the waste, which in any case should not be left lying about because it causes accidents though it may pay to store a limited number of handy sized off-cuts of various weights which could be useful later.

Bar is normally bought in the longest possible lengths, though in some circumstances it may be possible and advisable to get it in exact cut lengths.

Extra thick plates

On craft over about 50 feet it is necessary to put in thicker plates at high stress points. The larger the ship, the more important these plates become, and the more numerous. They tend to be more important on hard-worked commercial boats than on more delicate craft which lead a sheltered life.

These plates are normally at least 25 per cent but seldom more than 50 per cent thicker than the surrounding plating. They are located under towing bollards, at the bow where the anchor and chain wear, by the A-brackets and by rudders. Where stresses are particularly high there will be other stiffening components like extra frames, additional carlines under towing bollards, or intercostal stringers by propeller shaft brackets. On the smallest craft these internal stiffening bars are fitted without putting in the thicker plates.

Lightening holes

As a basic precept, lightening holes are a waste of time and money in small steel ships. The percentage of weight saved by cutting away the centres of floors and brackets tends to be very small on most ships under 60 feet, so that it rarely makes a significant difference to their speed or load carrying ability.

The cost of marking and burning or cutting out lightening holes is not compensated by the off-cuts produced. The pieces are so often too small to be useful or to have a reasonable scrap sale value.

In addition, as far as floors go, lightening holes increase the rate of corrosion slightly. This shortens the life of the floors because without lightening holes there is ample strength left even when the total surface is corroded.

On racing yachts or river boats which have a limited draft matters are different. Here weight-saving must be pursued with fanatical enthusiasm, so that lightening holes are a valuable way of reducing the displacement. Allied with ply decks, small batteries, wood toe rails instead of steel bulwarks, and all the other weight-saving ploys, lightening holes help to make a significant difference. It is the old story, which reappears over and over again in boat-building: no single action produces a miracle in the desired direction; it is the accumulation of steps, little jobs aggregated. This dictum works whether the aim is more speed, more seakindliness, easier handling or a dozen other objectives.

A side asset of lightening holes is that they improve access. Painting is made easier, and the job of putting in electric cable or piping simplified. To this end lightening holes are normally aligned. In some mould lofts shapes and patterns of lightening holes are kept for drawing round, so as to save time and give a neat uniformity.

Lightening holes can sometimes be put in bulkheads, not only in the bilge but high up, where they improve ventilation. They may be in brackets, floors, in tank baffles and in vertical plate keels. Just occasionally they are seen in web frames and beams, where these items are made with extra depth and strength to cope with high local loadings, such as at masts, by powerful engines or adjacent to massive winches.

Limber holes, mouseholes and cropped corners

Puddles lying inside a steel vessel are the cause of its death. Time and again a fine old steel

Fig. 9 The top sketch shows quarter circles burned out at the corners for limber hole and mousehole. This is the traditional style but it may be quicker and therefore cheaper to crop the corners with shears as shown in the lower sketch. A cropped corner has a smaller area and is therefore more likely to become silted up with dirt in the bilge. For this reason the sides of the cropped corner should never be less than $1\frac{1}{2}$ in $\times$ $1\frac{1}{2}$ in. An exception might be a small boat, perhaps under 30 ft, where 1 in $\times$ 1 in corners might be acceptable.

Just as important as the passage of bilge water which these holes allow is their other use: this is to avoid welds meeting.

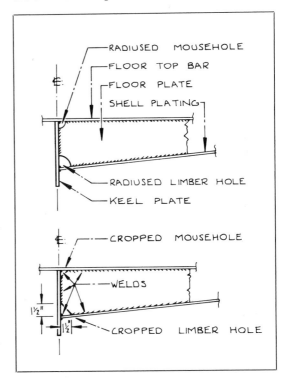

ship is held up as an example of longevity. It is found, on inspection, that she has no crevice where water can lie, and her skipper has been an enthusiastic bilge-cleaner and painter. Such men earn and get their reward, though not always in financial terms.

Regardless of the size of ship, the smallest limber hole should be 1 inch $\times$ 1 inch, and this may be in a triangle shape. In practice it is far better to go for an absolute bottom limit of $1\frac{1}{2}$ inches $\times$ $1\frac{1}{2}$ inches, with every possible hole larger. Small holes get blocked by all sorts of rubbish which accumulates in the bilge of every ship, even well-kept craft. A single toffee paper, which is by design waterproof, can lodge across a small limber hole and form a dam for the mud brought aboard by the anchor chain. If this occurs somewhere out of sight— such as under an engine—the life of the whole ship may be reduced.

When fitting floors, baffle plates in tanks and similar plates, it is usual to cut off the bottom corners. This is to avoid a convergence of welds, but it has the secondary effect of forming limber holes, sometimes called 'mouseholes'. If this procedure is carried out boldly on a frame-to-beam bracket the result is that the bracket becomes a parallel sided strip, a length of flat bar (or angle-bar if the bracket is flanged). The lesson here is to use pieces of flat bar (or angle-bar) where applicable. Cropping the corners of frames gives a useful series of apertures for electric cable or just occasionally for small pipes.

In tanks the mouseholes at the corners of the baffles allow the liquid to flow from the ends to the outlet. Since the baffles have the double purpose of supporting the tank sides and preventing the liquid surging from end to end when the sea is rough, there is no reason for

Fig. 9b Typical of the modern style of easy, fast building is this double chine 34-foot (10 metre) cruising cutter. To simplify ordering and save money the scantlings are kept down to the minimum number of different sections. For instance the main frames and beams are the same section, the bulkhead pillars are the same section as the deck stringers, and the brackets are made from offcuts taken from the plating.

To speed up construction and gain extra interior space the topsides are raised and given tumble-home. This gives a smart appearance and is easier to build than a cabin top. It also gives a wonderful amount of clear deck space.

Fig. 9a Mid-ship section of the 30-foot (9.2 metre) vehicle carrying landing barge *Salmo*. Construction was simplified and speeded up by the use of a limited number of very strong transverse frames and close spaced light T-bar stringers. There are no internal bottom stringers, but instead the two skegs and the external heavy T-bar keel strengthen the bottom plating.

Pillars to support the deck load of a vehicle are made from the same section as the transverse frames. A double chine form with no curved plates proved successful on trials and during the subsequent hard-working life of this boat, owned by Golden Sea Produce.

the mouseholes to be small. They can have sides equal to about one-sixth the length of the edge of the baffle. This makes internal cleaning and painting easier.

Where cementing or other filling occurs in pockets, notably in the bilge, it is no good putting limber holes at the bottom of the cavity prior to filling. Such holes will be covered, and it is always hard to know just how high the filling will finish. A series of staggered drilled holes up the floor or a deep lightening hole are the answer. The cementing must be sloped, even if only slightly, towards the centreline, otherwise puddles will lie at each side after the water has in the main flowed through the lightening hole. What has to be remembered is that a puddle $\frac{1}{32}$ inch deep is almost as destructive as one 24 inches deep.

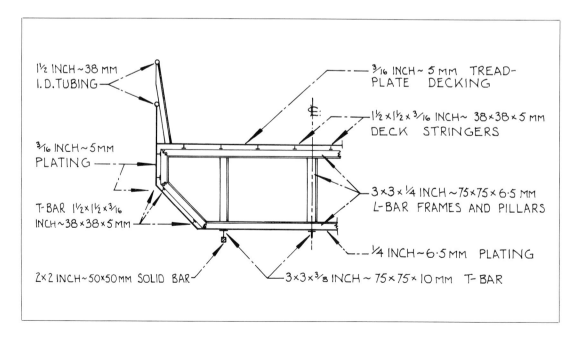

1½ INCH ~ 38 MM
I.D. TUBING

³⁄₁₆ INCH ~ 5MM
PLATING

T-BAR 1½ × 1½ × ³⁄₁₆
INCH ~ 38 × 38 × 5 MM

2 × 2 INCH ~ 50 × 50 MM SOLID BAR

³⁄₁₆ INCH ~ 5 MM TREAD-
PLATE DECKING

1½ × 1½ × ³⁄₁₆ INCH ~ 38 × 38 × 5 MM
DECK STRINGERS

3 × 3 × ¼ INCH ~ 75 × 75 × 6·5 MM
L-BAR FRAMES AND PILLARS

¼ INCH ~ 6·5 MM PLATING

3 × 3 × ³⁄₈ INCH ~ 75 × 75 × 10 MM T-BAR

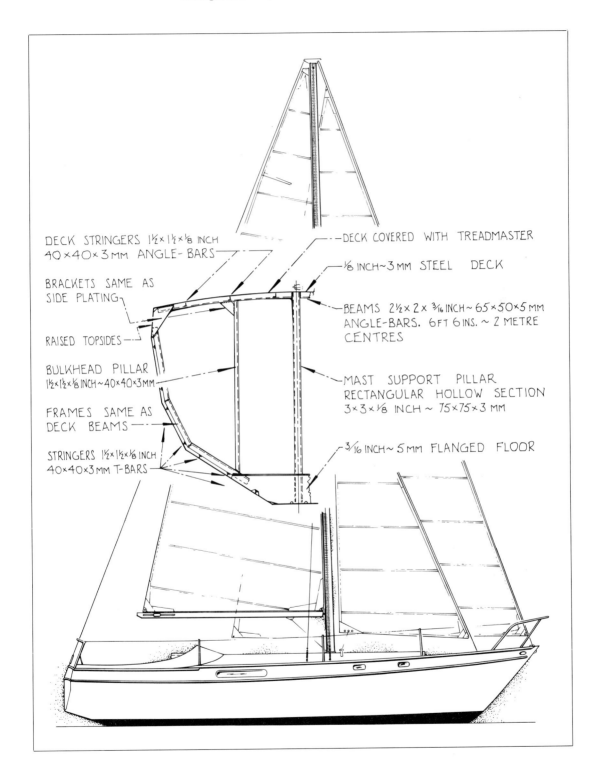

DECK STRINGERS 1½ × 1½ × ⅛ INCH
40 × 40 × 3 MM ANGLE-BARS

BRACKETS SAME AS
SIDE PLATING

RAISED TOPSIDES

BULKHEAD PILLAR
1½ × 1½ × ⅛ INCH ~ 40 × 40 × 3 MM

FRAMES SAME AS
DECK BEAMS

STRINGERS 1½ × 1½ × ⅛ INCH
40 × 40 × 3 MM T-BARS

DECK COVERED WITH TREADMASTER

⅛ INCH ~ 3 MM STEEL DECK

BEAMS 2½ × 2 × ³⁄₁₆ INCH ~ 65 × 50 × 5 MM
ANGLE-BARS. 6 FT 6 INS. ~ 2 METRE
CENTRES

MAST SUPPORT PILLAR
RECTANGULAR HOLLOW SECTION
3 × 3 × ⅛ INCH ~ 75 × 75 × 3 MM

³⁄₁₆ INCH ~ 5 MM FLANGED FLOOR

special scantlings

Cor-Ten and similar steels

This is a low alloy corrosion resistant steel containing traces of copper. Its great attraction is that it has been shown to have between five and eight times the resistance to corrosion of mild steel. For the record mild steel is calculated to lose up to 2 mils per annum due to corrosion if it has no protection, though this figure varies widely according to local conditions. Cor-Ten is so much better than this that it is sometimes used ashore unpainted. On ships this is unthinkable, except perhaps for dumb barges.

Cor-Ten has an ultimate tensile strength of 31 tons as opposed to about 28 tons per square inch for mild steel. Its yield point is 22 tons per square inch. There are rumours that Cor-Ten is noticeably harder to work than mild steel, especially with limited facilities: but it bends well enough, up to $\frac{3}{4}$ inch thick, and will work round an inside radius equal to the thickness of the material, which means that flanging presents no problem. It is true that Cor-Ten has properties which need understanding before it is worked, but the manufacturers are keen to talk over these characteristics with anyone interested. Makers include the Appleby-Frodingham Steel Co. of Scunthorpe and Colvilles Ltd of Glasgow in Britain. In the United States the firm to contact is the U.S. Steel Corporation.

Ample evidence points to a recommendation for Cor-Ten steel, or its equivalent, for small craft construction. In steel ships of this size the greatest weakness is the tendency to corrode. This fault lies behind the thickness of plating and the size of other scantlings which have to be specified. If steel which corrodes slowly is used then scantlings can be reduced. This lightens the whole ship, giving more speed, lower fuel consumption, better manoeuvering,

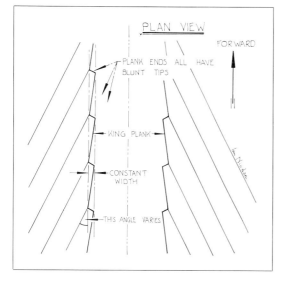

Fig. 10a The king plank. The swept deck planks should nib into the king plank so that no deck plank tapers to a fine tip. This is to prevent splitting and to give a good appearance. Great care is needed to make sure that each plank end tapers to the same width, even though the planks come in to the king plank at a different angle, according to their distance from the bow. See also page 55.

better load-carrying and so on. As Cor-Ten costs only slightly more than mild steel it is obviously in an owner's interests to specify it. The exact increase in cost depends on the tonnage and type of scantling bought.

It has to be conceded that T. Howard Rogers, in his comprehensive book *Marine Corrosion*, is not so enthusiastic about steels with copper alloyed in small qualities. He argues that the rate of corrosion of this type of steel is lower in industrial atmospheres, but possibly not all that much better in marine conditions. However he agrees that the rust formation is more protective than the rust on ordinary mild steel. Most important, he points out that this steel when rusted forms a better base for paint. Cor-Ten has the reputation of standing up to scratching well, as the rust at a chafe does not tend to creep under the surrounding paintwork and cause it to flake off.

Stainless steel

There is a firm trend towards using this material more and more. On good quality commercial craft and particularly on yachts it is seen. Its main use is for deck fittings such as chain plates, bollards, stanchions and so on. Window frames are occasionally made of this material, and I have seen hatches made of it in one case.

There are many types of stainless steel, but most are not fully stainless. Unless they are polished to a high finish they become dulled by a tea-coloured sheen. They are mostly hard to work. What is worse, it is often difficult to get small quantities to just the specification a boat-builder wants. For this reason it is a good idea to design round common popular items. For instance when drawing out a fore hatch the hinge pins might be made from an easily

obtained size of bolt. To be safe it is often worthwhile ordering the bolts first by phone, to ensure they are in stock, and then doing the design round the available bolts. This practice is sometimes useful when designing in other materials.

The same approach applies to things like chain plates. It is no good designing them to be made out of $1\frac{1}{4}$ inch $\times$ $\frac{5}{16}$ inch bar unless this is held by a nearby stockist. Provided it will fit the rigging screws it is better to go for $1\frac{1}{2}$ inch $\times$ $\frac{1}{4}$ inch bar, which is commoner. If even this is not available then mild steel sprayed with stainless might be considered as a substitute.

At present there is controversy concerning the place of stainless steel in small craft. Various researchers have shown that this material is subject to crevice corrosion and some have suggested that it is more prone to this trouble than other marine metals. One body of opinion holds that no stainless steel should be used anywhere afloat except below decks where sea water is not expected to penetrate. This view is not widely held, but there is a growing feeling that stainless steels should not be used at all below the waterline.

Probably the generally accepted, middle of the road, feeling is something like this: stainless steels are attractive and strong, normally long-lasting and certainly fashionable on yachts and similar prestige craft. They should therefore be used because owners want it, but only with care, only above the waterline, and only provided a range of precautions are taken. These include regular inspection, careful painting over joins to other metals and very full use of bedding compositions to exclude water from under flanges of deck fittings. There must be nowhere for water to lodge under bolt heads, welds should be fully ground and polished—in short there must be no crevices.

Tubes and bars for chines and sheerstrakes

It is quite common to see round bars used to form chines or at deck edges. For a given outside diameter a tube is naturally easier to bend and lighter, so it would be a first choice. There is some risk that the tube will corrode from the inside outwards, but as the walls are likely to be thicker (often much thicker) than the hull plating, this seems a fairly small risk.

Where a boat is built for arduous conditions such as fishing, with the added hazards of taking the ground at each low tide at the moorings, the chine should be of bar, not tube. Daily there will be a tendency to grind and wear the exposed angle. Commercial fishing boats live such frantically rugged lives that maximum strength at every point takes precedence over other considerations.

Where tube is used the ends must be well sealed. Both bar and tube should be tapered to fair into the stem and normally the aft end will be covered over by the transom. When this section is used at the deck edge it will be in conjunction with a toe rail or bulwark set inboard. On tugs and pilot boats, which lead lives almost as rough as fishing boats, it is essential that deck fittings such as bulwarks be set inboard otherwise they will be shoved inwards every time the craft is taken alongside a bigger ship in a lumpy sea. Under these conditions the slight rounding of a bar or tubular deck edge is a special advantage, as it will slide easily up the vertical steel wall of the bigger ships' topsides, on those occasions when fenders fail.

Rectangular hollow sections

This is a type of tube which has a square or rectangular section. It is not a normal shipbuilding section, but is gaining a lot of following ashore because of its strength, good appearance in many situations, and the many convenient ways it can be used.

In Britain the sections are made by Stewart and Lloyds, who provide ample technical data about the many available sizes. Not only are there different external dimensioned sections to choose from, but also different wall thicknesses for each size of tube.

Probably the two biggest advantages this section offers is its neatness and the fact that the flat sides make joins simple by welding, bolting or riveting. For stiffening which is visible in accommodation compartments, these sections, known as RHS, are always worth considering. They can be made to serve two purposes at once, being both stiffeners and vent trunking in one. Or they can carry electric cable or piping, while doing the work of bulkhead stiffeners or even hull framing.

On a 60 ton ketch we used it to support the main mast, which was stepped on deck. The main passageway through the accommodation passed beneath the mast, and if we had used round section tube these supports would have been 5 inches diameter each, so that their total width would have stolen 10 inches from the passageway. Instead we used a pair of 3 inch × 6 inch rectangular hollow sections set with the narrow dimension athwartships. This increased the usable passage width by 4 inches, and the sections were painted the same as the adjacent bulkheads so that they were unobtrusive. The beam across the top was of the same section, so joining was very easy.

On a 70-tonner we used much smaller RHS to make up a combined pulpit and feathers (davits across the stern to take a boat hoisted athwartships across the transom). As the pulpit had to have an opening for a Mediterranean gangway and also had to take the loading of the mizzen backstays, there were a lot of diagonal bracings, not to mention cleats for the dinghy hoists, integral davit blocks, backstay plates and so on. If we had designed the structure in normal round tube I believe it would have taken 20 per cent more man-hours to make.

RHS is excellent for the framework for a deckhouse or cabin top which is fabricated mainly of wood and glass or Perspex. The sections can be given beam camber without difficulty, and bent round fairly sharply when needed.

Stewart and Lloyds will supply data relating to the minimum radii round which the various sections can be bent. In special circumstances it will pay to make one or several saw cuts almost through the RHS, leaving just one side intact. Then slightly bend the tube and weld over the slits. It may even be worth cutting out a small V, bending it closed and welding up again. These bending techniques are useful where the bending machinery is inadequate or non-existent, but they do not always give a perfect bend, and should not be used on a large scale.

On a motor cruiser we went to town with a pair of RHS pillars. They were the aft corner posts of the deckhouse, and it was easy to bolt the wood aft bulkhead to them. They extended from the ship's bottom to the deck, being welded at both places, and on up to carry the load of the deckhouse top. An aperture well above deck was cut to let in air, and the bottom was cropped diagonally to let the air out into the engine space. Because these pillars were welded both to the yacht's bottom and to her deck carline, they carried the load of the main deck.

In another instance we used RHS for the side stiffeners of a wheelhouse. On top of each we designed a pair of welded straps which clasped the beams. Wood beams were specified, with bolts through the straps to hold them at each end. When an engine had to be removed the wheelhouse top deck was lifted off, the beams unbolted, and there was plenty of space to lift the engine up. As the beams were wood we made them deeper in the middle than at the ends, to get the maximum strength without loss of headroom. No lining was needed under the beams or at the sides, and the appearance was clean, modern and easy to maintain, yet the cost was small and there was a minimum of top weight.

Ton for ton, this section is more costly than angle-bar or bulb bar, but the ease of working often offsets the extra price. It has to be remembered that steel is so cheap that a builder will sometimes pay double the normal price for a short length of special section and still save handsomely on labour. This is a feature of small craft, where the total amount of steel purchased is often tiny compared with the final cost of the vessel. It may be worth buying in quite a small amount of RHS to make up a simple space-frame type of engine bearer, which is easy to make, light, yet rigid.

Dexion and perforated bars

Dexion is the trade name for a type of angle-bar which has continuous rows of perforation throughout its length in both flanges. The bar is available in different sizes, painted or galvanised, and with a variety of ancillary

Fig. 10b To convert inches to centimetres the decimal point must be moved ONE figure to the left. To convert to metres it must be moved THREE figures to the left.

Example: $4\frac{1}{2}$ inches = 11.43 centimetres and 0.1143 metres.

INCHES AND 16THS CONVERTED INTO MILLIMETRES

Ins.	0	1	2	3	4	5	6	7	8	9	10	11	Ins
	. .	25.40	50.79	76.19	101.60	127.00	152.40	177.80	203.20	228.60	254.00	279.39	
$\frac{1}{16}$	1.587	26.98	52.38	77.78	103.19	128.59	153.98	179.38	204.78	230.18	255.58	280.98	$\frac{1}{16}$
$\frac{1}{8}$	3.174	28.57	53.97	79.37	104.77	130.17	155.57	180.97	206.37	231.77	257.17	282.57	$\frac{1}{8}$
$\frac{3}{16}$	4.762	30.16	55.56	80.96	106.36	131.76	156.16	182.56	207.96	233.36	258.76	284.16	$\frac{3}{16}$
$\frac{1}{4}$	6.349	31.74	57.14	82.54	107.95	133.35	158.75	184.15	209.55	234.95	260.35	285.74	$\frac{1}{4}$
$\frac{5}{16}$	7.937	33.33	58.73	84.13	109.54	134.94	160.33	185.73	211.13	236.53	261.93	287.33	$\frac{5}{16}$
$\frac{3}{8}$	9.524	34.92	60.32	85.72	111.12	136.52	161.92	187.32	212.72	238.12	263.52	288.92	$\frac{3}{8}$
$\frac{7}{16}$	11.112	36.51	61.91	87.31	112.71	138.11	163.51	188.91	214.31	239.71	265.11	290.51	$\frac{7}{16}$
$\frac{1}{2}$	12.700	38.09	63.49	88.89	114.30	139.70	165.10	190.50	215.90	241.30	266.70	292.09	$\frac{1}{2}$
$\frac{9}{16}$	14.287	39.68	65.08	90.48	115.89	141.28	166.68	192.08	217.48	242.88	268.28	293.68	$\frac{9}{16}$
$\frac{5}{8}$	15.875	41.27	66.67	92.07	117.47	142.87	168.27	193.67	219.07	244.47	269.87	295.27	$\frac{5}{8}$
$\frac{11}{16}$	17.462	42.86	68.26	93.66	119.06	144.46	169.86	195.26	220.66	246.06	271.46	296.86	$\frac{11}{16}$
$\frac{3}{4}$	19.050	44.44	69.84	95.24	120.65	146.05	171.45	196.85	222.25	247.65	273.05	298.44	$\frac{3}{4}$
$\frac{13}{16}$	20.637	46.03	71.43	96.83	122.24	147.63	173.03	198.43	223.83	249.23	274.63	300.03	$\frac{13}{16}$
$\frac{7}{8}$	22.225	47.62	73.02	98.42	123.82	149.22	174.62	200.02	225.42	250.82	276.22	301.62	$\frac{7}{8}$
$\frac{15}{16}$	23.812	49.21	74.61	100.01	125.41	150.81	176.21	201.61	227.01	252.41	277.81	303.21	$\frac{15}{16}$
Ins	0	1	2	3	4	5	6	7	8	9	10	11	Ins

products which mate with the perforated bars. It is not a shipbuilding section at all, and is not truly even a construction section.

Its basic advantage is that it can be assembled quickly, with little skill and no drilling or welding. Dexion is made into all manner of things such as storage shelves or beds for an auxiliary generator. One of its special assets is that it is easy to join wood components to it. Another is the ease with which electric cable and piping can be fastened to it. As a result, in some small yards it is stocked instead of the normal cable tray for electric wiring.

Like so many special sections, the cost per ton is high compared with common scantlings. But this cost is negligible when compared with the saving in labour which results from its use.

It is not unfair to describe this type of bar as industrial. No yacht owner would wish to have it showing in any of the cabins or on deck. But in the engine room, in a store, or concealed behind panelling it is not offensive to the eye.

Dexion is intended to be bolted together, but naturally where it is to be joined to the ship's structure it can be welded. It would not normally be used for structure because the sections are thin compared with shipbuilding scantlings, so there is little margin for corrosion. But in special circumstances it has its uses. For instance sole bearers and cockpit bearers of a racing boat must be very light and they should not be often wetted, so they should be slow to rust. In any case racing boats are not expected to have a long life.

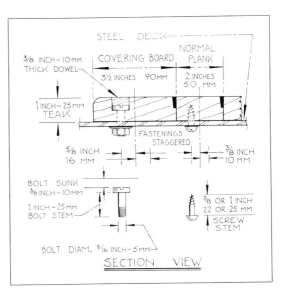

Fig. 10c It is important to have the deck planking thick enough to take good fastenings. Sketched here is the layout for a typical 45 foot (14 metre) boat. The bolts give much the best method of holding the planks down but they are considerably more expensive than screws. Quite often bolts and screws are used together, perhaps with two screws for every bolt. There should be insulating washers under the main metal bolt washer and also under the screw head. The seams between the planks are filled with a proprietary compound which remains slightly soft so that, in hot weather, it expands, but never squeezes out of the seam. When the planks cool, the compound contracts yet still remains tightly glued to the seam sides. Each plank is laid in a waterproof compound to give double protection against water seeping under the wood deck. See also page 58.

Fig. 11 Draughtsmen use these symbols to show the builder the type and location of each weld. This chart is based on British Standard 499 (Part 2) and is reproduced by permission of the British Standards Institution, 2 Park St, London. Copies of the chart can be obtained from them.

British Standard Welding Symbols

Based on B.S. 499 'WELDING TERMS AND SYMBOLS' Part 2 'Symbols for welding'

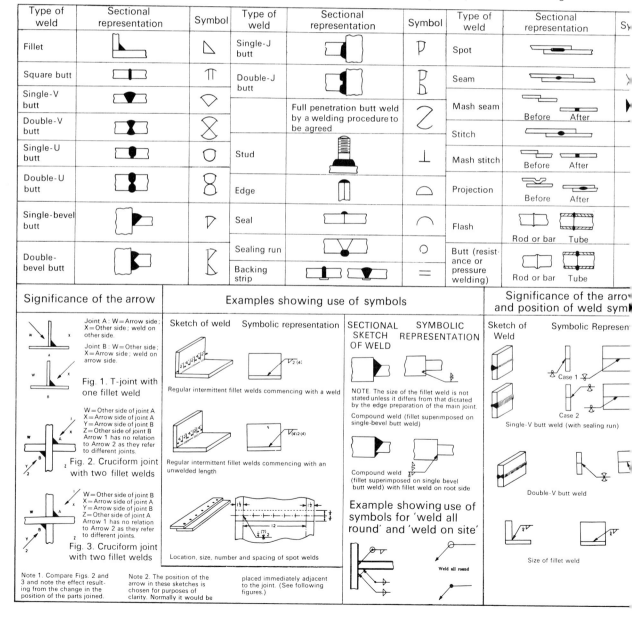

Special scantlings

LOCATION SIGNIFICANCE	FILLET	PLUG OR SLOT	SPOT OR PROJECT⁹	SEAM	FLASH OR UPSET	GROOVE								BACK OR BACKING	SURFACE	FLANGE	
						SQUARE	V	BEVEL	U	J	FLARE-V	FLARE-BEVEL				EDGE	CORNER
ARROW SIDE													GROOVE WELD SYMB⁹	NOT USED			
OTHER SIDE													GROOVE WELD SYMB⁹	NOT USED			
BOTH SIDES		NOT USED	NOT USED	NOT USED									NOT USED	NOT USED	NOT USED	NOT USED	NOT USED
NO ARROW SIDE OR OTHER SIDE SIGNIFICANCE	NOT USED	NOT USED			NOT USED EXCEPT FOR FLASH OR UPSET WELDS	NOT USED	NOT USED	NOT USED	NOT USED	NOT USED	NOT USED	NOT USED	NOT USED	NOT USED		NOT USED	NOT USED

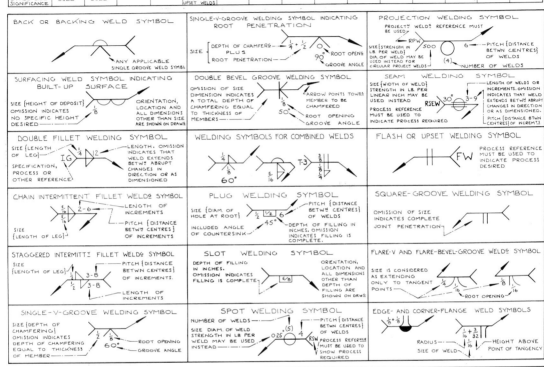

American Welding Society standard welding symbols

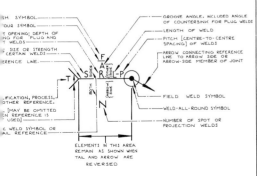

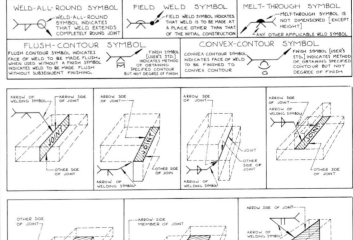

working steel

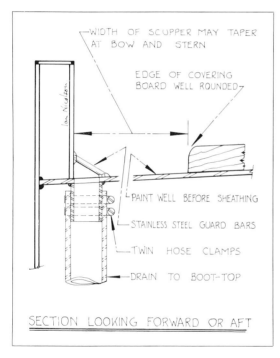

Fig. 13a *Scuppers with a wood sheathed deck.* Very often the wood sheathing on a steel deck is not carried right out to the toe-rail. This gives a good drainway for water running off the wood and means that the scupper drains are set well down direct on the steel deck. Some designers like very narrow scuppers, too small for a foot to slip into, whereas others go for quite wide scuppers and have them painted a contrasting colour. The guard bars are best made of stainless steel, like the top bar of the toerail.

Welding only

Small craft of steel are entirely welded. No other method of joining is used, except just occasionally in special cases bolting may be found. For instance if some deck fittings are galvanized, then the coating of zinc will be burnt off at the weld. In such a case the fittings might be bolted down to the deck, with ample bedding compound under the base flange to ensure the bolt holes remain watertight. But even with galvanized fittings it is not unusual to find that welding is used. The galvanizing ceases to be effective just above the weld, but that has to be accepted.

Since welding is used throughout, it has to be of a high standard. The quality of welding seen on motor cars, for instance, is totally un-acceptable. (In fact it is not good enough on cars, and rally drivers sometimes entirely reweld their steeds to prevent breaking up when the going gets tough.)

Welding is not difficult, but it takes practice, and becomes more difficult once 'off the beaten track'. For instance it is harder to weld plates below $\frac{1}{16}$ inch than $\frac{1}{8}$ inch thick and upwards, but then very few boats are built with anything below $\frac{1}{8}$ inch. Then again stainless steel is harder than mild steel.

'Stick' or MIG welding

These are the two methods of welding which are used in small shipbuilding. 'Stick' welding is the traditional procedure. In making a weld with this type of equipment, the welder has a simple electrode holder which is little more than a handle with a spring-loaded clamp to hold the welding rod — the 'stick'. He puts an electrode into the clamp, and welds away, taking current through the cable which is attached to the handle. As the electrode is used, it gets shorter so the holder gets nearer and nearer the job, till at last there is only a stub of the electrode left. A new rod has to be put into the holder, and the procedure starts all over again.

Each electrode is sheathed in a special composition which excludes oxygen during the weld. The formula of the flux, which has other jobs to do as well as exclude oxygen, varies from manufacturer to manufacturer, and according to the price, the kind of work and the quality of the electrodes. However all electrodes have to be kept in good conditions and away from moisture.

Stick welding is widely used, has a low first cost, and cannot be faulted. However it falls far short of MIG welding. This procedure uses CO_2 gas to shield the weld and prevent oxidation of the molten metal. It is quicker, spatters less, is less tiring, can be continuous since there is no pause to fit a new electrode, and so on. If it was cheaper it would sweep the board. The electrode is a thin wire (as opposed to the much thicker stick electrode) which is fed by an electric motor to the work. The distance from the hand to the work-piece is constant, which in itself is a help both for reducing fatigue and easing the job. Under expert guidance unskilled girls have been taught from scratch to make good welds using this equipment in a few hours. Naturally this does not mean that they could make perfect up-hand welds in difficult conditions, but it does indicate the ease with which this equipment can be used. However it cannot be used out in the open. MIG welding is incidentally used in a zig-zag pattern to fill a hole or bridge a gap. This unconventional approach can be most useful in some tricky boatbuilding situations.

Welding instruction and progress

Several big companies have welding schools. As an example, British Oxygen Company Ltd at the Technical Centre, North Circular Road, Cricklewood, London NW2 runs courses on stick and MIG welding for beginners and specialists. Course duration varies between one and six weeks; also there are refresher courses.

There are also films available from this and other companies both for instruction and entertainment. BOC loans its films free for short periods.

When a MIG welding set is bought it is usual for the company selling the equipment to give demonstration and instruction at the buyer's yard. This is not usual when stick welding equipment is bought. However stick welding instruction is widely available at night schools in Britain. MIG welding is less often found at these institutions.

The Training Division of the Welding Institute, at Abington Hall, Cambridge, also runs courses in welding for both operators and inspectors. The courses cover a broad range of welding, including relatively sophisticated techniques, testing methods and design knowledge. The attraction of these courses is that they up-date anyone whose knowledge of welding is getting obsolete. They teach the best methods of both welding and testing, and they have access to very new research.

Welding is taught to older children in some schools, and of course there are innumerable industrial apprenticeships and similar training schemes. Plenty of cities have night school welding courses, as well as day release classes for learning the art. Once the basic technique has been mastered it is a matter of practicing on scraps of material until a useful standard is achieved. Thereafter it is mainly a matter of self-discipline and supervision to keep the standard up.

For anyone starting steel shipbuilding, whether on a professional or amateur basis, the best approach is to follow the example of apprentices through the ages: build a small version of the product first. Mistakes made on a 15-footer seldom matter because they can be quickly and cheaply rectified. From that size the next step might be to a 28-footer, and so on. This procedure of starting modestly and working up in size applies to companies as well as individuals.

Welding equipment

For welding small ships there is a large variety of equipment available. In Britain alone there are seven major manufacturers of welding sets and many more smaller firms. Because of this big choice there is ample price competition, but it also makes it impossible to cover the whole market, especially as this is a typical commercial situation, with models and prices varying frequently.

Typical welding sets made by the British Oxygen Company Ltd are detailed because this firm has four regional sales offices which cover the whole of Britain, as well as associated companies in many countries across the world. This company, which has its head office for welding products at North Circular Road, Cricklewood, London NW2, is big enough to be well aware that it cannot allow its equipment to be below standard. It is also large enough to have a big array of peripheral branches such as a welding school, research departments, after-

sales service and so on. All this makes it a good 'guide' in this instance, but there are other companies in the field of welding equipment and materials which are equally up-to-date in their products and research.

Basic equipment

A small welding set, such as is often found in a car repair shop, is suitable for welding thin plating only. A typical example is the keenly priced BOC type Transarc 200, which is air cooled and considered light in weight. However they scale in the region of 300 lbs, so they are not easily lifted onto the deck of a small craft. This limitation applies to all welding sets, which escalate in weight as the power increases, so that overhead lifting tackle is often handy. These small sets use 16/8 swg electrodes and have a primary voltage range of 190/240 volts, and 380/480 volts while the maximum continuous welding current is 131 amps.

Full scale welding sets

For serious small craft construction just about the minimum size of set is the BOC ACP 334. It has a maximum continuous amperage output of 250 at 80 volts and 200 at 100 volts. Electrode sizes range from 16 swg to 4 swg. This set is oil cooled and like its smaller brother is mounted on wheels, which is significant because the weight is 700 lbs.

Output can be varied between 335 and 20 amps, with 49 different current selections. Normally a secondary voltage of 80 volts would be used, but for some corrosion-resistant steels and for deep penetration welding 100 volts is better.

Where a small shipyard is being equipped with welding sets, something like a BOC multiple-arc welding set would be selected. With six regulators the cost should be a saving on six individual ACP 334s. Moreover, the six regulators are more compact, and give a better balanced load to the main supply, as well as increased efficiency. These transformers are especially designed for the rugged conditions of shipyards and are intended for outdoor work.

This equipment is available in two sizes, one up to 350 amps and the other to 450 amps per welder. If the welding current has to be higher then two regulators can be used connected in parallel. A disadvantage of this equipment from the point of view of a small yard is that it is heavy and not so easily moved about.

The electrode sizes vary from 14 swg to $\frac{1}{4}$ inch and in special cases $\frac{3}{8}$ inch for the ACM 350. For the ACM 450 the top limit is $\frac{5}{16}$ inch electrodes, but again there is an extension to $\frac{3}{8}$ inch electrodes if there are only three operators.

MIG welding equipment

All the foregoing relates to stick welding sets. For a MIG set at the lower end of the price bracket (consistent with quality) there is the BOC Lynx II B/MRCS 225 which comes complete with wire feeder, torch and rectifier.

This set has a wire feed speed of between 100 and 600 in/min (2.5–15 m/min). The LT-3 torch is rated at 200 amps, and there is a comparable model of torch, called the LT-4, which is rated at 300 amps. The latter is recommended where aluminium alloys are to be welded, so that it is of interest where lightweight deckhouses are to be fabricated.

Electrodes

Each welder and shipbuilder will have his own preference in the matter of welding equipment and materials. In the matter of electrodes, as in other spheres, it pays to keep abreast with developments and read technical magazines regularly. To build the finest craft constant study is necessary.

Electrodes illustrate the situation well. There is a BOC stick electrode called the Radian, which is recommended for all-round work. It is available in sizes ranging from 16 swg to $\frac{1}{4}$ inch and is typical of the electrode which is used by small craft builders.

In contrast the same company make the Ferrolux 170 at more than twice the price. This much developed electrode deposits about 15 per cent more metal in a given time. It is a high quality electrode to give quicker welding and hence less fatigue for the operator. Its good arc characteristics, neat finish, and general 'good manners' make it worthwhile for any shipyard trying to boost efficiency. But for an amateur, or a small yard where production rate is less important than maintaining low cash outgoings, it will probably pay to stick to the more primitive type of electrode.

Bolting and riveting

Bolting is used to join aluminium deckhouses and casings to their steel coamings. Bolting is also practised over engine rooms, so that the deck structure can be taken off to change a main engine, or lift out a generator for overhaul. More rarely, bolting may be used where welding would cause unacceptable distortion, or where the welding heat is unacceptable.

On large ships riveting is used in such

Steel plates are shaped with a reciprocating machine. The weight of the plate is carried by a chain sling hung from a swinging arm or travelling hoist. For different amounts of curvature the tools in the machine are changed. The same machine can be used for shaping bars.

locations as the securing of the propeller A-bracket legs. But riveting is seldom seen on small craft. There is no justification for having the tools and rivets in the yard, bearing in mind the very small percentage of joins which might be made this way.

Where possible it is best to drill bolt holes prior to erection on the ship. However it may be risky drilling the bottom of a deckhouse sideplate and the coaming bar before the latter is welded to the deck. It still pays to drill the coaming bar in a press drill (or better still a multi-head drill) prior to welding in place. This results in half the drilling being done in ideal circumstances, even though the remaining half of each hole has to be made when the deck-house side is clamped to the coaming bar on deck.

Plate thickness	Bolt or rivet diameter
Up to 0.14 inch	$\frac{1}{4}$ inch
0.15 up to 0.22 inch	$\frac{3}{8}$ inch
0.23 up to 0.29 inch	$\frac{1}{2}$ inch
0.29 up to 0.35 inch	$\frac{5}{8}$ inch
0.36 up to 0.51 inch	$\frac{3}{4}$ inch

Spacing

For watertight work	4 diameters
For other sealing joints	5 diameters
For stiffener connections, etc.	6 diameters

Edge distance
The distance from hole centres to edge of material should preferably not fall below 2D, though $1\frac{1}{2}D + \frac{1}{8}$ inch is sometimes seen. (D is the diameter of the bolt or rivet.)

Packing
The faying surfaces of a bolted joint must always be coated with a watertight non-hardening compound.

Lifting tackle

It is no use denying that steel is heavy. Just as inescapable is the conclusion that the best way to build is to assemble parts into the biggest possible sections before adding each section to the main hull. And then again, plates should be as big as possible to minimize the number of seams and butts.

All this means that good lifting equipment is desirable for any builder, even an amateur making a 30-footer for himself. The more serious the builder, the more he should arrange to have elaborate lifting arrangements. The firm which can turn over whole hulls will be able to complete the main structure upside down, which means that all the shell plating will be down-hand welded. Just as important, it can be ground off down-hand, which is so very much less exhausting than working upwards and gives a better finish.

Fixed lifting tackle is not satisfactory, though it might be used for a single small boat. It is general practice to have a pair of steel joists running the entire length of the building shop. They should be high enough to lift in engines and superstructure assemblies. Running on these joists there will be a travelling beam, or better still three such beams. Each of these will have a chain hoist on it, electrified for economical commercial production. The beams should also have their own motive power in a fully established boatyard. The cost of fitting electric motors on the travelling wheels of these overhead beams will soon be offset by the savings in any yard involved in continuous building.

For heavy lifts two of the lifts will be used together, and they will also be used in conjunction for turning over big assemblies. Lifting

Fig. 13 A single screw naval harbour launch LOA 52 ft 6 in, Beam 15 ft 10 in, Draft 3 ft 7 in. Admiralty small craft naturally live a hard life in crowded naval harbours. Constantly coming alongside ships and quays calls for an extra strong structure, so this vessel was built with four bulkheads and twenty-two deep frames as well as a multi-plicity of longitudinal stringers. This type of construction is particularly favoured at the present time for naval craft but it calls for very careful design and construction if pockets of water are to be avoided at the intersection of each stringer and frame. Such pockets will cause rust and call for expensive early repairs.

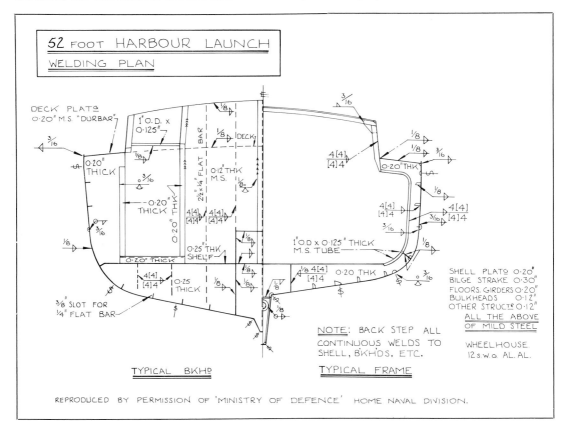

gear will also be valuable for straining plates and parts into place for welding, so it is doubly essential to have overload switches on all motors.

keels, backbones and ballast keels

Solid bar stems

If the boat is small enough, the bar stem can be made without special bending equipment. Two vertical pillars set a foot apart and well held, perhaps by being cemented deep into the ground, are enough. The bar to be bent is put between the two pillars and pulled to the correct shape. A certain amount of persuading with a 14 lb hammer may be needed, but the bends will not be sharp and provided the job is done without rushing, it is not hard. Frequent reference to the template is essential to avoid over-bending, because straightening can be more difficult.

A bar stem tends to look 'mean'. For so long now a well rounded plated bow has been fashionable, accompanied by flares which have got bigger and more sweeping, till they have become excessive. Even when it was realised that the flared bow was being overdone, and the knuckled bow came in, designers retained a full stem above the waterline.

An exception to this is in sailing yachts, where there is a strong reversion to fine stems. Experience afloat has shown that a fine entry wins races when beating, especially if there is anything of a sea. The vogue here is for very sharp bows, so that a bar stem would have to be quite a light section, perhaps $\frac{3}{4}$ inch diameter on a 14-tonner, to suit up-to-date lines.

Below the waterline a bar stem is acceptable. It is probably true to say that the majority of all types of craft are fairly sharp at the entrance, below the LWL. Big ships of all sorts sport bulbous bows, but off-hand I can think of only one ship of less than 60 tons with this type of forefoot.

Because bending is not easy with large sections, it helps if a square or round rather than a rectangular section is used. Bending a 3 inch × 1 inch bar in the 3 inch direction, even with furnacing facilities, takes a little practice, because it is essential to keep the bar flat in the 1 inch direction. If a frame is just a tiny bit kinked in the fore and aft plane while it is being bent to the correct athwartships curve, the matter is not serious. Certainly on commercial craft it is generally tolerable. A quarter of an inch adrift in four feet will seldom be noticed. And on high quality vessels the frames are usually well hidden by panelling so that minor deviations are not visible.

One reason why the bar stem has dropped out is because it has the reputation of being hard to repair. This applies more to big ships, though there is no doubt that a dented bar is a shocker to straighten.

Tubular stems

Some of the remarks relating to solid bar stems apply here. If a bending machine is available it may be worth using, first finding out the biggest diameter of tube the machine will handle and then designing to that size.

Some care is needed designing the join of the tube at the bottom. A straight cut across the tube may result in a sharp discontinuity of strength, yet a well sloped cropping may prove awkward to blank off. If the stem is carried above deck it is easy to envisage the problems when it comes to fitting and welding the deck all round the stem. It is advisable to stop the tubular stem at deck level and even here the forward face will be hard to weld to the deck.

There are times when a designer is tempted to specify a tube cut lengthways and opened out. This seems a handy way to join the stem foot to the keel. Sometimes the suggestion is put

forward that the whole stem should be made up from a piece of pipe bent to shape, then sliced lengthways from top to bottom. It seems a clever technique, cutting out weight, giving a simple join of stem to keel and plating, making painting easy. Where is the snag? It is in the nature of piping, which if sliced lengthways will twist and distort. This is not just the result of the heat from the burning torch, it is also due to the locked-in stresses in the pipe when it is made, whatever fabrication method is used.

Tubular stems have something in common with tubular chines, in that they are not acceptable to some construction supervision authorities as unseen corrosion can take place inside.

Plated stems

On small craft up to about 40 feet the side plating may be run together with no special stem bar at all. This construction, which incidentally finds no exact parallel in any other form of construction regardless of material, is beautifully simple. Care is needed to ensure that the plates lie properly before they are tack welded. Due to the meeting of the two sides and the mutual support of the plates, plus the inherent strength of the steel, this arrangement works well in practice.

A more normal type of plate stem is formed by a curved plate which extends from the forefoot to the stemhead. The curve is usually tight near the bottom, but quite open at the top, giving an increasing flare towards the deck. This same plate may sweep aft round the forefoot and curves out forwards at the top to give a 'clipper bow' effect. This involves curvature in two directions with a vengeance, making the stem plate the most difficult plate to form. To ease the problem some plated stems are grafted

A hard-chine tug is seen being built upside down. This form of construction is known as 'egg-box' because it consists of floor plates at right angles to fore-and-aft stringers, each plate being slotted half its depth to receive the plate crossing it. Forward of the watertight bulkhead the construction is much simpler, being flat bar frames and unflanged plate floors. The 'egg-box' construction is to support the two heavy diesel engines.

A neat anchor recess which covers the flukes when the anchor is hauled right home. At the bottom of the recess there is a well rounded horizontal bar to take the wear of the chain. This photo shows how a neat transformation is made from rounded plate stem to a round stem bar. It also shows the proper harmony of well faired joggled plating seams.

on to a stem bar above the turn of the forefoot. In practice this join is unsightly, and every effort should be made to blend the plate to the bar as gradually as possible. In any case the join should be well below the waterline to preserve the ship's good looks.

Big ship practice is to have an angle-bar down the inside of the plated stem, but such a bar is not necessary on most craft under 40 or even 50 feet. However, fishing boats, which are so hard used, and so often jostled together in harbours, need such an internal stiffener. On other ships it may well be called for by the construction rules which do not take into consideration the amount of curvature of the stem and hence the amount of 'shape strength' on a particular ship.

A special virtue of the plated stem is the ease with which it can be repaired. Of course, compared with a flat shell plate amidships, no stem is easy to renew. But a widely flared plate stem, with easy curves and plenty of space inside, will be much simpler than a fine bow with a recalcitrant stiff bar or tube up it.

Plate stems are also credited with greater resistance to damage during collision. The theory is that a plate buckles in fairly smoothly, absorbing the blow, whereas a stiff bar severs. What is certain is that a plate stem does less damage to another ship during a collision.

Skegs

It is usual to have some form of skeg on most power driven vessels. Often taking the form of a single plate, it is usually the aft end of the flat plate keel. Sometimes the skeg is in the form of a fairly short plate, not extending more than one-quarter of the length of the ship. Such a skeg is there chiefly to support the

rudder and propeller shaft, and to give some protection to these moving parts when in shallow water. Ships which take the ground at low water, in harbours which dry out, virtually always have some sort of protective skeg, though the precise shape and material vary. For instance occasionally a pair of massive tubular skegs are fitted to give good protection to a propeller, without disturbing the flow of water as it contracts in from each side, as well as from below, to feed the rotating propeller. These tubular skegs will be arranged so that the ship sits on them when she takes the ground, so ample strength is essential. In practice vessels over about 36 feet seldom have this type of pipework skeg because the loads are too massive.

An interesting special case arose when we were doing the early drawings for a proposed lobster fishing boat. The owners wanted every quarter knot of speed we could give, so we were taking a lot of trouble to save weight. We first drew in a fairly conventional fishing boat keel, extending from the forefoot to the heel of the rudder in a straight line. At the aft end this gave us a keel plate depth outside the hull of some 36 inches. It looked a lot of plate, and it had to be $\frac{1}{2}$ inch thick. Anything else would have been too flimsy. It was impossible to reduce the plate depth outside the ship, because of the required propeller diameter. Very tentatively on the drawing we scalloped away a big piece of the keel plate in a smooth curve starting just aft of amidships, up two-thirds of the depth, then down to a point on the original keel line about 2 feet ahead of the propeller. We sat back to consider the results of this heresy. First, it looked good. It saved about 200 lbs of plating and reduced the wetted surface. There was still ample strength, but what about when the ship took the ground at low water? We started to think about this from first principles. Any thin keel would sink into soft ground so that a muddy bottom need not be considered. A hard bottom is very seldom perfectly flat and straight, so that the long straight-bottomed keel would never rest evenly throughout its length. It would be supported only at two points. The ship had to be strong enough for these two points to be at bow and stern. Provided we retained enough strength in our scalloped keel, we could have its advantages and there would not be any worry about grounding at low tide.

An incidental advantage of this scalloped keel would be a shorter turning circle, which is a great asset in so many of the cramped fishing harbours from which lobster boats operate. There is no reason to expect the ship to be less steady on course with the cutaway skeg, so it seemed to be a total gain.

A hollow skeg, made up of two plates, is usual for ships over about 45 feet, because a single plate may get bent over. The aft end of a hollow skeg tends to be narrow, otherwise there will be a wide vertical plate aft which will cause a lot of drag. If the skeg is in the form of a narrow hollow box its inside will be inaccessible. This means that the stern gland may be hard or impossible to reach if it is at the aft end of the skeg, so a stern tube is fitted extending to a plate floor forward of the skeg.

Hollow skegs are sometimes filled, usually with cement, as it is so difficult to get inside them to paint. They may need athwartships stiffening, and this is done by techniques used to make hollow keels.

Lead ballast keels for sailing yachts

Either lead or iron can be used as ballast for a yacht. Lead is almost twice as heavy, and therefore much to be preferred since its centre of gravity will be lower. This makes the keel more effective and hence the yacht's ability to windward is appreciably better than if she has an iron keel.

Lead prices fluctuate, so that the economics of the argument vary every working day, as the price rises or falls in the market. But in general the price of lead is not so vastly higher than iron. As lead is easier to handle and work it is often found that a lead keel is only a small percentage more costly than iron. For a serious racing boat lead will be used unless the rating (handicap) rule favours iron markedly. In this connection it is worth remembering that the advantage of lead only applies when sailing to windward or reaching in fresh or strong breezes. Therefore iron-keeled boats with a rating advantage will do especially well in a race with little or no windward work.

If a lead keel is selected it should not be bolted on outside because there will be electrolytic action. In theory one can thoroughly paint the hull and the keel, fit a thick gasket between the two, put on sacrificial plates, and all will be well. However the sea is all-penetrating, and no paint film remains fully intact year after year, even with careful maintenance. So if the keel is to be lead it is safest inside the hollow steel fin. This is a pity in several respects: lead crushes easily so it acts as a shock-absorber when grounding; it is soft, easily cut and shaped either to alter the shape a little or to smooth away unfairness, and it is easy to reduce the total weight by removing a segment. Admittedly lead can easily be dug out of the inside of a fin to reduce the ballast.

Even when lead is put inside the hollow steel keel it needs some thought to achieve trouble-free ballasting. The top of the lead must be sealed when dry. Any sealant must be effective indefinitely and must be thick enough to withstand even abnormal wear and tear. A layer of bitumastic is probably the best 'icing' to use, better than cement or glassfibre, which have been tried, not always with entire success.

The lead will probably not all be put in at once. Even in quite a small boat, the fin will be divided up by floors so there will be a series of deep narrow boxes. In each relevant one the builder must mark the height which the designer shows on the plans as the level of the top of the lead on completion. After carefully cleaning out each well, lead will be put in each one except the first and the last. Even these may be partly filled. No bay will be completely filled to its mark. The yacht is now launched, and incidentally this will be facilitated by the absence of 15 or 25 per cent of the ballast. The rest of the lead can now be loaded into the fin, taking care the weight is as low as possible, but above all, that the yacht is correctly trimmed. By leaving the end bays of the fin empty it is possible to bias the last lot of lead to give the precise trim, which is a rare luxury for the designer and builder, and a bonus which the owner of a steel yacht will welcome.

It is important to get the lead into the fin without any air holes. This is done by putting in only a few small pieces in each bay. A steel drain-pipe is rigged so that it slopes down to a bay, the slope being of the order of 20°. Lead pieces are put on the drain-pipe while one or more blowlamps play on the underside of the pipe. As the lead melts it trickles into the iron fin. Once the flow gets going solid lumps can be put in the fin to quicken the rate of filling up. But if lots of big cold pieces are put in too quickly the molten lead will harden too fast

and cavities will develop in the lead. This is madness, because it eliminates the advantage of the costly lead, namely its great density.

Dishonest builders have been known to buy only half the quantity of lead needed for a particular yacht, and bury lumps of iron, or even concrete, in the molten lead. If after the lead has been poured in (without supervision) there is a suspicion that the keel is not solid lead throughout, a few drillings down into the lead will be revealing. Unless of course the wily builder has put the adulterant material right at the bottom. Supervision is, as in so many matters, the solution to this conundrum.

Putting in part of the lead after launching calls for skill in proportioning the amount in each bay. The aim must be a series of steps downwards towards the sump where bilgewater should collect for pumping out. Unless the placing of lead aboard is worked out in detail it is easy to end up with a sump forward, so that water coming through the forehatch or in through the chain-pipe accumulates in an infuriating puddle forward. This puddle will slosh about, unable to reach the main sump which is almost always at the aft end of the fin keel.

Pouring lead should not be undertaken lightly. When molten it splashes like water, so that special care is needed putting solid chunks into the fin on top of molten lead. When I was apprenticed a man working behind me tripped with a ladle of molten lead. The liquid metal splashed on my back but cooled and hardened as it flew towards me. Later I combed lead slivers out of my hair, which had been just thick enough to hold the metal away from my scalp.

When buying lead some excess over the quantity needed should be purchased, if the lead comes from a scrap merchant, because there will be a small quantity of dross which will float to the surface and if possible should be skimmed off. In spite of the inclusion of impurities it is often cheaper to buy lead from a scrap merchant than from a metal dealer.

Iron ballast keels for sailing yachts

It is important to remember that the 'scale effect' operates on sailing yachts. This means in effect that in general the bigger the boat, the better she will sail. She will not only go faster, but will be steadier, be stopped less by head seas, turn with more certainty and so on. All this assumes that every other factor except size is constant.

The larger the yacht, the more an iron keel may be tolerated. And of course a yacht with a powerful and reliable diesel can afford to be less efficient in beating to windward off a lee shore. Here again the bigger the boat, the more space there is for a good diesel with ample fuel capacity.

An iron ballast keel may be fitted on the outside of the shell of the hull, or put inside in a similar way to lead. Where building headroom is limited the former approach has advantages. On a boat say 40 feet long the ballast will be about 18 inches deep. If this is left off, the under side of the plate keel will be flat, and can be right down near the ground with only a low cradle beneath it. This may make all the difference to getting out through a low doorway or under a low bridge when moving to the water on a lorry. For there is no reason why the ballast should not be put on at the very last moment. The crane which is to lift the boat into the water can first lift the ballast off the lorry on which it arrives, then lift the

hull onto the ballast, and after the two are joined finally lift the completed vessel into the water. This procedure will save a deal of humping and heaving to get the ballast under the ship. It means that the bolt holes must be pre-drilled and a template is needed. This template is first put on the keel plate for drilling prior to plating up, and later onto the ballast for continuing the bolt holes down.

An outside ballast keel could be taken off and altered, but not cheaply, not easily. Inside ballast is easier to change, provided it is put in place with this possibility in mind. Inside iron ballast will be put in piecemeal so that the boat's correct trim, both in depth and fore-and-aft level, can be precisely achieved. But outside ballast will give a marginally lower centre of gravity. Generally inside ballasting is cheaper, but there is a possible exception. On some craft, where there is a long straight keel, it may be possible to use a heavy rolled steel section bought by the foot and cut off the desired length. This form of ballast is wonderfully strong, and it makes a useful stiffener to the longitudinal rigidity of the boat. But these sections are only available in relatively small sizes, so that this idea seldom applies. It works best on motor yachts which need some ballasting, perhaps to carry sail, possibly to ease the motion, maybe to give self-righting in event of a capsize.

Bolts through an outside keel should have a factor of safety of about 18. One bolt alone should be ample to support the keel if all the others fail when the boat is upright. The reasons for this super-safe approach are that these bolts corrode unnoticed, and also they have to withstand unknown severe stresses if the yacht goes aground when heeled.

There have been some frightening troubles

with stainless steel bolts, which anyhow are pricey. It seems to make sense to use galvanised bolts, and to take trouble to seal both ends so that water cannot get at the bolts. Some builders put them in with a bedding of white lead round to exclude water. A heavy layering of grease inside the hole before putting the bolt in, and on the bolt, would seem as effective.

In any case keel bolts ought to be examined every four years. Only one need to be taken out, in theory, but human nature has its weaknesses. Too often the same bolt is removed each time, the easily accessible one. For this reason, when I do a survey, I often ask to see two bolts. Other times I specify which one is to be withdrawn. This precaution is not excessive, because if the bolt taken out for examination is just slightly corroded, the surveyor may pass the keel bolts, but ask for the one removed to be renewed, since it is out anyway and corrosion has just started. If three surveyors in succession adopt this attitude, the other bolts may be in a dreadful state, while the tested one is renewed thrice.

Though I know of a machine-shop owner who had his own ballast keel machined perfectly flat on top, it is usual for the keel to be put on 'as cast', with the inevitable slight unevennesses on the faying surface. This must be dealt with by putting ample bedding on top of the ballast before it is drawn up. Before fitting, too, it is useful if the correct weight is found, for the designer's records. Only the very naive think that a keel comes out at the designed weight. Finding its exact centre of gravity is a fiddling job, but the information is valuable for the designer.

Bolting external ballast keels

If there is any centreline structure, then bolts cannot be fitted down the centreline. This is not necessarily a disadvantage, as bolts offset each side work to advantage when the yacht heels.

However at each end of the fin the keel may be too narrow for this technique, so the bolts have to be put in at an angle, or steeved. They start at the top, off the centre, and angle inwards so that the nut is on the centreline. As the bolt is not vertical a wedge-shaped washer must be put under the ends.

In practice it pays to reduce the size of the bolts at the ends, otherwise there will be insufficient width at the bottom of the keel to pocket in the bolt head. It will normally be necessary not only to have space for the head but also a socket spanner, if the head is formed by a clenched-on nut.

This problem can be overcome by putting in bolts with small counter-sunk heads at the bottom. To hold the bolt so that it cannot turn while the nut is being tightened, all that is needed is a slot for a big screwdriver.

Naturally there must be a clear space between the ground and the bottom of the keel to get the bolts in, if they are driven upwards. In some yards it is regular practice to dig holes to get the bolts in. A better approach is to use short bolts, with the head (or bottom nut) half way up, in a horizontal slot in the keel. These bolts are driven downwards. Full length bolts may also be driven downwards with the nuts on the bottom.

Drilling big holes in a keel is a slow job. It may pay to drill a fairly small hole first and enlarge it in stages. Cast holes and cast pockets for the nuts save a lot of work. The holes must be undersized when cast and drilled out to fit the bolts exactly. Oversize holes are sometimes cast, but this must be risky. A leak through a keel bolt is frightening, if not all that serious. In theory it should be easy enough to stop, since the hole can be made tight both at the top and the bottom. But if the bottom is oval and rough, it is a poor seating for water-excluding washers. And as for the top, it is a basic principle of small boat work that stopping a leak from inside is seldom effective, always much harder than the evidence suggests, and the result invariably looks a 'dog's breakfast'. The blindest surveyor will spot an internal leak-stopper and will quite rightly become highly suspicious. The crew should be too.

Low quality ballast and motor-sailers

It is not unusual to discover steel punchings, steel scrap and odds and ends of metal put inside fin keels. This heterogeneous mixture is held in place by a covering of tar or cement or the builder's favourite mixture. Some use glassfibre and have problems getting it to adhere truly, so that water seeps down the edge and rust lifts the covering off. The result is messy and dangerous, because if the boat heels excessively the ballast may spill out.

There is some excuse for using punchings of steel provided that the boat is not expected to perform well when sailing to windward. But these days owners consider that a fifty-fifty, or motor-sailer, should go well on the wind. They want to race, often enough. Wily designers, noticing the craze for motor-sailers burgeoning, have put powerful but fairly light diesels into moderate but not corpulent hulls. The result has been a breed of boat which sails fast and goes well under power. They may be called fifty-fifties, but they sometimes behave 110-110. As a result no designer or builder can afford to turn out low performance motor-

sailers, and so light, ineffecient ballast can only be tolerated in power boats that have a little sail.

Bilge keels to reduce rolling

Bilge keels are generally fitted on all types of power boats. They are monuments to hope, a reminder of just how uncomfortable and infuriating rolling is. They are virtually always of little use, less effective for instance than a steadying sail (when the right wind presses on it).

The plain fact is that the only effective way to stop a ship rolling is to put her aground. Designers aim, with varying degrees of unsuccess, to reduce rolling. They all fit bilge keels because they make a slight difference to a harsh condition. A roll damping fin is vastly more effective than bilge keels, but even the smallest can easily add 3% to the cost of the ship, and the price spirals up with size. To be sure, this is a small price to pay for the added comfort, and craft used for surveying, fighting, or other purposes where steadiness matters simply must have roll damping fins.

Bilge keels are normally about one-third the length of the vessel. They should taper smoothly at each end, and a quick initial check on how well a ship is built is to glance at the bilge keel endings. For economy some yards just slice the bilge keels diagonally each end.

In an athwartships plane they ought to be located clear of the ground when the vessel sits on a flat sandy bottom. A cautious experienced designer knows that no sandy bottom is ever perfectly flat. It is like all inanimate objects perverse, often shaped to be as inconvenient as possible. For this reason the bilge keels must be given a good clearance above the ground.

They should also be tucked well within the

maximum beam of the boat, otherwise they will get damaged and cause damage when lying alongside. These limitations result in bilge keels being quite small. On a 30 foot vessel it is unusual to find a pair as much as 7 inches wide, or a width of more than 12 inches on a 50-footer. Yet width is what matters. Bilge keels are like every other plane acting in a fluid. They are cousins to aeroplane wings, to ships' rudders, to sails and to hydrofoils. They obey the same laws, and as with all these objects, a high aspect ratio is what gives the maximum effect for the minimum area. So if bilge keels are to be of real use they ought to be like stubby wings projecting from the bilge about one-eighth the ship's beam, and about half this dimension fore and aft. From the point of view of strength long winglets would be risky, but a second set could be well aft the forward pair, set far enough away to be clear of interference from the forward set. What has in fact been described is the size and proportions of roll damping fins.

In practice bilge keels are made a little more effective by cutting slots in them throughout the length, against the ship's side. This has the effect of a row of very short stubby wings, and it also helps bend the keels round the fore and aft curve of the bilge. The outer edges of the keels are sometimes stiffened, occasionally with a round bar welded on, or by using a bulb bar for the keel, fitting the bulb outwards.

At first sight bilge keels appear to be useful longitudinal strength members, coming at the most convenient position over the middle third of the ship. But in the first place there is seldom need for longitudinal stiffening in small ships of under 60 feet. More important, because of their vulnerability bilge keels call for stiffening inside the hull to take care of stresses

Fig. 14 When tank testing to discover the correct line of the bilge keel is too expensive, this technique may be used. The aim here is to locate the keel so that it is as effective as possible in resisting rolling. It is easy to follow on plenty of commercial small craft, but for other types the topsides are often not straight or nearly vertical. The same can be said about the deadrise.

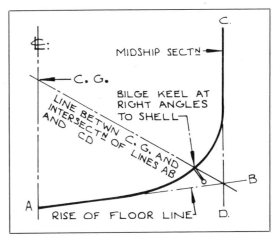

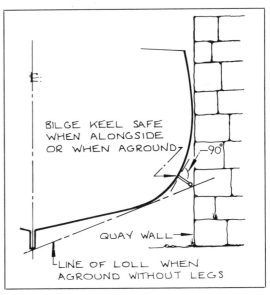

Fig. 15 Because so many small craft take the ground and have to lie alongside rough quays the bilge keels are sometimes located solely to minimise the chances of damage.

set up when one of these projections bumps.
Also, for all their relative ineffectiveness, they
do work hard, as a calculation will show. In
4 seconds a ship may roll through 40°. She will
roll about her centre of gravity, so that the
travel of the bilge keel through the water can
be determined. The speed of roll builds up to
a maximum in say half the time taken to
complete the half roll, all of which gives the
rate of acceleration, and the force on the bilge
keel. This force is not to be despised when it
comes to welding on the keels, especially as
there can be no athwartships or diagonal
support for the keels.

In addition, when going hard into a head sea
the keels will tend to slam, especially in a light,
fast, buoyant craft. For this reason they should
not be carried too far forward. It is said that
they are most likely to be effective forward
where the water flow is smoother, less
turbulent.

Keel roll damping flange

This device has been attributed to John Bain,
the Scots designer of motor cruisers. It consists
of a horizontal flange across the bottom of the
keel (see illustration). Like bilge keels it works,
but does not produce a miracle. It mitigates
rolling a little, but like bilge keels it can only
work when rolling is present, and it can only
cut rolling by a given, fairly small, percentage.
A modest 15° roll can be extremely trying.
The amount of such a roll that can be ironed
out from such a small inclination may be
perhaps 20 per cent, though this is highly
unlikely. That still leaves a roll of 12°.

The damping flange on the keel is not
suitable for vessels which frequently take the
ground, and it should be marked on the

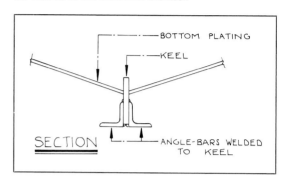

Fig. 15c The keel roll damping flange described in
the text. An alternative type consists only of a flat
bar welded to the bottom of the keel.

docking plan. There is a dilemma for the
designer here: should the flange be very
strong to resist unfair stresses or should it be
lightly fastened so that it fails long before there
is any chance of twisting the keel? A partial
answer to this conundrum is that it is probably
better not to use it at all where the keel
consists of a single vertical plate which is deep
relative to the size of the hull. If there is a box
keel, then the bottom plate of the box may be
extended sideways to form the flange. It should
be well faired at each end, and it appears
without any additional work.

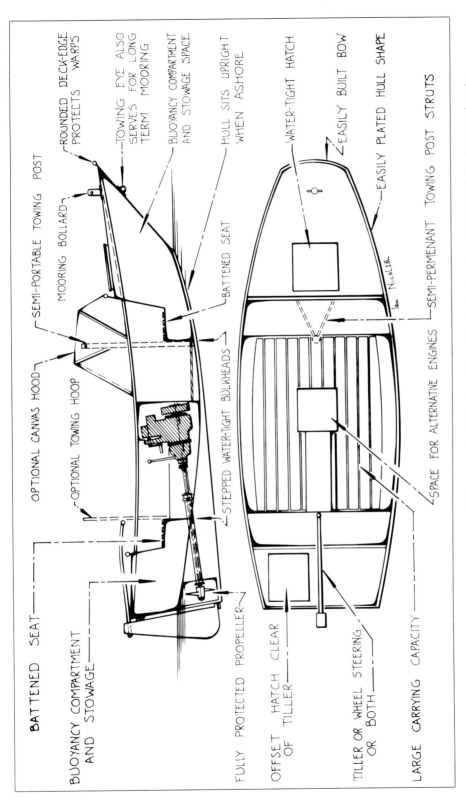

BATTENED SEAT

OPTIONAL CANVAS HOOD

SEMI-PORTABLE TOWING POST

MOORING BOLLARD

ROUNDED DECK-EDGE PROTECTS WARPS

TOWING EYE ALSO SERVES FOR LONG TERM MOORING

BUOYANCY COMPARTMENT AND STOWAGE SPACE

HULL SITS UPRIGHT WHEN ASHORE

WATER-TIGHT HATCH

EASILY BUILT BOW

EASILY PLATED HULL SHAPE

SEMI-PERMANENT TOWING POST STRUTS

BATTENED SEAT

OPTIONAL TOWING HOOP

STEPPED WATER-TIGHT BULKHEADS

SPACE FOR ALTERNATIVE ENGINES

BUOYANCY COMPARTMENT AND STOWAGE

FULLY PROTECTED PROPELLER

OFFSET HATCH CLEAR OF TILLER

TILLER OR WHEEL STEERING OR BOTH

LARGE CARRYING CAPACITY

Ian Nicolson.

Fig. 16 Motor flattie. This is a very simple but useful boat. Hull construction is designed for anybody who is not used to boatbuilding because there is a particularly easy form of double chine. The bottom is flat and horizontal athwartships so that this boat sits upright when aground. If she has to be moved by lorry she does not need any chocks or supports. When she is laid up ashore she needs no supports because she sits secure and safe on her flat bottom. There are three versions, one 22 ft. long; a bigger version, 25 ft. long and a smaller version, 19 ft. long. A variety of engines can be fitted since there is plenty of space amidships. The two big water-tight compartments confer a good margin of safety. This boat can be used for fishing, for towing, as a club launch, for angling, as a contractor's launch, and so on. Though a canvas hood is shown up forward, a small cabin could be fitted quite easily; in short this is a versatile craft, cheap to build, strong and reliable.

frames, floors and stringers

Framelessness

Some boats are built without frames. A set of
moulds has to be erected to build the hull, and
this is generally done with the keel uppermost,
to give down-hand working. Moulds are made
fairly close together, 2 feet apart or less, and
have stringers to hold the moulds rigid. The
stringers will be spaced about 12 inches apart.

Setting up the moulds has to be done carefully, and of course making them involves more
trouble than making a collection of frames.
The point is that frameless boats are built in
batches, so that the moulds are used repeatedly,
which is where the very real saving in time and
material is achieved.

Once the hull is welded up it is lifted off the
moulds and this needs adequate tackle.
However anyone building a batch of boats will
anyhow want good lifting gear. Someone may
even wish to build a single craft without
frames. The sort of situation that comes to mind
is a small barge for carrying a cargo which is in
bulk and has to be removed by grab-crane or
suction pipe. If no frames are fitted then the
crane can get the cargo out easily, whereas with
frames someone will have to be inside the barge
with a spade clearing the cargo from behind
each frame.

Another case might be the building of a
steel fast motorboat, where every effort is
being made to save pounds. The weight of the
frames might be put into slightly thicker plating.
To stop the plating from being dented in by
crashing into waves the bottom of the hull may
be filled with poured-in foam plastic. In these
cases it might be policy to build the boat the
right way up, but this will seldom be the case.

A boat without frames is easier to maintain
inside. The difference in the amount of work

Fig. 17 A special high-strength frame. In some
locations, such as under a yacht's mast or in way of
a large winch, an extra strong frame is required. It
may be made by fitting a deep section frame plating,
finished with a flange on the inner side. The flange
has no sharp curves and is continuous, with tripping
brackets extending from the shell to the flange.
Lightening holes are not always found, but they
make sense since this type of frame is heavy. It has
extra stiffening where it is weakest, at the inner edge
of the side deck.

is startling, since the preparatory work can be
done by machinery, working over the un-
interrupted smooth surfaces. The paint can be
applied by roller, and there is little risk of
missing an inaccessible corner.

Just as important in a small boat, there is the
gain of usable width. It may not seem much to
have $1\frac{1}{2}$ inches more width on either side of the
yacht, but so often naval architects are
struggling for just that amount when working
on the accommodation plan.

Frameless boats are common up to about
28 feet for sea work and 35 feet for inland
waters. Sailing yachts of this size, often with
single or double chines, having absolutely no
plating stiffeners, or rods or tubes at the chines,
are quite common. These boats usually have a
moderate but not undersized sail area and are
not designed for hard racing or for extended
cruising. They are popular for charter work and
family cruising.

Builders of framed boats sometimes scoff at
these unframed boats, but it is hard to see the
justification for their attitude. Provided the
unframed boat is not much over 30 feet it is a
sound proposition for work which is not too
rigorous. The charter fleets are good examples.
These boats are in use for about six months each
year, not just at the weekend like most yachts,
but every day of the summer and autumn
months. They are often in unskilled hands, so
that collisions with quays and other craft are
frequent. They stand up to this rough usage
well, and having inspected two charter fleets at
the end of a full season I can see why the fleet
owners like unframed boats.

Both these fleets were in the Sneek region in
Holland, which is a popular and busy centre
of yacht chartering, so that the fleet owners
were experienced, and not likely to stick to a

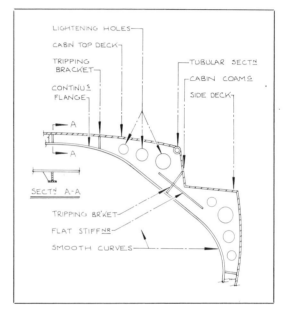

form of yacht which could not stand up to
hard work. Another consideration is that in this
area, among the Friesian lakes, there are
frequent bridges. Plenty of these bridges are
big ones, some carrying rail traffic, so that they
cannot always be opened just as soon as a
yacht heaves in sight, trumpet blowing
fortissimo. One result of this is that yachts
have to circle in the canal waiting for the
bridge to open. The canals are not all that wide,
and are heavy with barge traffic, much of
which passes under the bridges while the
yacht has to circle waiting for the bridge to
open. This is just the sort of situation which
invites frequent collisions, and of course the
barges are massive, often laden till their decks
are literally awash and so they are both
unmanoeuverable and possessed of fearsome
momentum. If they strike a yacht, or she

strikes a barge, the resulting bump demands a rugged hull to take the blow.

There are other considerations. Some of the minor canals have bridges round blind bends, and the charts are not all so detailed as to warn the skipper of the impending obstruction. Avoiding action has to be taken at the last moment, in very confined spaces. Power is often by outboard, which means that engaging astern gear is relatively ineffective for stopping headway. It all adds up to the fact that these charter yachts must often get badly bumped yet they take it all in their stride, so it seems unfair that they should be strongly criticised.

Flat bar frames

This is the easiest form of framing because this type of bar is easiest to bend and to weld. Naturally it is used on edge, but it is still simpler to bend than angle-bar, especially where mechanical bending equipment is limited or nonexistent. As there is no flange, it is easier to get the welding rod into the join on both sides.

Builders of rugged commercial craft look down on this form of framing because they are aiming at a very high standard of strength. They are seldom worried about the extra weight of the flanged frame, and they have proper frame benders which will cope with the heaviest job quickly and effortlessly.

Amateurs and small yards regularly use flat bar frames and have thorough success with it. They occasionally call it hoop iron section. It is easy to paint and maintain and if a bit of additional local strength is needed, this is easily added.

It is not usual to see this type of frame used on craft above 50 feet, in fact few boats over

40 feet have it. One disadvantage is the floppiness of the frames while they are being set up. Sometimes a temporary diagonal angle-bar stiffener may have to be tack welded or bolted from the frame top to near the garboard area, to keep the flat bar rigid.

At first sight the flat bar section might seem a disadvantage when it comes to fitting lining or ceiling. However it is unusual to fit any panelling or battens to the fore and aft flange of an angle-bar frame. Almost always wood strips, which have different names in different areas, are bolted or screwed to the standing flange. These pieces of wood, which some people call cleating or groundings, take the screws which hold the lining.

The floppiness of a flat bar frame can be turned to advantage. For instance the hawse-pipe through the ship's side may come in way of a frame so that at first sight it seems necessary to stop the frame short, and add additional short lengths of frame each side of the hawse-pipe. This can be avoided by cranking the frame, so that it avoids meeting the hawse-pipe, and continues in a line of unbroken strength from deck to keel.

Angle-bar frames

This is the conventional type of framing, the one on which Lloyd's rules are based, the one favoured by builders who aim for strength and simplicity. It is seen in the majority of commercial craft and in the typical yacht over 45 feet. In short, this is the safe choice. In small craft it is rare to find unequal flanges of angle-bar, partly because this type of section is not commonly stocked or rolled in small sizes. However, where weight is to be saved it is an obvious choice. A good case can be made for using two sizes of unequal angle-bar as the main scantlings for all craft built in a yard. Where strength is the prime consideration the fore and aft flange will be welded to the top flange of the floor, and possibly to the flange of the bracket at deck level.

As with other types of frame, it is usual for the standing flange to be exactly athwartships. Occasionally this means that welding on one side would be very difficult, so the frames are put at right angles to the plating. This situation occurs at the aft end of round-sterned craft, and just occasionally at the bow. This disposition of the stiffening, known as cant framing, gives the plating better support. If there is a tendency for frames to meet at the bottom in an inconvenient way, with too many angle-bars competing for limited space, then the usual thing to do is to crop alternate frames short.

Alternative frame sections

Just occasionally a T-bar section is used. Where maximum strength is wanted for a given weight, it is useful, so not surprisingly occurs in naval craft and ocean racers. As the standing flange does not protrude much from the athwartships flange, it is easier to weld than under the flange of an ordinary L-bar. This matters on naval craft where there are continuous welds between the frames and the plating. Before designing T-bar into a boat, make sure it is available as the supply has been irregular. Bulb bar is not extruded in sizes small enough for the craft covered in these pages, as a general rule.

Longitudinal framing

This is really a misnomer, because it suggests that all the frames run the length of the ship, instead of round the girth. In practice there are a few widely spaced strong frames, with lighter frames fastened to them running fore and aft.

This type of framing probably started out under the name of the Isherwood system, after its inventor. It was first applied to big ships, notably tankers, and is gaining popularity for the construction of big ships. The reason is that such ships tend to be weakest in a longitudinal direction, so that the normal framing athwartships, though convenient for the builder, does not make the best use of the weight of material built into the vessel.

Quite a different situation exists with the size of craft we are discussing. In general they have ample strength in the length of the ship, because the shell plating is relatively thick. Their framing is designed mainly to support the shell plating, so that the aim is to have the smallest size of unsupported panel possible. On this basis it does not matter which way the frames run, provided their distance apart is correct.

Just very occasionally fore and aft framing is used, yet logic suggests that it should be more frequently employed. The athwartships frames take a relatively long time to make, to erect and fair up. In the longitudinal system these athwartships frames are widely spaced and few in number. There will probably be one in the place of three or four when conventional framing is used. The longitudinal frames are largely fitted without any preparation. They are simply wrapped round the previously erected heavy athwartships frames, with no special previous bending, except perhaps at the ends. They have to be recessed into the athwartships frames, tack welded at each intersection and later fully welded. This process is quick, and for anyone familiar with building in wood it can be compared with bending in timbers as opposed to putting in sawn frames. Only, of course, bending in the steel longitudinals does not involve any steaming—with the scalded hands, and the rushing from steamer to boat before the frame cools and hardens.

It is very hard to see why longitudinal framing is not more used. It is tempting to suggest that builders and designers do not appreciate the advantages. Certainly one builder for whom we drew up plans using this system would not consider any other system for the subsequent boats he built to our designs. Is it significant that he is young and decidedly go-ahead?

The main disadvantage of longitudinal framing is that ample precautions have to be taken to prevent water lying on top of each bar. If each fore and aft frame is well sloped throughout its length, then the problem is half defeated right away. Limber holes are obviously essential, and if in doubt a few extra holes take very little time to cut. It is a good idea to have these limber holes even when the whole hull is sprayed with rigid polyurethane foam, which sticks tenaciously to the steel and prevents any water condensing on the inside of the shell.

It may be worth fitting the longitudinals on a slope just to make it easier to bend them round the hull. Studying the lines plans will not help everyone, and this is an instance where a half model repays the few hours needed to make it. Half models are not much in fashion, partly because people feel they take a long time to complete. However my partner, Alfred Mylne, produces beautiful examples in relatively few evenings. Much of the time is taken with the painting and polishing, which naturally is not

needed prior to planning the run of longitudinal frames.

When working out the construction plan it will be important to remember that the longitudinals generally go in without any previous bending if full advantage of this system is to be gained. This means that it will be better to use something like 1 inch × 1 inch × $\frac{1}{8}$ inch L-bar rather than a 2 inch × $\frac{1}{8}$ inch flat bar, for ease of bending. In addition the L-bar will need less of a deep slot cut in the athwartship frames, so these frames can be smaller in the athwartships dimension. Sometimes there will be difficulty getting longitudinal stringers fully fair, because of a tendency to kink at the athwartships frames. A little pre-bending helps. Ample use must be made of a wood batten for fairing, but this is essential with all types of framing.

It is not necessary to recess the longitudinals at all. The athwartships frames can be set inboard by the athwartships dimension of the longitudinals, which are simply laid outside the frames and welded to them. This is quick and easy, but has disadvantages. For a start, the athwartships frames no longer support the plating, so that the longitudinals have to be slightly closer together. It is hard, once the plating is on, to paint the outboard face of the frames.

Frame spacing

The spacing of the frames, like so many other questions on construction, will be settled by consulting Lloyd's rules. Alternatively previous experience will be a guide. If the designer is short of precedents, there is a lot of information in the illustrations in this book.

However, before blindly following some rule

or recommendation, consider what follows after the frames have been fitted. In time there will be the accommodation bulkheads and furniture. It is normally convenient to fasten these components to frames, so the spacing may be considered with this in mind.

For instance if frames are spaced at 20 inch centres, then four times the interval gives us a good berth length of 6 feet 6 inches with 4 inches for the bulkhead, plus its sound-proofing, lining and so on. Then again, twice a 20 inch spacing makes a toilet compartment just long enough to contain a w.c. with basin folding over, or pulling out over the w.c. like a drawer. And again, a single interval of 20 inches is about the minimum width for a good wardrobe. So where initially it might have seemed about right to have the frames at say 18 or 19 inches, a good case can be made for widening the interval and compensating, for example, by now going for marginally thicker plating or adding a bilge stringer. Just occasionally it may seem as if there is no way to achieve a 20 inch interval. In this situation it is sometimes possible to have 17 inches forward, and at high stress points such as in way of the engines, and 20 inches elsewhere. Incidentally, bulkheads are fastened on the forward or aft face of a frame. This will be a convenience when a compartment has to be lengthened just a little during the design stage.

Frame forming

One of the advantages of building a hard-chine ship is that the majority of the frames will be straight, or very nearly so. Round bilge boats require a lot of shaping in the frame making stage, and this can be a slow job. It used to be the practice to heat each frame and while it was soft force it to shape on a steel floor which was pitted all over with square holes. Massive steel clips, called dogs, were wedged into the holes to hold the frame rigid, while it was coaxed to the right contour, using rather primitive hand tools.

Nowadays frame bending is done cold using hydraulic press machinery. Once, where no machinery was available, I saw the frames burned out of plating. This will sound like a lot of tedious burning, but it was not as bad as all that. For a start the inside of one frame forms the outside of the next, its handed mate. Then as the shape of the ship does not change all that fast between one frame and the next aft, the cut edge of the plate left by burning out one frame will often almost serve for the next frame. Another approach is to hammer the edge of a flat bar frame. This is a slow way to make it bend, but then many sections, especially forward, have relatively little shape in them.

Yet another approach is a combination of the last two methods. The straighter part of each frame is made from bent bar, and the curve of the bilge is dealt with by cutting sections of plate.

Cant frames

At each end of many ships the plating curves in quite sharply. This is especially true in the region of a cruiser or canoe stern. If normal framing is used in this location various problems arise. For a start the angle between the frame and the plating becomes so sharp that welding in the interior angle is hard or impossible. Then there is the problem of unsupported plate area. The length of plate between frames may be as much as 40 per cent more than amidships where the plating runs approximately parallel with the centreline. Another source of trouble is the tendency for the plating, as it is being hove up in place, to force the frames out of line. This is because frames before being joined to the plating are not rigid in a fore-and-aft direction. If they are of flat bar they are positively floppy in this plane.

Cant frames are introduced to deal with these various contingencies. They are set approximately at right angles to the plating, and not at right angles to the centreline of the ship. In practice they form a fan shape when seen from above, the last spine of the fan being the stem or sternpost.

It is not unusual for the frames, where they meet at the bottom, to crowd together, competing too strongly for the limited space available. This trouble is especially prevalent where angle-bar frames are used rather than flat bar. One way to cure this trouble is to keep alternate frames short, or keep one-third of the frames slightly short and one-third very short, leaving one-third the full length.

Cant frames may be topped by cant beams. These will be welded to the frames, or to brackets on the frames, and extend to a deep main beam set at right angles to the centrelines. However the need for cant beams is less strong than the need for cant frames. As a result cant frames are found in association with normal beams.

Floors

One university summer vacation I worked for a shipbuilding company which had just completed three up-river gunboats. The day I arrived in the drawing office, the whole place was in a subdued technical uproar. All three ships had just returned to the yard after getting only a few hundred miles on their way to their destination in South America. These ships had been designed for work in sheltered waters and they did not like the thrash into a head sea at the beginning of their Atlantic crossing. The bottom plating forward and the floors from the bow aft could not take the pounding, and though no leaks occurred, there was a lot of tortured metal. The metal had to be straightened and stiffened before the gunboats set out once more to join the South American navy to which they belonged.

Some years later I surveyed a yacht, and among other defects, I had to condemn the floors along the middle length of the boat. The ship basically was not in bad order, and once the floors were renewed, she was likely to last another twenty years or more. I found out that her floors had been renewed once before, so the floors I specified would be the third set in the life of the yacht. This certainly emphasises the importance of keeping a dry bilge and the frequent painting of the area below the sole. But it also suggests that floors need a lot of planning.

As floors are low down, a bit of extra weight here is seldom much of a disadvantage. Extra thick plating is advisable for floors, to allow for corrosion. The extra thickness may well obviate the need for flanging or fitting a stiffener along the top. In practice small yards do not often flange, but it is a good way to stiffen floors. It is quick and cheap and not likely to retain pockets of corrosion. Where a stiffener bar is welded on top it is usual to weld intermittently on each side. To make this easy the bar is middled on top of the floor, so that it forms a T. This top bar need not be as thick as the floor itself. To be fully effective it should be welded to the fore and aft flange of the frame.

The bow of this superbly finished Akerboom 20 ft
launch shows the sensible mooring bollards,
massive enough to deal with any crisis, and doubling
as supports for the raised forward toe rail. The bow
fender of plaited rope is tensioned by stainless steel
rigging screws which are held by welded lugs at
their aft ends. The toe rail is topped by a continuously
welded round bar which is also used round the rim
of the small hole fairlead at the aft end of the toe rail.

However the join can be made so effective that a 'hard spot' or local area of excessive strength occurs. If there is a straight line of these there could under severe conditions be a risk of plate buckling. To avoid this situation, which admittedly is rather remote in the size of craft under discussion, the floor tops must not be in a straight line.

It is generally not worth cutting lightening holes in floors except in large boats where access fore and aft may be needed. However a row of holes for piping is often an asset, and of course large limber holes are essential. They will normally be at each side of the bottom of the floor, and should be at least $1\frac{1}{2}$ inches × $1\frac{1}{2}$ inches in size. Anything smaller, regardless of the size of the ship, can get blocked by bilge sludge.

Where weight matters have floors assembled from L-bar. The top one will be a sole bearer, and the bottom one will be toe welded to the keel. It will be worth making the latter out of thicker bar, of greater size than the framing. An intermediate bar or diagonal stiffeners may be called for to complete the floor. Even a slightly complex assembly of L-bars may be a little cheaper than a shaped plate floor with lightening holes and top stiffener. If in doubt try making one of each type and timing the fabrication.

On big ships it is usual to weld the foot of each frame to its floor in such a way as to avoid high local stress concentrations. The technique is to taper the toe of the frame. On the size of craft we are dealing with this precaution is seldom necessary. The usual procedure is to lap the frame onto the floor, and weld all round both sides of the join. But on boats under about 36 feet, if the join is not fully welded, provided there is no chance of corrosion, it will normally be strong enough.

It is an attractive idea to have the tops of the floors in each compartment in line in the horizontal plane, so that they can act as floor bearers. However a slight misalignment of one floor, so that it is a tiny bit too high, ruins the whole scheme. Also the floor-frame-beam hoops will normally be made up on the mould loft floor, so that lining up the floor tops will be difficult. Slight variations caused by welding, the need to fair up the frames and so on will make it hard to align the floor tops. A better idea is to keep the floor tops about 1 inch low, then cap each floor with a wood packing piece which is easily planed to the precise thickness to give a level support for the sole.

This assumes that the floors have top stiffening flanges. An idea which I have not seen, but which seems attractive, consists of bolting a fairly stout wood beam to the forward or aft face of a plane plate floor. The beam both supports the sole and acts as a floor flange. Where the floor is made up of angle-bars the top bar may be left off when the hoop of floor, frame and beam is being assembled. The top bars of the floors are then carefully aligned on the ship so as to be level sole bearers, and welded in place before plating begins.

Floor-frame-beam hoops

Plating up is not a delicate job. There will be a fair amount of hammering and muscle-work to get the plates in place and fair. It is therefore essential that the basic framework is strong and firm. The obvious way to get the required ruggedness is to make sure the skeleton of the ship is tough. If the frames are not tied at the top, they will be all too floppy for the energetic work they have to resist. In addition it is much easier to assemble the floors, frames and beams

Frames, floors and stringers

Every pair of frames is joined by a floor which is
welded for at least a short length to the flat bar keel.
The very short intermittent welds, common in small
steel motor cruisers, are seen at each frame.

into strong hoops while they are lying flat on the ground.

These hoops are usually made up on a scrieve board, so that the fairness and accuracy can be checked and rechecked. In some yards the standard of experience and skill is such that each hoop is welded together before being hoisted up on the keel. This leaves little room for error and changes are awkward. It is indefensible to pack out even one frame to achieve fairness, so a good case can be made out for a more cautious approach. In this the frames are welded to the floors, but the beams are only held to the frame heads by a single bolt on each side. This bolt passes through a hole which is an easy fit in the flange of the beam, but a very sloppy fit in the flange of the frame. By loosening the bolt the frame can be eased in or out a little, also the beam can be raised or lowered a trifle. This allows fairing to be carried out without cutting welds or steel. Once the skeleton is fair each join is welded up, then the bolts removed. This will reveal a big hole on top of a smaller one, and a run of welding should be put in to prevent moisture from entering between the two flanges.

The foregoing assumes there is no bracket between the beam and the frame. If there is, the procedure is the same except that the bracket is *welded* to the frame head, but *bolted* to the beam, again using a large and a smaller hole. The finishing procedure is the same.

When designing the ship, it is possible to make building simpler by arranging the beam flange and floor flange to face the same way, so that assembly of the hoops on the mould loft floor is easier. This is not in accordance with big ship practice. However, small craft construction in many aspects is ahead of big ship building, and is less hidebound. (Big ship

Fig. 18 The big ship way to terminate a frame on a floor is shown here. The same procedure may be used at the top of the frame where it joins the beam bracket. The purpose of the tapered scalloped toe is to avoid the meeting of welds. It also allows welds to be carried right round plate rims and bar ends, to seal the edges and in this way minimise corrosion. The tapering of the frame is to avoid a high stress area. This frame ending is seen on craft of about 55 ft length but seldom on smaller vessels.

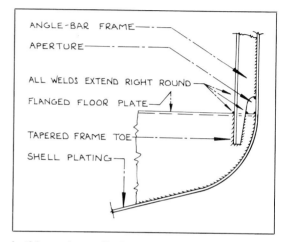

builders admittedly lead in one field by far: they are much quicker and more adept at demanding government help. But then of course they tend to achieve more financial losses more often. This ability is not confined to one country.)

Rub rails

On almost every type of craft some form of protection is desirable, and often essential, to prevent the topsides being battered and dented, scratched and torn.

Fishing boats regularly lie alongside each other, sometimes twelve abreast when they all pour into one small harbour to escape a storm. Tugs jostle in locks, nudge each other as they lie adjacent in harbours, and shoulder against heavy merchant ships. Pilot boats have as part of their daily work to go alongside ships which may be rolling and heaving in a seaway, sometimes with a wicked cross-wave which hurls the little pilot boat against the unyielding mass of freighter. Barges are edged, shoved and thumped about to get them under cranes, into locks, out of confined docks. Every working day they are biffed and bumped deliberately.

Yachts, directors' launches and similar 'delicate' vessels are not supposed to be subject to punishment. Their topsides glisten with expensive enamel, their plating and frames are often fairly light. So they need rub rails to prevent accidental damage to these light yet pristine topsides.

It boils down to the fact that only racing craft and those built extremely lightly may be left without rub rails. It usually is not a question of whether rub rails should be fitted, but how heavy and numerous they should be. On fishing boats, especially seiners which work in pairs, it is common to have one rail at deck level and another down at water level. Between these two horizontal bands there are vertical or diagonal rubbing strips spaced every few feet along the topsides except at the bow. They extend across the transom on stern trawlers and similar craft.

When immersed the vertical type of rub rail puts up a notable resistance, and even when set at 45° it still churns up a lot of water. Occasionally this patterned rubbing strake is seen on ferries, and on a few yachts where it is made a 'feature', partly to give the yacht character but mainly for practical considerations.

Vertical or angled rubbing strakes are important when the vessel is alongside and is rolling. A plain horizontal rubbing strake will catch above or below any obstruction such as the deck of another ship, the edge of a pier, or the rub rail on another vessel. One result of this can be that the whole rolling momentum of the boat suddenly tries to tear off the rubbing strake. The ropes supporting fenders may be chopped through or the fenders pushed aside.

Under these conditions the vertical or semi-vertical rubbing strake comes into its own.

Various materials are used for rubbing strakes, from wood to steel. The Dutch buy stock rubbing strake sections in 1 metre lengths. This is a C-shaped pressing, with the top horizontal, the radius fairly tight and the bottom sloped, as shown on page 113. It is very strong, easy to fit, and it looks right.

Various forms of coping are used but they seldom fit the bill. They are solid, and so very heavy for their size and effect. They tend to be too thin and deep, and they give too easily under severe stress.

A special asset of a good rubbing strake is that it supports the topsides and behaves like a horizontal frame, fitted externally to be sure, but none the worse for that.

The Dutch type of section can easily be tapered away at each end, either very gently or quite abruptly according to the style of the vessel, the need to save weight, and the designer's eye for beauty. Like all rub rails it often looks good painted a contrasting colour, usually a dark shade. It takes the scratches which would normally be on the lighter painted topsides. Due to the dark paint the scratches are normally easy to patch, paint neatly and do not show so badly in the interval before a touch-up is possible.

Where wooden rub rails are used they must not be bolted horizontally because:

1 Leaks will occur at the bolt holes.
2 When severe bumping occurs the bolts will get bent even when well recessed, which will make them very hard to remove when renewing the rub rails.
3 When wood gets deeply scored the bolts will stand out end on and cause severe damage to other craft.

These contingencies are eliminated by fitting a pair of horizontal steel bars, with the wood between them. The bolts extend vertically down, with nuts on the bottom. Good practice consists of copious greasing of each bolt to make it easy to remove. The grease also preserves the bolts which is a double benefit because a rusting bolt is hard to get out.

Oak should not be used for rubbing strakes because though it is very tough, it reacts adversely with steel. Elm is good, tough, stringy, but may rot, especially at the inboard face of the rubber where water is likely to lodge for long periods. Teak is best for quality ships, but expensive. It will not rot unless neglected for a long long time. In contrast few soft woods have the toughness required, and the various mahoganies blacken then soften when the paint or varnish is scuffed off and the wood stays wet for a matter of weeks.

Scanning the market for a suitable wood a conclusion which comes up in many areas is that the situation changes monthly. Certain woods are suitable, and their characteristics are listed in those handy publications put out by the Forest Products Research Laboratories. Often historically 'new' to shipbuilding, they have been brought in because of the shortage of traditional timbers. They tend to come from tropical Africa, and include such generally useful examples as afrormosia and iroko. When looking for a tough hard-working wood for belting round a boat contact two or three local wood yards. Talk to whoever seems to speak with authority on the subject, discover if he has knowledge and sympathy for the problems of small ship builders. Learn the sizes of the suitable timbers in stock. It may well pay to change the rub rails from say 4 inches × 4 inches to perhaps $3\frac{1}{2}$ inches × $4\frac{1}{4}$ inches at

the design stage, to suit supplies available at the critical time.

Wood makes a cheap form of fender belting, but it is not the longest lasting or the smartest. Pride of place goes to the various extruded rubber fenders that are sold by the major tyre companies. These continuous lengths of fendering are available in different sizes but they have this in common: they are costly and mostly a bit tedious to fit. Most of them are a hollow D-section, with greater or lesser flanges along the top and bottom. However the flanges are not for the fastenings. These pass through the vertical straight part, and instead of large washers under each bolt head there is generally a continuous metal strip extending continuously through the section. Fitting this strip causes a fair amount of trouble and bad language.

Plastic continuous fender stripping is also available, but in smaller sizes. One company which sells it is Camper and Nicholson Ltd of Gosport, Hants. In the very small sizes both rubber and plastic fendering can be bought from local chandlers.

There used to be a practice of using rope all-round fendering. Coir was usually selected because it is lighter than most rope, is springy and not expensive. Rope is seldom seen now because it does not last long under rugged conditions. It looks dreadfully straggly once it starts to chafe and even when new never has the sort of appearance which a critical board of directors would tolerate on their own launch.

For tugs the world over a row of worn-out motor or tractor tyres is usual. To support them nothing is better than chain, and there should be drain holes at the bottom of each tyre. This may sound primitive, crude, amateurish, coarse and a host of other derogatory adjectives. In fact it is just common

Fig. 19 A strong ship needs a rugged fender. This shows the construction of the solid half-round bar on the 53 ft vessel built for the National Environment Research Council.

Fig. 20a Various techniques are used to extend the accommodation as far forward as possible, yet give the maximum safety with an effective set of water-tight bulkheads. One way of extending the safety afforded by the bow bulkhead is to locate tanks forward. Damage is more likely to occur below the waterline and is in any case less serious if it occurs higher.

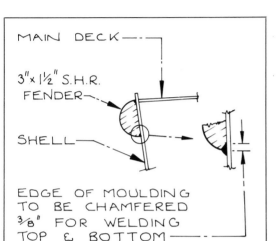

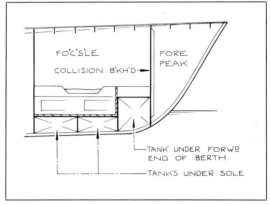

sense and good economics. Tyres are cheap and easy to obtain, to renew and to fit. They suit pilot boats and fishing boats as well as dredger tenders and any other commercial craft which must constantly work alongside other ships, quays and rough stonework. Tyres are doubly effective because they are rubber and hollow. They squeeze closed to take the first shock of impact, then the rubber's resilience comes into play. Sometimes they are used cut into segments, especially round the bow and at the corners of the transom. At such locations rigging screws are needed to haul them up dead tight against the ship.

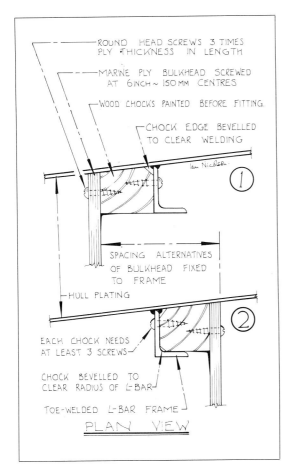

ROUND HEAD SCREWS 3 TIMES PLY THICKNESS IN LENGTH

MARINE PLY BULKHEAD SCREWED AT 6 INCH ~ 150 MM CENTRES

WOOD CHOCKS PAINTED BEFORE FITTING.

CHOCK EDGE BEVELLED TO CLEAR WELDING

Ian Nicolson

①

SPACING ALTERNATIVES OF BULKHEAD FIXED TO FRAME

HULL PLATING

②

EACH CHOCK NEEDS AT LEAST 3 SCREWS

CHOCK BEVELLED TO CLEAR RADIUS OF L-BAR

TOE-WELDED L-BAR FRAME

PLAN VIEW

Fig. 20b *Fixing a wood bulkhead*. Where possible a designer arranges the bulkheads in a boat to occur near a frame, so that special steelwork is not needed for securing the bulkhead. He still has some variation in the precise location of a bulkhead because it can go on the forward or aft side of a frame.

In Sketch No. 1 the bulkhead is secured to the forward side of the frame with a chock or packing piece which is put on first. In practice, the chock may be made up of short lengths of wood, typically about 1 foot (300 mm.) long with at least three screws holding it to the frame. If the bulkhead is to contribute to the strength of the vessel bolts through the frame the chock and the bulkhead will be used and there should be large washers under the bulkhead to prevent the wood being crushed.

Sketch No. 2 shows how the same frame can be used for a bulkhead located substantially further aft than in Sketch No. 1. Here again a spacing chock, or series of chocks, is used and they should be very well painted on all sides before fixing in place.

bulkheads and pillars

Weight and cost saving

A good way to save weight, and incidentally building costs, is to eliminate bulkheads. This is done on craft like ocean racers, and to a lesser extent on some charter yachts. Where privacy is needed curtains are useful, and they do not restrict ventilation through the ship the way bulkheads do. When drawn back a curtain opens the hull out, giving a pleasant feeling of spaciousness.

A half-way stage involves using only partial bulkheads, which extend from the ship's side in to about the cabin coaming. They help support the side decks, act like very deep frames, and are useful for hanging furniture on to, quite apart from their basic function of dividing the ship up. They are also used in conjunction with the concertina type plastic bulkhead. However this modern version of the folding screen is not an unqualified success afloat. The plastic used is too often flimsy and tears at the edges after a short time.

Wood bulkheads are light, simple to fit, and are pleasant in accommodation spaces. It is easy to get attractive wood finishes, though the current tendency is towards Formica faced ply. Owners are asking for easily maintained ships so many craft are being bulkheaded with factory finished ply which needs no more than a wipe with a damp cloth and never needs painting. This ply has Formica or a similar substance bonded on both sides. It is expensive to buy, but in the end there is a saving since no painting or other finishing is needed.

Designers try to locate wood bulkheads at frames, and the bulkheads should be bolted not screwed to the frames. A spacing of 9 inches between fastenings is quite large enough. Where the bulkhead simply cannot be arranged to come at a frame, lugs are needed, welded to the shell. Each lug should be pre-drilled for its bolt. It should be about five times as wide as the bolt diameter and extend in from the shell far enough to make drilling the bulkhead with an electric drill easy. Naturally the lugs must be welded in place before the ship is shot-blasted

Watertight bulkheads

One of the advantages of steel ships is the ease of fitting watertight bulkheads. These not only reduce the chances of sinking when an accident occurs, they limit fire damage and confine the oily bilge water which so often collects under engines to the engine compartment. This type of bulkhead, or indeed any steel bulkhead, enormously strengthens the hull in an athwartships direction. Subsidiary advantages flow from this. For instance a powerful winch on the foredeck needs a rugged structure beneath it, but the number and strength of the special beams can be reduced if not eliminated where there is a collision bulkhead adjacent to the winch. Another example is on a tug, where great strength is needed in the area of the towing bollard or hook. This towing point is normally located near amidships, to help manoeuverability, so the bollard may be fitted over one of the engine room bulkheads.

It is far from common practice to fit water-tight bulkheads in small ships, apart from life-boats such as those operated by the Royal National Life-boat Institution in Britain and the equivalent bodies in other countries. However an owner with even the minimum of watertight bulkheads, namely a collision bulkhead forward, could reasonably ask for a reduced insurance premium on the strength of this safety factor.

The collision bulkhead is quite close behind the forward end of the waterline, with nothing but the chain locker ahead of it. It is fitted vertically, but common sense suggests that it should slope from the top aft, so that in the vital area by the waterline it is as far aft as possible. This arrangement would in some cases give increased accommodation.

On big ships the bulkheads are sometimes stepped, but there will seldom be occasion to use this technique on small craft. Better arrangements using fuel and water tanks are as shown in the illustration on page 91.

After the collision bulkhead, the next logical one to fit is at the aft end of the engine room. In practice it is rare to find a bulkhead only at the aft end, because this would be taking half a bite at a cherry. With a bulkhead at each end of the engine space, as well as the collision bulkhead, the ship is divided into four water-tight compartments, and it should be reasonably easy to ensure that she does not sink if any one of these spaces becomes flooded. It is not a long job to work out the results of flooding each compartment in turn to see if the loss of buoyancy is fatal. If it is, and the ship will sink, the designer may be faced with a difficult, perhaps an impossible decision in regard to which bulkhead to move. Almost as bad, the ship may float with one compartment flooded, but at an outrageous angle, with her bow or stern pointing to the sky. Often enough this possibility is discovered after a great deal of the planning, perhaps even when the building is complete. The situation is saved by filling part of the over-large compartment with rigid polyurethane foam. (In passing, the skilled naval architect or builder is not the one who never makes a mistake: he never existed. No, it is the one who recovers from an awkward situation without serious cost and before anyone is aware that an error existed.)

Though steel bulkheads are cheap and easy to fit, there are additional costs to consider. For instance glands are needed for the propeller shafts and the steering rods or wires. However these glands can double as plumber blocks, supporting the shafts.

As an economy the bulkheads can be fully welded all round, and made watertight except at the propeller shafts, keeping the gap between each shaft and the bulkhead as small as possible. In this way an efficient fire barrier is provided in most circumstances. Also, provided adequate pumps are available the ship has a chance of staying afloat even after serious holing. Bilgewater will seldom be allowed to rise as high as the shafts (because if it does the whirling shafts will throw it everywhere) so that oily bilgewater will not escape from the engine compartment with this economy type bulkhead.

For small craft with limited horsepower a simple gland is made from Ferrobestos or Tufnol. This particular kind of gland will work for propeller shafts or steering rods.

After a few years a watertight bulkhead is often found to be in perfect condition except for the very bottom. Here, where puddles lie simply because the bulkhead is doing its work, corrosion is common. This trouble is counter-acted by making the bottom of the bulkhead of thicker plating than the rest. The stouter plate need not extend up more than a few inches. If a piece of heavier plate cannot conveniently be found for such a small area, then a thick gauge of L-bar or flat bar should be used.

Bulkhead stiffeners

A glance at Lloyd's rules shows that even a small bulkhead requires stiffening. In practice builders not working to Lloyd's avoid the expense of stiffeners by exerting a degree of cunning, up to a certain size of ship. For instance if the bow bulkhead is not very wide, it may be adequately stiffened by the flange round the access door. A bulkhead further aft may be stiffened enough by bars welded on to take the sole and the settee ends or even by simple ventilation trunking.

On big ships, notably tankers and other bulk cargo carriers, the bulkheads are corrugated to save the need for stiffeners. Seldom practical on small craft, because of the absence of suitable plate-flanging equipment, a comparable approach is often almost accidentally used. If a bulkhead is located at the forward or aft end of a deck saloon or wheelhouse, then the stairway may be recessed through it. This has the effect of a big corrugation. If in addition the bulkhead turns through two right angles, perhaps to steal some engine room space to make room for a berth foot, then again the result is a corrugation.

The location of bulkhead stiffeners should *not* follow any blind rule like: all stiffeners on the aft side aft of amidships. Such rules have no place in thoughtful small craft design. A constant appreciation of detail is the only way to survive commercially or to produce light, economical, successful craft. For example, the stiffeners on an engine room bulkhead will normally be on the engine side. Here they will be useful for carrying the loads of ancillaries like lube oil tanks, generators, work bench or vice. In addition their appearance is unimportant in the engine room, and they may be useful for supporting electric wiring or piping or acoustic tiling. However, at times the stiffeners are better situated on the the accommodation side of the

Bulkheads and pillars

Fig. 21 A. Balfour of Rhinefield Rd, Brockenhurst, Hampshire, designed *Zephyr* for cruising and occasional racing. Dimensions are: LOA 30 ft, LWL 24 ft, Beam 10 ft, Draft 5 ft, Displacement 4.5 tons. Sail areas: main 192 sq ft, foresail 172 sq ft. Fig 22 An advantage of steel construction is that engine noises and smells can be entirely cut off from the rest of the accommodation by a watertight bulkhead. The same bulkhead also reduces the fire risk, provided the engine room is well ventilated.

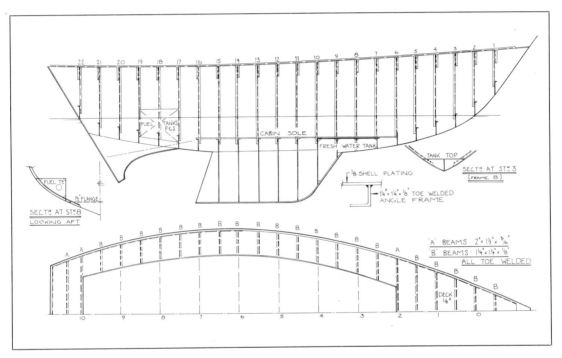

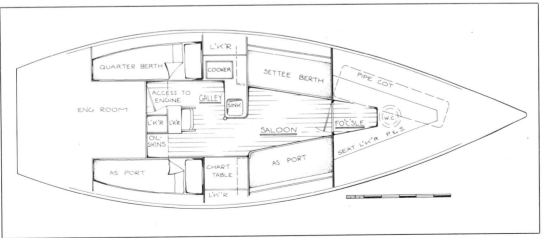

bulkhead, then the cleating for the linings can be fastened to the protruding bars. As a general rule it is bad to drill holes in a bulkhead for bolting on strips of wood, to take lining or anything else. Such holes are always a source of rust and are likely to fail if the bulkhead has to be tested for watertightness, even if the through bolts have watertight washers and bedding and so on.

The stiffeners on the forward bulkhead should be on the aft side if the chain is stowed forward. Chain has a devilish ability to get fouled on any protruding structure, though admittedly vertical stiffeners are hardly likely to foul chain except perhaps if the chain lodges or jams at the bottom of the stiffener.

Generally the stiffeners will stop short of the boundary of the bulkhead, to make it easier to weld round the edge of the bulkhead. This is in contrast to big ship practice, where the stiffeners are carefully bracketed to the hull, to the deck and any other adjacent structure.

Where possible stiffeners should be positioned so that they can serve a double purpose. For instance in the fo'c'sle of many boats there will be seats or berths. To carry these a stiffener can be arranged athwartships at the right height on the aft face of the collision bulkhead. In the same way some of the stiffeners may be used as the boundaries of watertight doors and hatches. This technique saves building time, material and weight, but it does require extra designing time and skill.

Bulkhead stiffening brackets

Brackets joining bulkhead stiffeners are not usually fitted to the hull shell or to the deck; except in craft about 60 feet or over, or ships used on arduous service. There are exceptions

to this principle. For instance the engine bearers need ending with care, and what better method than to join them to bulkheads, with stiffeners extending up from the bearers. If the bearers do not extend down to the skin (and this is rare except in very light craft) then the bulkhead stiffener will reach from the engine bearer down to the shell.

Also, where a bulkhead is located under a mast or powerful winch or some such high stress item, there will normally be bracketing. This is to carry the strains gradually from deck to bulkhead, and possibly, but less often, there will be brackets at the bottom.

Traditionally all brackets are triangular flanged plates. However there are virtues in other types of bracketing. For instance if a triangular plate is used, the inner corner should be cropped to avoid a meeting of three welds. So why not chop away more than just the corner, and we end up with a bracket formed by an angle-bar. Where the bracket is in the accommodation it will have to be covered with lining or some such if the ship is to have a high finish. This is a fiddly, expensive job so a half-way house is to make the brackets out of tube or RHS which when painted looks reasonably smart. The tubular type is also less wounding to crews being thrown about in bad weather.

Watertight doors and hatches

A steel door or hatch is offensively heavy. Even when it is situated where the crew can open it easily the weight is a nuisance. In a bad sea the sheer momentum of a steel door is frightening, and accidents of the most painful type occur. Trying to open a steel hatch from below, especially if burdened with a coil of rope or even a couple of fenders, is awkward. Once the hatch has been lifted to the vertical position from below it is hard for anyone, even a strong man, to prevent it crashing over onto the deck. If chains are fitted to prevent the hatch going too far they get in the way and frequently catch across the coaming, preventing the hatch from closing and damaging the sealing rubber. In short heavy doors and hatches are to be avoided.

Teak doors and hatches look lovely when properly varnished. However they are expensive, and still fairly heavy. If they are not maintained leaks occur at the seams because though teak is one of the most stable woods, it still swells and shrinks with changes in temperature and moisture.

Light alloy or plywood doors and hatches are good alternatives. Attractive stock hatches can be bought for yachts. Some have transparent tops and cast aluminium frames, but for many commercial craft they are not rugged enough. When making an alloy hatch, or indeed any type of watertight closure, it is important to design the closure so that a sharp edge of metal bites into a rubber seal. At one time seals were made by forcing the rubber down onto a flat surface, but this is unsatisfactory because water seeps through. Admittedly a ridge of metal biting into rubber has a destructive effect, so that after a few years the rubber needs renewing. For this reason the rubber should be retained by glue and stainless steel bolts. If a ply door or hatch is being used then the bolts can be brass, or better still bronze.

The ridge of metal, which will be about $\frac{1}{8}$ inch thick, is best on the hatch or door, with the rubber on the deck or bulkhead. This is the reverse of common practice, but it avoids the unpleasant sharp edge round the hatch coaming or door surround, which may cause injury and is anyway so objectionable to climb over. If the metal biting edge must be on the deck, then it should have a second, wide coaming just outside it, which will take away the discomfort.

Light, inexpensive hatches and doors are commonly made of plywood. For virtually any yacht except one used for ocean cruising, and many small commercial craft, both hatches and doors are conveniently made from $\frac{7}{8}$ inch marine ply with no stiffening or framework. Unless very skilfully finished, the raw edge of the ply offends the eye, and should be covered. In spite of numerous often-expressed opinions to the contrary, edge sealing is seldom fully effective against the ingress of water after a few years. But then the ply must be of full marine quality, even for a well-sheltered door below decks, so the edge seal is not vital. Ply as light as $\frac{1}{2}$ inch may be used on boats if weight is being saved at every turn, but some sort of framework will be needed.

On commercial craft it is not unusual to see hinge pins and locking bolts made of mild steel. This is poor practice because the steel rusts, then wears rapidly. It means that the door or hatch no longer clamps tight shut. Some builders go to the trouble of fitting grease nipples, but small craft are often hard used so that the crew have little time to attend to greasing hinges, even when there is adequate supervision for this sort of maintenance.

Pillars

Builders of small craft tend to use pillars infrequently. In large ships the problems of accommodation and space are less pressing, and strength has to be sought more keenly. Living space is so short in little ships that designers are loath to lose any by setting pillars in the middle of what little space there is, and so they struggle to achieve adequate beam strength.

On naval ships pillars are regularly fitted beneath guns. Commercial and fishing craft have them under heavy winches and similar loads, while sailing yachts have them under masts where these are stepped on deck.

Pillars need not be placed exactly down the middle line of the ship, if they interfere with hatches, holds or accommodation. A single pillar offset right outboard has some effect since it reduces the unsupported span of the beam. Lloyd's rules are a handy guide to the valuable effect even one lone pillar well off centre can have. Of course if a pillar is too very far off the centreline it may be simpler to increase the size of the beam end-brackets.

A pillar is not fitted at every beam, even where great strength is required. A common technique is to support every other beam, or even every fifth one. Usually, but by no means always, there will be stringers running fore and aft in way of the pillars, distributing their usefulness over the maximum length of the ship.

In certain circumstances it will make sense to pillar at every beam. For instance where there is a central passageway down the ship below deck with some heavy load above, it will be worth fitting double pillars at every beam. These pillars support the bulkheads each side of the passageway, and are unobtrusive, since they are bulkhead stiffeners.

Keeping pillars out of the way is quite an art. Sometimes they are used as corner posts to wardrobes, or as the inner edges of partial bulkheads. I have seen them used in a big aft cabin at the inboard corners of the berths.

They made each bunk have the feeling of a four-poster bed. This is subtlety in design which paid off in added headroom, lighter (and incidentally cheaper) beams and an all-round gain.

Where bulkheads are quite light, perhaps of thin ply backed with decorative panelling and sound-proofing tiles, a pair of strong pillars are usefully worked in each side of the doorway. They will support the bulkhead and the door, as well as the deckhead over.

Just as the purpose of the pillar is to reduce the unsupported beam length, so in turn the pillar should be made as short as possible. It may be welded to a sole bearer, or a deep floor, or to both. At the top, where there is room there may be a bracket onto the beam, but this is unusual except where an especially heavy load is being carried. Bracketing either at the bottom or the top should be both fore-and-aft, also athwartships. This is not always convenient, so a compromise may be the use of a single flanged bracket, with the flange welded at each end.

To be effective pillars must be straight but they need not be vertical. For instance a small sailing yacht may have a pair of pillars supporting the mast. If they extend vertically down, and are far enough apart to give a passageway through, then at the bottom they may land on the shell, whereas they should pick up a strong floor. In these circumstances the pillars might be set at an angle so that they are perhaps only 14 inches apart at sole level. Provided they are about 26 inches apart at shoulder level they will not obstruct a man walking between even if he is padded out with bad weather clothing.

Pillars may be of rod, tube, rectangular hollow section or angle-bar and occasionally of some other section such as T-bar or channel.

Rod tends to be heavy and its minimum diameter is seldom needed. Tube is better, and serves well in accommodation spaces, since the absence of sharp edges and the easily grasped shape make it popular with passengers and crew. It should be welded all round at top and bottom in theory, but seldom is. Provided the foot is well above bilgewater level, and the top is not likely to be corroded, quite a thin wall of tubing serves most purposes. However in practice few builders will want to go to the trouble and expense of finding special thin wall pipes, and virtually all builders use the common commercial grades.

Where bulkheads or furniture have to be fastened to the pillars it will often be more convenient to use a rolled section, such as an angle-bar. However this particular bar does not look attractive, so it needs either lining or facing with timber, or otherwise concealing in the accommodation spaces of good quality craft. Further details concerning rectangular hollow sections are given in chapter 5.

The purpose of pillars is to help out the beams, and in this respect they tend to reduce the total displacement. A wide ship, a shallow draft river boat for example, will need beams which are very much stouter than her frames. Judicious pillaring will reduce the beam size to that of the frames and so minimize the number of different sections which have to be bought.

Just occasionally pillars are used to support the bottom. For instance very flat-bottomed river boats will pound in a bad sea. Deep floors provide part of the answer, but often when building this type of ship displacement has to be minimized, so big heavy plates are not acceptable. In these circumstances pillars are used to stiffen athwartships or longitudinal bottom frames.

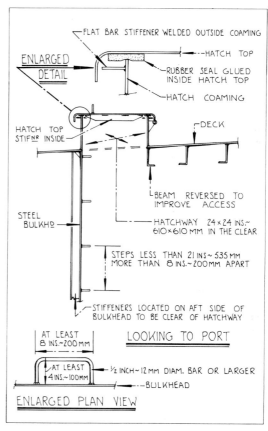

Fig. 22a If a fo'c'sle hatch is located by a bulkhead, the steps can be welded to the bulkhead. For reasonable access a man wearing winter clothes and oilskins needs quite 24 × 24 inches (610 × 610 mm) so the stiffeners on the bulkhead have been put on the aft side, and the beam just ahead of the hatch-way has had its horizontal flange turned forward.

In the enlarged detail at the top the hatch coaming is shown biting into the semi-soft rubber seal. This is glued inside the flanged top, safe from chances that it will be scuffed or torn away by accident. The hatch top stiffeners are inside, away from the weather and so the hatch top is smooth and smart. It is shown with a handle identical to the steps, made from bent steel bar.

By putting the hatch coaming stiffeners round the outside the access through the hatch is made easier and water deep on deck is less likely to get below.

plating and transoms

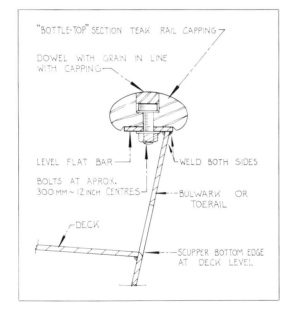

"BOTTLE-TOP" SECTION TEAK RAIL CAPPING

DOWEL WITH GRAIN IN LINE WITH CAPPING

LEVEL FLAT BAR

BOLTS AT APROX. 300 MM ~ 12 INCH CENTRES

DECK

WELD BOTH SIDES

BULWARK OR TOERAIL

SCUPPER BOTTOM EDGE AT DECK LEVEL

Fig. 22b Fine finish. This section shows one of the traditional ways of finishing a toerail, or bulwark or cockpit coaming. The 'bottle top' section looks very smart and does not allow water to lie on top so that varnish lasts longer.

Not shown in this sketch is the semi-hard washer under the metal washer of the bolt, to insulate the bolt from the flat bar. On some boats this flat bar is made of stainless steel because it is inaccessible and therefore hard to paint. The wood section can be shaped with a mechanical router or the top bevels taken off with a tilted circular saw, the final finish being done by hand.

Plating

The most usual method of plating is by flush-butting the seams and butts, so that they are welded edge-to-edge, then ground flush. This gives a smooth external surface, but calls for accurate fitting of every plate. The smooth surface is easy to maintain and there is nowhere for water to lodge and start corrosion.

Flush butts with joggled seams are found on some craft, mainly commercial vessels. The joggling is done with a hydraulic press, and is outwards, so that there is no need to joggle or notch the frames at the seams. On a frameless boat there is no reason why joggling inwards should not be used, but this technique is not seen.

The line of the joggled seam is like a stringer, being twice as thick as the plating. The width of the joggle is about eight times the plate thickness. The outer edge of the joggle is continuously welded, but the inner one is sometimes only intermittently welded, even on well-built craft. The idea of this intermittent weld is not just to save time: an important object is the restriction of welding heat and hence distortion.

Joggled seams show quite prominently so they must be absolutely fair, sweeping attractively from bow to stern in harmony with other lines but especially in sympathy with the sheer. There is an argument here in favour of making a half model, to plot the seams. Until a fairly high degree of skill is achieved it is best to make the model quite large, say over 3 feet long. The seam lines are best selected by pinning stiffish battens on the half model.

A great advantage of joggled seams is that the edges need not be precisely parallel. Naturally there must not be serious discrepancies, but a variation of $\frac{1}{8}$ of an inch is acceptable, and cannot be detected. Because joggling is so convenient, it is sometimes the practice to joggle below the waterline and flush-plate above. This technique is favoured on round bilge motor cruisers as it gives a smooth yacht appearance afloat with relatively economical plating.

On flush-plating the internal welding is sometimes discontinuous, again to get fair plating. On good, but perhaps not the very best quality craft, the inside welding may be $1\frac{1}{2}$ inches long with gaps of the same length.

One way to achieve smooth plating is to cut down the number of joins. In this connection, as a basic rule it is better to have the minimum number of butts. An extra seam or two will show less, since the lines of the seams will sweep in harmony if not parallel to the sheer. In practice plates are made as big as possible to save welding. The limitation in size is firstly the swallow of the press available, and the lifting tackle capabilities. But most important is the convenience of the platers. If an individual plate is so large it can only be manoeuvered with a struggle, then it is better to accept an extra butt or seam.

Plating thickness will depend on the service which the ship has to perform. On a typical 40 foot cruising ketch, not intended for ocean-crossing, though capable of it, the keel might be 6 mm, the garboards 5 mm and the majority of the plating 4 mm. Sometimes 3 mm plating is used, but it is generally considered a bit light and tends to be more expensive to work than the thicker plating. This is borne out in part by the fact that superstructures often cost more per ton of steel worked than hull plating, and super-structures are often in 3 mm plating. But of course there are other considerations here.

Superstructures often need more grinding off. Against this they tend to need less shaping, and they seldom have curvature in two directions except along a rolled edge.

The lower plates are normally made thicker than the rest, since they are most subject to corrosion by bilgewater. On small launches the plating is generally all the same thickness, probably 3 mm. On very simple craft, where weight is not important it is more economical to buy in all the plating of the same thickness, rather than have a small quantity of heavier plating for the garboards. In this case the whole hull will be made up to the garboard thickness, and so the framing spacing can perhaps be widened a little.

One highly successful 25 foot racing (sailing) yacht was plated in 2 mm steel recently. She had great success in the first year of her life, but this was in part due to her subtle shape, good sail plan and hard-driving owner, just as much as her lightweight shell. With the advent of ever more efficient paints and plate preparation this light plating may find increasing favour.

Plate fairing techniques

Design

Where there is choice a designer should introduce curvature into the plating. This shaping need not be such that it has to be worked in by machinery, since plates will curve easily to segments of cones or cylinders merely by hand bending. The point about this curvature is that it costs nothing, except perhaps a little more shaping to the frames, but it makes the plating start and continue to look more fair.

Naturally there are limitations in this matter,

Fig. 23 This technique may be used to fair up a sheer without burning off the top edge of the sheer plate. As the top edge of the sheer plate is inboard, it cannot be seen. The gunwale bar must sweep curvaceously from bow to stern, but it can be faired at the ship by measurement and then by sighting. To do this it is essential to stand first well aft fairly close to the boat, looking forward, then forward close in, looking aft. This must be repeated, and the bar adjusted, till the sheer is a perfect curve.

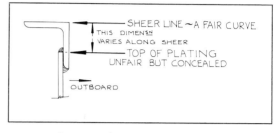

since so many conflicting requirements crowd the designer's mind when he is working on the lines plan. However plate fairness matters mostly above the waterline, and here the designer normally has a degree of choice. For instance it matters little on a great many craft whether the topsides aft are flat or curved. Often it is not vital whether there be flare, flam or tumblehome at the quarters. Here the designer so often has choice, on the type of ship where plate fairness truly matters. He should grasp the heaven-sent opportunity and go for bold shaping. It looks better anyway, and it will certainly help with the initial and final smoothness. If this recommendation seems like heresy, it can be asked, 'Does a few degrees of flare forward or tumblehome aft seriously affect speed, manoeuverability or seaworthiness — or indeed seakindliness?' The answer must be that, in moderation, minor changes to induce more curvature have only a minimal effect on the ship's performance. So, with ships as with women, the more curvature the better.

Thick plating

Where there is a choice, the thicker the plating the fairer it will be. Thicker plating distorts less when welded and bends more fairly. However this is not the way to build a fast boat, since it will be heavy. To be sure if the plate thickness goes up the frames may be further apart, but not enough to compensate for the added weight of plating. Lloyd's rules provide a handy basis for increasing frame spacing as the plating is thickened. Carried to its logical conclusion the plate thickness is increased, and the frames spaced ever further apart, till the first frame is the stem and the next is the transom. This is the frameless ship, known in other technologies as *monocoque*

construction. Few boats over 35 feet are built this way, even for inland waterways. It has the added advantage that as there are no frames there are none of those weld marks which show outside the plating even though the weld is inboard. They show even when the weld is very discontinuous, with quite short welds staggered each side of the frame.

Putting the plate thickness up to help achieve fair plating can rebound. If unfairness appears, then the thicker the plate, the more difficult it is to smooth out undulations. However this is a very minor consideration because in practice the increase in thickness will not be much over 25 per cent, and this addition will not make so great a difference to the work of fairing up after plating.

Minimum welding

The more welding there is between the frames and the shell, the more the ship will 'look like a hungry horse'. This phrase is actually used in Japan to describe the condition in which it is easy to count the frames from outboard because the ship looks starved and shows her ribs. Due to the welding heat the plating contracts and bellies in between each frame. This can be mitigated by using discontinuous welding, which explains why frigates often look so dreadful. They are plated lightly, but have full continuous welds each side of each frame.

Plating and transoms

In the past a few builders have welded the plating butts, then riveted the seams to seam battens or used joggled riveted seams. The riveting was normally confined to the area above the waterline where plating fairness tends to matter most. The builders would rivet the frames to the plating too, and the results were smooth and fully acceptable. But of course this is no longer a practical way out because there are few riveters left, and it is a slow job even in those few yards which still have riveting equipment.

There is a simple technique which will suit small yards with limited equipment, or anyone building their first steel ship. The design of the plating must incorporate a seam parallel to the sheer, about one-third or one-quarter of the way down from sheer to waterline. This seam is sealed by a wide rubbing strake, which is in practice an external steel seam batten. It is bolted in place using countersunk bolts of small diameter, close spaced. They have to be small in diameter to ensure that their heads are fully countersunk without using an unacceptably thick seam batten.

The very act of tightening the bolts will fair the plating and incidentally most of the bolting is unskilled work. It will be essential to bed the seam batten thoroughly, and the outer edges should be ground round. As this plate will be both in fact and appearance a rubbing strake, it may be good policy to paint it a dark contrasting colour so that scratches on it show up less.

Correct welding sequence
The illustrations show the basic welding procedures. The essence of the problem is to plan the work beforehand. An hour spent drawing out the welding sequence will save

Fig. 24 The first drawing shows 'chain' welding, the second type is called 'staggered'. The least distortion is caused by staggered welding which is far more often used than chain. Notice how in both cases welding is worked right round both ends to reduce corrosion and gain strength. This feature is important, as is the length and gap size. Poor builders increase the gaps and shorten the welds till the former are twelve times the latter.

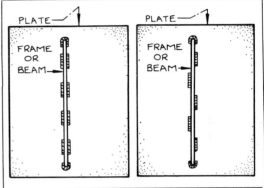

three correcting subsequent troubles.

In general the ship should be welded from amidships out towards the ends. The largest possible prefabricated units should be made and faired, then assembled into the final ship. Before making a seam or butt weld the plate should be tacked in place.

For all continuous welds the 'step-back' procedure is used. Where possible welds should not meet. In practice, a weld junction is often eliminated on the ship even though this chance has not been seen in the drawing office. If welds must meet, then the one which ends on the continuous line of the other is made first. When it is complete the end is chipped back, and the second weld is made across the end of the first.

Where possible seam and butt welds are made before welds to stiffeners, frames, beams and so on. This is because the plate edge welding may cause or result in an unfairness. By adjusting the stiffener this unfairness will be at least partly eliminated.

Because fairness of the topsides matters more than over the underbody, it is logical to get the topsides welded first, though other

Fig. 25 The numbering sequence for welding long seams. If the seam is a very long one, then each step may take an electrode.

Fig. 26 Where a set of plates are being welded, the 'stems' of all the T joins are welded first, in the sequence shown here.

Fig. 27 As far as possible lines of welding should not meet. When this situation is inevitable first weld the 'stem' of the T then cross it. In other words, in this sketch, weld from A to B, chip back the weld at A, then weld from C to D.

other considerations obtrude here.

Intercostal stringers

Where there is an unfairness between two frames, and this irregularity is serious, some builders fit a short stringer between the frames to get rid of the blemish. If the unfairness is inwards then the stringer is welded just a fraction clear of the plating, which allows wedges to be driven in. The wedges are hammered home till the fairness is away. While the edges are still in place the faying edge of the stringer is welded clear of the wedges, and these are then knocked out to allow the full length of welding to be completed. In some cases the welding will not be continuous.

If the unfairness is an outward bulge then once the stringer is in place, external force is used to drive the plate up to the stringer and welding is applied to hold the plating in.

This practice is not generally recommended because locked-up stresses must be left in the plating. Also the short intercostal stringer shrieks to anyone knowledgeable its true function, betraying the standards of the builder all too plainly. Where a stringer of this sort has to be used the ingenious builder makes it part of the cleating supporting an important fitting, maybe working in a tank side, or an engine bearer support, so that the stringer looks part of the original design. In such an instance it will be matched by a twin on the opposite side.

Using fillers

During the course of painting the topsides (and sometimes the cabin tops and deckhouses) it is usual to achieve a final fair appearance by using fillers. These are made by various paint manufacturers, the current favourites being special versions of the epoxides. This type

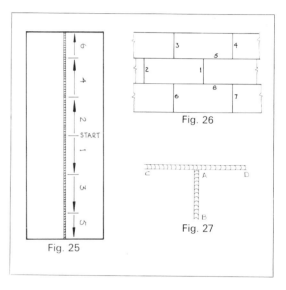

Fig. 25

Fig. 26

Fig. 27

requires a base and hardener to be mixed before application. Once mixed a chemical action commences, and when this is complete the filler is extremely hard and well bonded to the plating.

Whatever filler is used, the skill in applying it may be summed up in the phrase 'Lay it on thickly, then scrape it (almost) all off.' It is a painter's skill, and for the best results the work should be done by painters who are prepared to rub down and recoat several times, till perfection glints on every square foot of the topsides. Only on racing boats is it usual to fill the bottom.

Filler should not be asked to do the impossible, and should not be expected to fill hollows of more than $\frac{1}{16}$ of an inch deep. It should be applied and wiped off with enormously wide trowels, so that there is no chance of local hills or cavities. Frequently during the work the foreman should stand well forward, then well aft, and sight down the topsides to pick out defects.

Transoms

There is every reason for having a rounded transom. Curvature gives strength, vastly improves the appearance and is not hard to achieve. Just occasionally a Veed transom is seen. This shape for instance used to be popular for British Customs launches. It seems to have relatively little virtue, and looks odd to say the least. The larger the transom, the more important it is to round it, both for strength and looks. The amount of curvature need not be large, but anything less than about 1 in 9 is ineffective. On the other hand more than 1 in 5 is getting a bit 'apple-sterned'.

Some top quality builders of commercial craft edge their transoms with a solid round bar. The result is a very strong job which stands up to hard pounding which the stern receives. In locks and alongside docks the transom edge gets more thumping than any other part of the hull because a fender will not lie on a projecting edge. Fishermen in Scotland say that a major reason why they insist on having double-ended boats stems from this problem. They say a transom-sterned boat cannot take the hammering which occurs when a dozen of these boats are jostling alongside a fish quay.

After the transom has been erected, and the plating welded to the solid steel transom edging bar, a grinder is taken round if a yacht finish is wanted. The result is most attractive, and has the practical advantage that since there is no sharp edge the paint wears better. However for fast craft a rounded join between plating and transom is undesirable below the waterline. If the water is to flow away with the minimum resistance a sudden sharp cessation of the plating is necessary.

One or two horizontal stiffeners are needed to hold the transom to its curvature until it is welded to the plating, deck, stern, knee, etc. The top stiffener may take the form of the deck margin plate and the lower one is sometimes positioned for carrying the rudder. Normal transom stiffeners are vertical, and will probably be the same scantling as the main frames.

On stern trawlers and craft engaged in comparable work all the transom stiffeners, or most of them, will be put on the outside. They will be in the form of cope, which is solid half-round section bar, or they may be made of hollow half-round. They will protect the transom, and it will be essential that each one is carefully rounded at top and bottom, so that nothing can snag. Having the stiffness on the outside will tend to simplify the construction.

A sailing yacht may have the backstay chainplate extended down to form a transom stiffener. On some power yachts, and much less often on sailing yachts, there are steps on the transom. One popular arrangement is to have a wide step right across, well rounded at each end. It is convenient for getting from the dinghy to the parent yacht, for bathing and so on. Up the transom from it there may be a full-blooded ladder, or recessed steps, or individual folding steps. On any vessel some form of steps up the transom is a good safety precaution, because it can be very hard to get a man out of the water onto the deck without them.

Windows in the transom are well worth having, especially in a yacht where the aim should be to have a view all round from as

Fig. 27a A well-curved transom looks better than a flat one, and is less likely to be dented. To hold the transom to the correct curve while the boat is being built at least two transverse stiffeners are needed. The top one can double as the deck margin plate, and it will have to be cambered to the same curve as the deck. A flat bar stiffener under the margin plate is shown with its top edge cut to the camber curve, but the bottom edge is left straight to save work and to give extra strength at the centre.

many of the cabins as possible. They have the added advantage that they break up the over-large area of flat plating, and improve the appearance in almost every case. For safety these windows should be recessed. Where the transom is even moderately rounded there may be difficulty in arranging the windows because curved glass is expensive and hard to get. Perspex is not generally acceptable here because it scratches and crazes too easily, and is not easy to keep clean and clear.

The way round this dilemma is to make up a deep-section window frame to hold flat glass. The frame without the glass in is laid on the transom in its correct position, and a line drawn round it. Once the piece of steel has been cut out, the frame is put in place, almost entirely inboard, with the glass near the forward edge of the frame and hence well protected. The frame is then welded all round. The part which projects outboard can either be cut off flush, or cut parallel to the transom, leaving about $\frac{1}{2}$ inch standing proud all round. This technique is simple yet makes for strength, safety and ease of replacement of the glass.

Fit any decoration or lettering before erecting the transom. If this is left till the transom is in place, the work will have to be done on a vertical or overhanging surface, which is vastly more difficult.

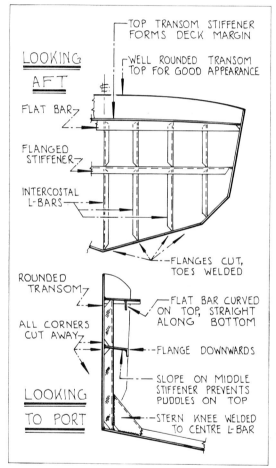

The mid-height transom stiffener does not need any camber, so it can be flanged, or stiffened with a welded flat bar. Its forward edge can be straight even though its aft edge must conform to the round of the transom.

The vertical transom stiffeners may be of flat bar or angle bar, and are shown here intercostal between the horizontal stiffeners. Two rows of welding should never meet if it is possible to avoid a junction, so the vertical stiffeners have their flanges cut back to be clear of the horizontal welds.

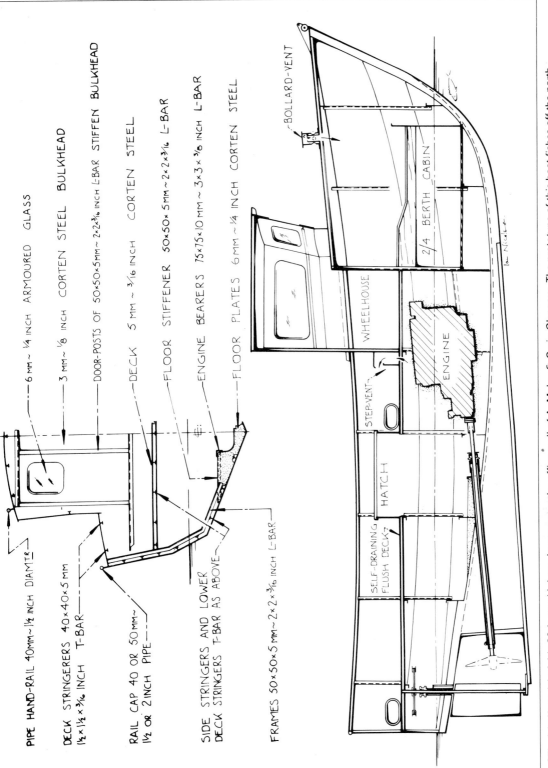

PIPE HAND-RAIL 40mm ~ 1½ INCH DIAMTR

DECK STRINGERERS 40×40×5 MM
1½ × 1½ × ³⁄₁₆ INCH T-BAR

RAIL CAP 40 OR 50mm ~
1½ OR 2 INCH PIPE

SIDE STRINGERS AND LOWER
DECK STRINGERS T-BAR AS ABOVE

FRAMES 50×50×5 MM ~ 2 × 2 × ³⁄₁₆ INCH L-BAR

6 MM ~ ¼ INCH ARMOURED GLASS

3 MM ~ ⅛ INCH CORTEN STEEL BULKHEAD

DOOR-POSTS OF 50×50×5MM ~ 2×2×³⁄₁₆ INCH L-BAR STIFFEN BULKHEAD

DECK 5 MM ~ ³⁄₁₆ INCH CORTEN STEEL

FLOOR STIFFENER 50×50× 5MM ~ 2×2×³⁄₁₆ L-BAR

ENGINE BEARERS 75×75×10 MM ~ 3×3×³⁄₈ INCH L-BAR

FLOOR PLATES 6MM ~ ¼ INCH CORTEN STEEL

BOLLARD-VENT

2/4 BERTH CABIN

WHEELHOUSE

STEP-VENT

ENGINE

SELF-DRAINING
FLUSH DECK

HATCH

Ian Nicolet

Fig. 27b A half model of this 30 ft. steel lobster boat graces the office wall of A. Mylne & Co in Glasgow. The prototype of this boat fishes off the north coast of Scotland in stormy waters. The same hull form can be used for a variety of jobs including different types of fishing, handling moorings, angling, as a fish farm tender, or yacht. The double chine hull is easily driven and also surprisingly easy to build thanks to the longitudinal T-bar framing. Unusual in a steel work boat is proper provision for ventilation both in the cabin and in the engine space. Another attractive feature of this style of boat is that she can be built with a relatively shallow draft simply by modifying the engine and stern gear arrangements. This typifies one of the great advantages of steel construction, namely its adaptability to different circumstances.

decks and beams

Beams

In some respects the beams are the most important part of a small steel ship. Steel will have been chosen for its strength, which will be particularly needed in locks and in similar places where groups of ships jostle together. A yacht for deep-water work needs good beam strength to withstand a heavy wave breaking on her. Since the deck has no appreciable curvature compared to the shell, it lacks the 'shape strength' of much of the hull. In addition the deck is pierced by hatches, the cockpit, it is cut away for the cabin top, and is generally less able to contribute to the resistance of massive waves than the hull plating.

All this is recognised in Lloyd's rules which call for beams to be heavier than the frames. In practice many small craft builders use the same extrusions for the beams as they do for the framing. This is to simplify steel purchasing and stocking in the steel store. An obvious exception occurs when flat bar frames are used, with a wood deck having no under-deck of steel. Here the beams must be L-bar, to take the deck fastenings. In this case it is worth trying to get unequal angle L-bar, using the small flange horizontally to take the fastenings and the stronger flange vertically. Weight is saved high up, and the cost reduced marginally.

Just occasionally wood beams are used. If they carry a ply deck, then no lining is needed. The beams are painted before being fitted, and the deck is also painted on the underside before being laid. Since at most only the final coat has to be painted on, time is saved. Even that may not be needed if true skill is being used. This saves all those paint drips which have to be cleaned off, apart from all the protective covers which must be laid everywhere to guard against paint splashes. The beam ends are bolted

Fig. 28 Section view. Wood beams mean that no under-deck lining is needed. The joining of the wood beams to the steel work calls for care and skill, but sealing the teak down onto the ply is an even more difficult job to do well. If the teak does not bed thoroughly on the ply then water will percolate into the gap. In frosty weather the teak will be lifted and rot usually occurs in the ply.

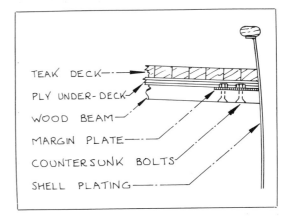

through the deck stringer plate, two bolts each end being needed as a minimum. This wood beam technique is likely to grow in popularity as builders come to realise how expensive it is fitting lining overhead.

The normal procedure is to have a beam at every frame. However where the frames are widely spaced and used in conjunction with multiple stringers, there must either be more beams than frames, or an arrangement of deck stringers. This is similar to the topsides framing. There must be deep strong beams to carry the lighter fore-and-aft deck stringers, which will be quickly fitted since they will bend to the sheer, whereas the beams need shaping to the camber.

Normally the beams will be part of the floor-frame-beam hoops which are made up before plating begins. Where this is not so, it may be possible to weld some of the beams to the steel decking before laying the decking. This has the advantage that the welding will be down-hand. It can be followed by partial painting. These beams will not be carried right to the deck edge, but will be joined to their frames, or to the topsides if they are not close to frames, by brackets. This idea is particularly attractive for the intermediate beams, where there are twice as many beams as frames. This situation may arise where headroom is limited. In order to keep the beam depth to a minimum, and hence the headroom to a maximum, some builders fit numerous light beams which have a small moulded depth.

Where beams and half-beams are spaced closely it is common practice to have no beam brackets on ships of up to 50 feet or more. The full weld between frame and beam is immensely strong, especially if backed by two or three bulkheads. An intermediate stage is to fit a few

brackets, usually at the ends of cabin tops and at the fore and aft ends of major openings like holds and big hatches.

Brackets may be made of triangles of plate, or short lengths of flat bar. The plate brackets are not usually flanged, but the best builders weld all round both sides of all bracket joins. Not often seen is the use of L-bar brackets, yet they make a lot of sense. They are quickly made, cropped from off-cuts of frame and beam material. They should be no heavier but stronger than unflanged triangular plates, and they should be cheaper to make than plate brackets.

When building a big light yacht, it is not uncommon to find that the deck has a tendency to be limber, due to the flexing of the long beams. This situation is especially prevalent on big motor cruisers, which these days have so much beam. If, as often happens, the owner is demanding an above-average speed, the designer has to reduce the weight of the scantlings to minimize the final displacement. One result is that those magnificent open aft decks seen at fashionable yachting centres are

Fig. 29 Deck edge construction of the 53 ft NERC research ship for South Georgia. Because the frames and beams are stopped short slightly, they are easier to make and fit.

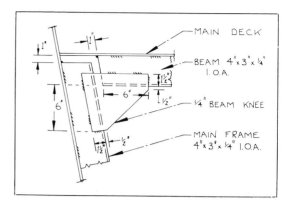

not truly rigid. Beneath there is generally a big aft cabin, whereas forward there are smaller cabins with more bulkheads. The bulkheads give the beams lots of support, and so the flexing is less noticeable.

One way round this problem is to fit pillars. But an owner who has spent £90,000 or double or triple that sum does not want pillars down the middle of his styled bridal suite. An ingenious way round this dilemma is to make the beds into four-posters, and carry the posts up to deck level, where they are fastened to beams. To be sure, these posts will be well outboard, but they reduce the length of unsupported beam substantially and do not spoil that sense of spaciousness in the cabin.

On sailing yachts of any size a comparable problem is met, but here the solution is often easier because owners, if they are experienced, do not want wide open spaces which are dangerous in a seaway because there is nothing to hold on to. Pillars in the centre of the saloon are usually acceptable, especially if they are kept fairly thin, and support the cabin table.

Beam support

Since it is all too clear that the weakness of every beam is its long unsupported length, cunning should be used to reduce the free span of most of the beams. In boats over about 45 feet there is a special reason for this. Boats of this size and bigger cannot normally use the same section for the frames and the beams. This means that relatively small quantities have to be bought of two different sizes of bar, whereas the aim must always be to keep down diversity.

Where there are fore and aft bulkheads, even though these are very light, maybe of only $\frac{3}{16}$ inch ply in an extreme case, the supports for

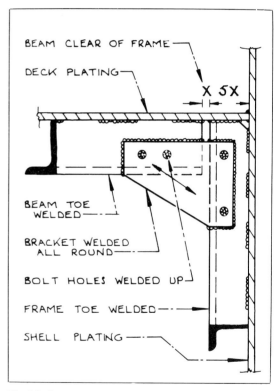

Fig. 30 Section view. Small craft over 50 ft regularly follow big ship practice. The frame and beam are bolted to the bracket before being set up. If either are unfair in relation to their neighbour, they can easily be adjusted. Once fairing up is complete the bracket is fully welded, including at the bolt holes. This not only gives great strength, it also minimises corrosion.

the bulkhead may be pillars extending from the beam to the frame or floor. These pillars need not run down the centreline of the ship: the aim is to reduce the length of beam without support.

Where the space right outboard under the deckhead is not used it does not matter if the beam brackets are large. No one wants to put in enormous plate brackets, and it will be better to use angle-bar, with the top end as far inboard as possible.

Beam camber

A flat uncambered deck is seldom acceptable on any craft. Camber not only adds strength by virtue of its curvature, it improves the appearance, speeds up the drainage of water off the deck, and gives a little extra headroom without raising the sheer.

Normal camber is the arc of a circle. If this is changed to a parabola with straight sides, the side deck beams will be straight. This will result in a useful saving of time. On frigates and similar craft the camber is made up of three straight lines: the middle third is a horizontal line, and the outer thirds are straight lines sloping to the sheer. This configuration is adopted for economy and ease of repair. It does not look too offensive on frigates because they have long deckhouses, with a great deal of paraphernalia over the remaining deck area. If this idea is followed then it is worth taking some trouble to round the top of the transom bulwark, so that the knuckles in the camber cannot be detected from aft. If a curvaceous breakwater or even a pair of them — a low forward one and a higher main one — sweep over the foredeck then the knuckle sheer should be hard to detect even for an expert.

Stiffening set on top of the deck

This type of deck stiffening is seldom seen, probably because there are still influences of traditional wood shipbuilding in most steel yards. Many designers of small craft have learned their basic craft first in wood, or maybe in fibreglass, so that a technique which is particularly suitable for use on steel decks is likely to be relatively unknown, or maybe less trusted.

Deck stiffness is a special problem for the size of craft we are considering. In every case, with a negligible proportion of exceptions, headroom will be a constant worry during the design stages. This will encourage the cutting of beam depth to a minimum, yet there is a limit to how much this can be done, even with pillars. If a way can be found of spreading deck loads over a lot of beams the battle is half won. Intercostals between the beams are part of the answer, but to be fully effective they need full continuous welding which is not convenient as it will normally all be up-hand. Some longitudinal stiffeners can be welded to the underside of the deck before the deck is fitted.

By putting the stringers on top of the deck the required stiffness is achieved in the simplest possible way. Naturally no owner is going to accept massive angle-bars wandering down the middle of the deck. But toe rails set inboard are a different story. They will have solid round rod or tubular tops, fully welded. The toe rails themselves will be fully welded to the deck for maximum strength, with just a few scuppers which will be located towards the ends of the deck where the break in strength will be acceptable.

Toe rails are not the ideal solution because they cannot be located very far in from the

Fig. 31 This simple deck edge treatment is used by Yarrows on the frigates they build. The deck toe rail or spurnwater is bolted through the steel deck and looks very neat with dowelled bolts. Where it is discontinued, to let water run off the deck, there are rubber tongues extending clear of the topsides so that water drips clear of the hull plating and does not leave dirt marks on the topsides. These rubber 'gargoyles', being fully flexible, are not damaged when the ship comes alongside.

Warships have to be wetted all over to minimise the effect of nuclear fallout, and so cannot normally have spurnwaters. However if a ship fitted with the Yarrow type is at sea when war commences the wooden spurnwaters are easily chipped away.

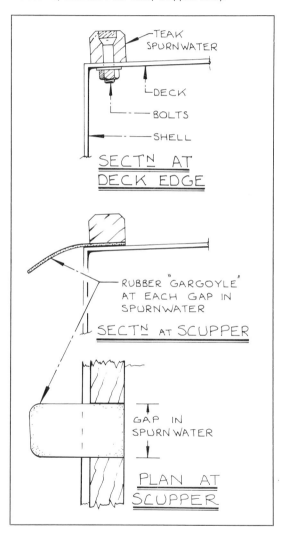

deck edge, nor can they be very high. Anything over 3 or 4 inches high on a 60-footer will look odd.

Where the strength is needed on a foredeck it can be gained by welding on one, and occasionally two, breakwaters. These are just the job, as they are by nature deep, with some form of stiffening flange such as a tube or solid round rod along the top. Breakwaters extend diagonally from the centreline to the deck edge, so if they are well and truly part of the deck structure they contribute handsomely to the stiffness.

Breakwaters have a limited use. They cannot be scattered about an aft deck without raising some sceptical eyebrows, not to say cynical laughs. But hatches can be used instead. The side coamings of hatches will generally be deep and strong. They can be carried forward to form deck boxes, or casings for Calor gas cylinders, or to form a mast tabernacle with integral ventilators, or some such. On a fishing boat the fish pens may be made from say 18 inch deep plating, suitably edged along the top. If the fore and aft sides of the pens are made permanent, well welded to the deck, and the athwartships sides are portable for easy deck washing, we end up with the deck stiffening we need, yet with no objectionable obstructions to frustrate cleaning up after gutting sessions.

Where possible these fore and aft on-deck stringers ought to extend to, and beyond, bulkheads for maximum effect.

Where the deck is mainly of wood, the stringers may be welded to the centreline deck stringer plate or to the deck edge stringer plate. Where the deck is laid in the traditional fashion, with planks swept to match the sheer, there should not be much extra work with these on-deck stiffeners. But where the deck is of ply, there will be extra edge seams when comparing the situation with a conventional deck.

Deck fairness

For yachts, directors' launches and similar craft where pride of ownership and prestige are concerned, it is essential that the decks be absolutely fair. This type of craft will normally have a teak deck, so at first sight the building procedure will be as follows. Erect frames and beams. Plate up. Fit deck sheer plates, centre-line deck plates, margin plates round hatchways etc. Lay teak deck. (This is of course an abbreviated list.) Examining this schedule, it is obvious that once the frames and beams are erected, they must be very carefully faired. It will be usual to have the frames and beams set up as complete 'hoops' welded together. If a beam stands too high, the way to fair it is to hammer it down; but this will spread the frames on the end of that particular beam, making them unfair. If the beam is low it is easy enough, if a bit tedious, to pack it up, as there will normally have to be packing on top of each flat beam flange, to bring the underside of the deck planks flush with those planks which rest on the margin and centreline steel plates.

A radically different approach is worth considering, namely the fitting of an overall steel deck sheathed in teak. The teak will of course be far thinner than if there was no overall steel deck. Now beam fairing is vastly easier. Beam flanges need not be packed up with tapered wood slivers. All the beams will be either flat bar on edge or a toe-welded angle-bar with the horizontal flange at the bottom. Life is now simpler since the part of

Fig. 32 Section view. There are dozens of ways of finishing off the deck edge. This one is seen on all types of yachts and commercial craft. It is not the 'highest yacht standard' because that would mean a teak rail cap. But it is a practical arrangement, with the rubbing strake made from the 1 m lengths of special bar popular in Holland.

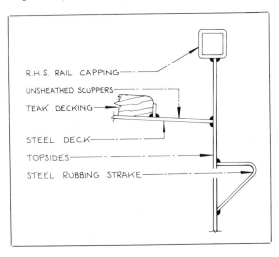

the beam which stands high or low is a vertical flange edge. If it is too high it is ground down. If it is too low the steel deck is laid on top and the gap is filled with a continuous weld. In any case the gap will not be large, because prestigious ships are not built by people who allow large gaps. The deck plating must be held level while it is being welded, or it may tend to pull down onto the beam. But this is no problem. Just insert steel wedges between beam and deck plate to maintain the distance while the weld is made.

All-steel deck versus wood deck
The strength factor

Wood deck planks are not physically joined to each other. They gain a certain amount of mutual support because they are jammed against each other, and the caulking acts like a long continuous wedge. As a result the beams are not helped much by the wood decking. Also the wood is fairly flexy, so that when a load comes on one beam, the decking

Fig. 33 Plan view. Where a curved coaming meets a straight one there would normally be a tapered deck plank. This form of 'sniped' end is bad, often resulting in splits. In this case big ship practice has been followed and a steel filler plate has been substituted. The deck planks end against a margin plank running athwartships so that the maximum number of end grain plank edges can be caulked easily. This layout is also the smartest.

does not transmit the load to the adjacent beams completely effectively. In short, from a strength point of view each beam is taken on its own.

A steel deck, with toe-welded angle-bar, is rather different. Provided the welding is sufficiently continuous, and there is a lot of evidence that it should be 50 per cent of the length, both sides, then the deck combines with the beam to form a strong homogeneous whole. In effect each beam becomes a channel on edge, the web being formed by the vertical flange, the bottom flange forming one side of the channel and the deck the other side.

When calculating the beam strength there are various views and techniques. Probably a good average consists of assuming that only half the deck, up to the next beam should be taken as the upper flange of the channel. Thus, when calculating the beam strength, if the beam spacing is 16 inches and deck thickness $\frac{3}{16}$ inch, the upper flange is taken as 8 inches × $\frac{3}{16}$ inch. In the context of the boats we are discussing, that is a very strong flange indeed. The beam's bottom flange is likely to be in the region of only 2 or 3 inches × $\frac{1}{4}$ inch or $\frac{3}{8}$ inch.

Where local stiffening is needed the steel deck is easily braced. Intercostals between the beams can be welded both to the deck and to the beams, so that again we gain a big advantage in modulus.

The headroom factor

If a deck is all steel, then the beams will be angle-bar toe-welded to the deck. As the flange is at the bottom and the steel deck forms another flange — in effect to each beam — the beams can be much lighter. The gain in headroom is achieved because the steel deck needs a much shallower beam. On a 60-footer

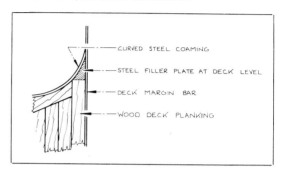

the beams on a steel-decked craft may be $1\frac{1}{2}$ inches less than on a wood-decked ship. Of course the wood-decked ship can have a bulb angle, to give the beam greater strength for a given depth, but in the sizes we are considering bulb angles are seldom found. Besides the bulb is not as massive as the bottom flange of an angle-bar, toe-welded.

An approach which does not seem to be much used is to specify channel for the beams of a wood-decked boat. With the deck bolted to the top flange, the bottom flange would give the equivalent strength to a toe-welded angle-bar. Drilling the bolt holes must be done from above because from below it would first be necessary to drill through the lower flange before getting to the upper flange.

Plywood decking

Only the best marine ply should be used, when it is specified for decking. It should be to British Specification 1088, and this qualification must be seen stamped on each sheet.

$\frac{3}{8}$ inch thickness

This is the thinnest practical material, and should be used on cabin tops of small light racing yachts. Beams are needed which do not give a gap of unsupported deck of more than 10 inches, i.e. 1 inch wide flanges with the beams at 11 inches is the maximum. It helps a lot if the cabin top is well rounded, to give curvature strength.

This thickness might also be used on the foredeck of a half-decked boat, especially if there is a raised king plank to act as a centre-line fore-and-aft stringer, together with inboard toe rails to act as extra fore-and-aft stringers.

$\frac{1}{2}$ inch thickness

This is normally the thinnest ply used. The thinnest Lloyd's allow is $\frac{9}{16}$ inch, on boats 20 feet long. This thickness will not dip when a heavy man treads on it provided the gap between beams is 13 inches or less. It is suitable for the main decks of racing yachts up to about 44 feet, long, though of course such a boat would be considered extremely lightly decked by most standards. It is suitable for the deckhead of a wheelhouse assuming this area gets little traffic (see notes about scantlings near compasses on page 123), but would not be used normally on deckheads of boats much over 50 feet.

Half inch ply is too thin for screwing up-wards through a steel beam flange, but it is suitable for use under a $\frac{3}{4}$ inch or $\frac{1}{2}$ inch layer of teak on boats up to about 45 feet.

$\frac{5}{8}$ inch thickness

This thickness is to be preferred for many of the jobs which $\frac{1}{2}$ inch ply will just about cope with. Though an extra $\frac{1}{8}$ inch seems very little, it is an increase of 25 per cent. It is still too thin for screwing upwards, since a $\frac{5}{8}$ inch screw through a $\frac{1}{8}$ inch beam flange will only go $\frac{1}{2}$ inch into the wood, and this means there will be very little useful grip, even using 12 gauge screws.

$\frac{3}{4}$ inch thickness

Lloyd's specify $\frac{21}{32}$ inch for yachts up to 40 feet in length, so one might use $\frac{3}{4}$ inch ply on racing yachts up to 50 feet overall. On ocean cruisers up to about 36 feet this is a good thickness, since it should be able to stand up to total capsize and heavy seas breaking aboard. This is also a sensible minimum thickness for commercial craft. Screws get a fair grip in this, though bolts are much better. A compromise towards economy, clean decks and quick building might consist of a mixture of bolts and screws. With $\frac{1}{2}$ inch teak on top this would be a suitable deck for craft up to 60 feet for light duties. Lloyd's call for $\frac{15}{16}$ inch decking but allow this to be 12 per cent lighter if teak is used, on craft up to 60 feet. (A 12 per cent reduction applies not only to teak, but to other hard woods having a density of 45 lbs per cubic foot.)

A layer of $\frac{3}{4}$ inch ply with $\frac{3}{4}$ inch hard wood on top makes a good deck for many commercial craft, up to 50 feet, but not for fishing boats, which need very special super-substantial decks.

$\frac{7}{8}$ inch thickness

This is suitable for racing yachts up to about 60 feet, and cruising yachts up to around 52 feet, but for ocean cruisers this would not be used on craft over 45 feet.

Ply decking techniques

To speed up decking in ply, and make the work simpler, the material is bought scarphed up in long lengths. In theory there is no limit to the length which the ply manufacturers will supply. Their machinery is designed to make pieces 8 feet × 4 feet (very occasionally 5 feet) wide. These standard sections are scarphed into long lengths only if the buyer makes a special request, and there can be delays. Also, once the scarph has been made the ply has to be re-sanded, and so there is a minute loss of thickness, which in most cases is not significant. However, where a ship is being built under Lloyd's or similar supervision, if the ply is already about 1 mm under the required size, this extra thinning down may result in the ply being rejected by the surveyor.

Ply manufacturers will use different scarph slopes, so that slightly different amounts of each sheet will be used for the scarph. As a result, the ply should be ordered to 'safe' lengths. If two 8 foot pieces are scarphed together the result will be at least 15 feet 6 inches, even with 1 inch ply. In practice three 8 feet sections $\frac{5}{8}$ inch thick scarphed together are about as much as two men can handle, and even three people will find this size is bordering on the over-awkward. Under special circumstances I have personally handled lengths 43 feet long with only one man to help, but we were going to very special lengths to avoid scarphing or butting on the job. When long lengths have to be handled overhead lifting gear is a great help.

Scarphs made in the factory are smooth and undetectable after painting, whereas only a good shipwright can achieve a comparable standard. Also he will take perhaps two hours or more on the job — what with mixing glue and so on — and in a properly equipped factory costs should be lower.

The whole point about ply decking, as opposed to conventional planked decking, is that it does not leak. But the seams and butts need careful making if there is to be absolute watertightness. It will seldom be satisfactory to butt the ply on a beam flange, since these are too narrow for two rows of fastenings well in from the edge of the ply. An alternative is to have steel stringers under each seam, but as a main reason for having ply decking is to save weight steel stringers are not popular. One technique is to put the ply down in two layers with butts and seams staggered. There is a theoretical weakness at the intersection of each butt over the seam below, and vice versa. However if the gluing is thorough, and the edges of each ply panel are glued, there should be no trouble.

This method of decking only works if the ply layers are well fastened together. During laying and gluing ample weights must be laid on the upper panels, to force them down on the lower layer. Where numerous weights are not available, sandbags make a reasonable substitute if used very liberally.

This double layer is particularly useful where a thick deck is needed. In some areas it is difficult to get ply over $\frac{7}{8}$ inch, and almost everywhere the top limit is 1 inch. A few manufacturers will bond layers together to make up thick ply, but there tends to be a long wait for this (as there often is for factory scarphing).

Another way to join the ply panels is with ply butt straps under the deck. These should be amply wide: *at least* twenty-five times the ply thickness is not a bad rule of thumb. To avoid having the edges of the butt straps showing, it is worth running each strap from beam to beam. This disguises the fact that there are butt straps, and altogether makes a neat job.

There must be well staggered fastenings through the butt strap: two rows staggered each side of the butt, except perhaps on small unstressed boats, where a single line each side is occasionally acceptable.

Ply edges are vulnerable and must be sealed. Herein lies a snag. If the edging is not perfect there will be a thin gap which will harbour water, and the last state will be worse than the first. Better an uncovered edge, which will dry out when the deck dries, than one which always has a little puddle lodging against it. If this puddle freezes, trouble follows.

The edging may take the form of a toe rail or a steel flat bar edge welded. If the latter, then the bar must be fitted first, and the ply laid tightly against it. Caulking between the steel upstand and the ply will usually be required. Alternatively the ply can be machined or planed along the edge to form a mouthing to take one of the modern deck glues. These compounds are not truly glues at all, but are rubbery compositions which are made by mixing two ingredients. A chemical action follows, not too fast, so that the liquid can be poured into the seam before hardening takes place. The result is a flexible sealer which takes care of movement of the boat's structure, changes of weather, the expansion of the decking and so on. These synthetic glues bond onto each side of the seam wonderfully and are much better than the traditional type of deck glue. They are sold by manufacturers of marine paints.

Screws into ply from below

These should be spaced at 6 inches or less along every beam and all round the edge. This is far below common practice, but in this department of shipbuilding, a standard practice is sadly lacking. Round-headed screws are used, and it is possible (in Holland at least) to get special nylon washers which are lipped especially for this job. The hole in the beam is drilled oversize as far as the screw is concerned. The washer insulates the shank of the screw

from the beam, as well as the underside of the head of the screw. This washer minimizes electrolytic action between the screw and the beam.

Very careful drilling prevents oversize holes being made. The only way to get exact holes is to have a stop put on the drill to prevent it going in too far.

Deck sheathing compositions

There are various chemical mixtures which are trowelled on decks, instead of using a wood sheathing. The work can be done by the builder, but it is more usual to call in specialist firms who are to be found at all the major and some minor shipbuilding centres. For instance Rowan and Boden Ltd of Paisley, Scotland have ten branches scattered over the British Isles.

At the design stage it is necessary to consult the suppliers of the material, because the various compositions have different weights, go on in different thicknesses, and have different insulating properties. Some of these sheathings are particularly good for weather decks, others better for covering tank tops which form cabin soles, and so on.

There is Airadek which is laid on $1\frac{1}{4}$ inch thick as a substitute for timber sheathing, and is half the weight of the wood it replaces. It bonds to the steel so that it prevents corrosion. As the sheathing is laid section by section, any damage caused to one part will not result in water penetrating all over the deck. In practice these sheathing compounds are tough, some quite incredibly so, others just thoroughly adequate. This particular compound is available coloured red, green or grey. It never needs painting, though it should be treated with a sealer twice a year, or once a year on yachts which are used for a summer season only. This sheathing can be repaired if it is damaged, it will not burn and its surface is not slippery whether wet or dry. As a square foot of this covering weighs $5\frac{1}{2}$ lbs, it does not add much to the top weight.

There are various sheathing formulae for use on cabin soles. Some may be laid over fuel tanks, others are no good for this job. They are intended to go under lino, vinyl flooring, carpets and so on, partly to cover unevenness in the steel surface, partly for insulation. Other assets are their resistance to corrosion and fire.

These various sheathings are laid much more quickly than a wood deck, though of course there is some drying time, when it is fatal to walk on the unhardened compound. Prices vary a lot, but a saving of 50 per cent of a comparable wood deck is sometimes possible.

The saving will be most where the deck has the greatest number of steps, bolt heads and obstructions. One advantage of a compound sheathing is that the deck can be clincher laid, so that time is saved fitting the deck plates precisely. At each clincher 'land' there will be a double plate thickness, which acts as a stringer, and this can be valuable where the beam spacing is slightly too large.

It is fairly easy to compromise between the attractiveness of a teak laid sheathing and a composition sheathing by having half of each. The strategic areas where the deck shows most are teak covered, the others have a composition covering. A particularly ingenious way to do this on a yacht is to have a breakwater forward. The aft deck and side decks are teak, but composition is put on ahead of the breakwater. From most positions on deck and in the deckhouse it will be impossible to see the composition.

Moored up stern to the quay, as most boats are in the Mediterranean, the whole deck will seem to be teak sheathed. Another approach, more difficult to pull off successfully, is to have the centre part of the deck and the other areas which are most often walked over in teak. Under the boats can be composition. A yacht with paid hands may have canvas runners laid on the composition.

Composition will adhere to aluminium alloy, so that where there is a light alloy deckhouse that top may be covered by one of these synthetic deckings.

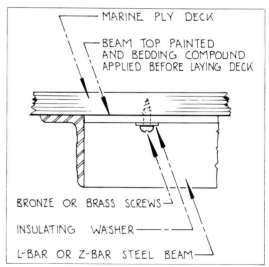

Fig. 33a One of the best ways to save weight in a steel boat is to fit a wood deck, Marine ply is quickly laid, usually screwed up from below, using round-headed screws to save the work of countersinking the horizontal flange of the beam.

The screws should almost extend to the top of the ply and the wood will need some form of protection, especially if the boat is used commercially, to prevent the top laminate from being worn away with use.

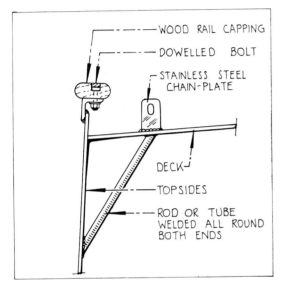

WOOD RAIL CAPPING

DOWELLED BOLT

STAINLESS STEEL
CHAIN-PLATE

DECK

TOPSIDES

ROD OR TUBE
WELDED ALL ROUND
BOTH ENDS

Fig. 33b Parts subject to wear such as chain-plates and bollards are best made of marine grade stainless steel, such as EN 58J. This is an expensive material, so only the minimum amount is bought. To stiffen the deck a round bar or tube works well and has no sharp edges to hurt the crew, or 'throw' paint.

The sheer is shown capped with an angle-bar for strength. Even if the sheer plate has been badly trimmed the angle-bar gives a neat sweeping sheer, though of course it cannot disguise serious mistakes in the sheer line.

Hardwood, ideally teak, is used to cap the rail, and there must be plenty of paint and bedding under the wood to prevent rust. Even so, after years of use the wood may need removing to clean up the top of the angle-bar and repaint it.

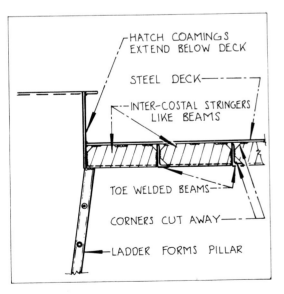

HATCH COAMINGS
EXTEND BELOW DECK

STEEL DECK

INTER-COSTAL STRINGERS
LIKE BEAMS

TOE WELDED BEAMS

CORNERS CUT AWAY

LADDER FORMS PILLAR

Fig. 33c A steel deck is supported by beams which are usually of angle-bar, toe welded. Between them stringers are made intercostal, often of the same size bar as the beams. These intercostal bars have their corners cropped so that there is no meeting of welds. The ends of the intercostals should be welded right round.

To stiffen the deck edge the hatch coamings are carried down to the same depth below the deck as the bottom flange of the beams, so the horizontal flange of the stringer bars can be welded to the coamings.

To save money, time and space the ladder associated with the hatch is made to do the work of a pillar. It is usual to locate a pillar at the junction of a beam and stringer.

deckhouses and cabin tops

General design considerations

As with other parts of the ship, the deckhouses and cabin tops are not so different in steel as in other materials.

Deck structures influence the appearance of a ship very much. When she lies alongside, in many situations only the deckhouses can be clearly seen. They should be sweetly shaped, which is the opposite of 'styled'. It is better to set a rectangular box on deck than to copy vehicle design features and fashions. One essential qualification of a car shape is that it should look dated within 24 months of being foisted on a public punch-drunk with advertising. Naval architecture succeeds when a design continues to look right, seaworthy and seakindly, from all angles, in all weathers, for fifty years.

As a rule deckhouse and cabin top sides should lie in. If in doubt, 8° off the vertical is a good angle. Anything less is a bit too fine to discern. For a boat which must stand all kinds of weather, up to 16° may make sense as it gives some triangulation. For a sailing yacht, where the aim will be to feed the air-flow smoothly up to the sails, 30° might be considered.

Avoid streamlining the fore and aft ends, because it merely wastes space. It either takes away useful deck area or it makes the internal space short of headroom towards the end of the deckhouse or cabin top. It is also a signal to the knowledgeable that the designer thinks, very wrongly, that he can cut down the ship's windage by this arrangement. To avoid a monotonous appearance the rake of the fore end should not be the same as the aft end. (Which rakes more and by how much is a matter of taste.) It is also something of a 'signature', so that it is possible to guess the designer just by

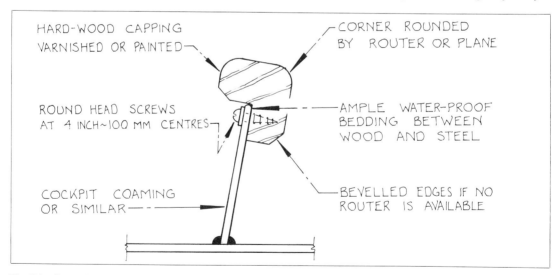

HARD-WOOD CAPPING VARNISHED OR PAINTED

CORNER ROUNDED BY ROUTER OR PLANE

ROUND HEAD SCREWS AT 4 INCH~100 MM CENTRES

AMPLE WATER-PROOF BEDDING BETWEEN WOOD AND STEEL

COCKPIT COAMING OR SIMILAR

BEVELLED EDGES IF NO ROUTER IS AVAILABLE

Fig. 34a Generally wood capping is not used except on yachts and high quality craft which are not subject to severe wear. Varnished hardwood, preferably teak, adds a lot to the appearance of a boat but it is often best to make the wood fairly easily detachable so that it can be taken off for painting or varnishing. The screws or bolts have to be arranged so that they are accessible and they should be non-ferrous. This sketch shows a typical cockpit coaming or toe-rail or even a handrail along a cabin top.

Deckhouses and cabin tops

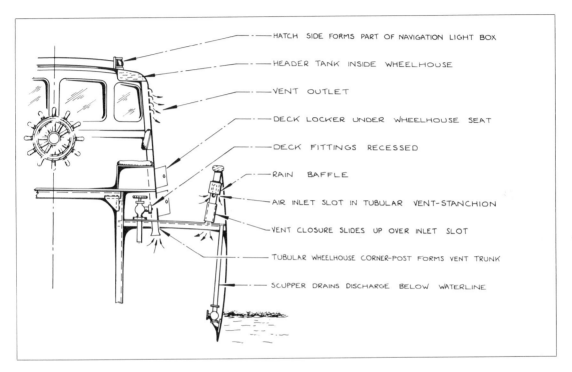

HATCH SIDE FORMS PART OF NAVIGATION LIGHT BOX

HEADER TANK INSIDE WHEELHOUSE

VENT OUTLET

DECK LOCKER UNDER WHEELHOUSE SEAT

DECK FITTINGS RECESSED

RAIN BAFFLE

AIR INLET SLOT IN TUBULAR VENT-STANCHION

VENT CLOSURE SLIDES UP OVER INLET SLOT

TUBULAR WHEELHOUSE CORNER-POST FORMS VENT TRUNK

SCUPPER DRAINS DISCHARGE BELOW WATERLINE

Fig. 34b A clean appearance gives multiple dividends. It makes the boat look modern, simplifies fitting out, maintenance and painting. It also cuts down the number of traps for dirt. The designer should make sure rain and spray, washing down the ship, do not leave dirty runnels or rust streaks. This is achieved by proper guttering, scuppers and the like. (On many naval vessels guttering is not fitted because they must be easily wetted all over to minimise the results of radioactive fallout.)

The smooth look is very much in fashion, partly because of the influence of industrial designers and partly because fibreglass is so much used for small craft. When building in steel the designer has to use the materials subtly to outbid fibreglass builders, so he must follow, or better still, improve upon the good appearance of their best products.

This sketch shows some ideas following this theme. Wherever possible fittings are grouped together into one component. Excrescences sticking out of the top of deckhouses, apart from giving a cluttered appearance, can be more expensive than integral equipment. For instance it may not be necessary to make up a navigation light box at all if the lights can be lodged alongside the semi-portable hatch in the top of the wheelhouse. (This is fitted for lifting out the machinery.) The internal header tank follows the same general idea and incidentally is less likely to result in a freeze-up in cold weather, or tepid water in hot climates.

Ventilators, which are so important, are also obtrusive. The idea of using the bulwark stanchions as ventilators has several merits, not least being the saving of labour and material. The ventilator shown is a simple tube with a slot near the top in the aft face to let the air in. To keep out rain and spray there is a larger tube over the vent slot. In very bad weather a close fitting sleeve is pushed up the vent tube to engage a clip and close the inlet. Water from bulwark scuppers can soil the topsides, so here large clog-free drains carry deck water overboard below the waterline.

studying these tell-tale rakes, though other confirming factors are needed.

For the best appearance a cabin top or deckhouse should not have a straight flat side. There should be harmony between the sweep of the deck structure and the sheer line, but they need not be parallel. One trouble this throws up is that the cabin top deck is likely to end up with curvature in two directions. However if curvature is kept to a minimum fore and aft, it is unlikely that the cabin top decking plates or ply will need much coaxing to the correct shape.

The top edges of deck structures may be of tube or rod, like chines. The same scantlings are sometimes used as corner posts, but if they are chosen, then they should not be left exposed to view inside in a good quality ship. The various sections used on other parts of the ship apply with suitable modifications to deck structures. For instance external stiffeners may be fitted in the form of handrails or lifebuoy brackets.

The 'total window' look

Modern design tends towards directing the maximum amount of daylight into a deckhouse or cabin. This demands the biggest area of windows and ports, which conflicts with seaworthiness. As any opening or area of glass or Perspex must be considered a relative weakness, the two requirements have to be reconciled.

On craft which are not expected to withstand the worst the weather can do, it is possible to make the whole of the upper part of a wheelhouse of glass or Perspex, apart from a few pillars. The effect can be very attractive from within and without. It is delightful as well as highly practical to be able to see through 360° from inside the deckhouse. On a tug, for instance, this facility is a great safety factor.

From outboard the whole vessel can be made to look longer, lower, sleeker. Where a short length of steel structure is unavoidable, it can sometimes be set inside a window. Apart from dead abeam, the eye will not pick up the structure, especially if there is a strong light reflection on the pane of glass outboard of it. The result is smart, clean-looking and practical, since the glass needs little maintenance. Incidentally this idea of 'total windows' all round may save some top weight, especially if part of the windowing is in Perspex.

It may also save money, if it is done with careful planning. For instance, if the windows are ordered as complete frames in single units for each side, then only the corner posts and inner pillars are needed from the level of the window bottoms upwards at each side. This presupposes that the wheelhouse door is at the aft end, which is no bad thing. Doors which open onto side decks too often leak in strong cross winds and can be hard to open in gale conditions even on moorings.

Rounded deckhouse corners

Every designer aims at producing a ship with a smart and 'finished' appearance. He will almost certainly want to have the corners – the vertical edges – of all his deck structures rounded, to make his current work modern looking. Then he may have doubts. Is he pandering to his own pride, prejudices, reputation and professional advancement? In passing, the designer who does not do everything to enhance these qualities soon becomes nothing more than a hack draughtsman, or worse. In practice, rounded deckhouse edges are much to be encouraged from almost every point of view.

They give 'curvature strength', round the full

curve, which means that the first stiffeners can be spread further from the corner. This, with the omission of an angle-bar at the corner, results in weight saving. The rounded edge is much less likely to have its paint chipped, and indeed from a maintenance point of view is much better. Painting inside an acute angle is seldom satisfactory.

The rounded edge gives both a feeling and an actual increase of deck space. If the side decks are a bit restricted rounding is doubly valuable. A rounded edge is important where warps, wires and nets have to be worked fore and aft. A sharp edge will tend to chafe or cut through whereas the rounded edge will ease the rope past.

Around the compass area

As normal mild steel, such as is used for construction, is magnetic, it will affect the compass. To get over this problem the structure and details in the compass area are made non-magnetic. On tugs and fishing boats the compass is often an overhead one. It is set on top of the wheelhouse, and the card is seen through a mirror or prism by the helmsman below.

The deckhead of the wheelhouse is sometimes made of aluminium alloy. The same material must be used for the beams and the wheelhouse front. At the design stage it is a good idea to put the compass in early, and draw a circle in plan, elevation and section view. The circle will be the 'contamination zone' and it will probably have a radius of about 9 feet. Everything within this radius must be non-magnetic, including small items like bolts and hinges. It may be necessary to move bridge ladders or the mast, or change the materials of the guard rails, since

the compass position is dominated by the location of the steering wheel and can normally only be sited in one exact position.

Partly because of expense, and partly because of the difficulty of getting light alloy plates and beams, some builders are using non-magnetic steel for the wheelhouse area round the compass. It costs more than mild steel, but nothing like the astronomical cost of light alloy. When light alloy is selected, it may be used for the whole of the deckhouse, to save top weight.

A builder with limited facilities could do worse than use wood beams and ply for the decking. Both are so easily obtainable, and even if no wood workers are available, this small amount of work will not be difficult to sub-contract. Wood has the advantage of being light, cheap and easily worked.

On sailing yachts the compass problem can be awkward. One type of compass has a prism for magnifying the figures as they swing opposite the lubber line. This compass is intended to be read by a helmsman several feet away, and is just what is wanted here. The compass is mounted on the cover over the forward end of the main hatch, where it should be safe from the rough and tumble of tacking and gybing in the cockpit. The cabin top can be made of ply since this material bends easily round the normal deck camber. Marine ply is available in thicknesses from $\frac{3}{16}$ to 1 inch, so that if the cabin top has a heavy camber, the builder can always put on two or three layers of ply instead of one thicker lamination.

Non-ferrous cabin tops and deckhouses

Where top weight has to be reduced, even if costs go up, it will normally be necessary to make the deck structures of some other material than steel. Probably light alloy will give the maximum weight saving, though wood and fibreglass will closely rival it. Much depends on the skill and experience of the designer and the craftsmen available, when it comes to the finer limits of weight saving. As a good basic rule, the more a man has worked with a material, the more he knows about saving weight in that medium. This applies both on the drawing board and among the sawdust, or chopped strand mat off-cuts.

When sheer appearance is the principal aim it is very hard to equal varnished teak. To be sure it is not especially light, it needs varnishing every six months, it may crack if the sun is hot, it blunts tools and needs experience to work it. But nothing has quite the same prestige, nothing else gets the same appreciative nod from the critical knowledgeable person.

Though teak is used raw, that is in the unvarnished condition (sometimes with a wipe over of oil), it is only in this form for seats, cleats, some rail caps and so on. It is not used raw for cabin coamings and would not look right.

Mahogany is used for cabin tops, but it does need careful maintenance. If it once gets saturated for a long period it goes black, and bleaching to an acceptable standard is hard to achieve. An owner trying to save weight might go for a mahogany cabin top, keep it varnished as long as he could, then eventually paint it. If mahogany is used it should be incorporated in such a way that there is no chance of a puddle lying against it even when the boat is laid up at an unusual angle.

With wooden coamings there will be wood beams and almost certainly a ply cabin top deck, in the same fashion as all-wood yachts are built. But occasionally a composite cabin top is seen. This has steel supports to the coamings tied across the top with steel beams. It is convenient where a lot of local strength is needed, under the mast step on the cabin top, for instance.

Experienced ocean-cruising owners know wooden cabin tops have been cracked through by heavy seas and the use of a steel inner framework will appeal to them. The steel work needs designing in such a way that it merges with the wood unobtrusively, and this is a good place to use rectangular hollow section.

Fibreglass cabin tops on steel hulls are more rare. They may be used to reduce maintenance, and where extra strength is required they can have steel framework glassed in or bolted inside. When a ship has to be built in a hurry, or where there is a shortage of steel-workers, it may pay to use a non-ferrous superstructure. Very occasionally it will save money, but not often because steel is so cheap and quickly worked. It is true that cabin tops and deckhouses cost more per ton of steel used than main hulls, but they are still very cheap made of steel.

For a one-off fibreglass cabin top the accepted method of construction is rigid foam/g.r.p. because this does not need a mould. If a mould has to be made the cost of the fibreglass cabin top must include the mould. I have found that one of the best ways of making a quick light and inexpensive cabin top is to combine marine ply with g.r.p. The ply forms the main areas, and the g.r.p. is used for the joins, holding together the edges and corners. It also covers the whole area outside, both for strength and to reduce maintenance. The wood forms an insulating layer, and when more people tumble to the simplicity, lightness and strength of this method, which can result in a completely watertight cabin top, it must become popular.

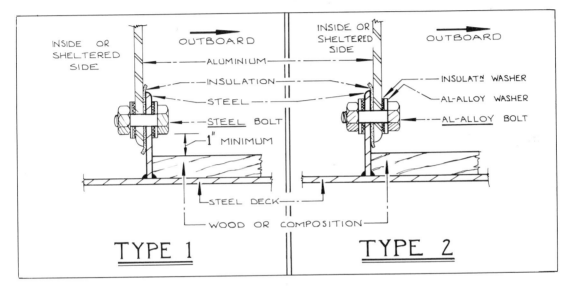

Fig. 35 Steel to aluminium joins. Fitting a light alloy deckhouse, skylight or other structure to a steel hull can be done in several ways. The two most common are shown here.

Type 1 has the advantage of cheapness since steel bolts are easy to obtain and inexpensive. Its weakness is that water may lodge at the protruding lip of the insulation. Type 2 will shed rainwater and spray, but before designing to this plan be sure that the aluminium alloy bolts are available.

In each case the insulation should be ample, to break any bridging flow of water which will set up electrolytic action. The use of rivets here does not make sense in most yards because of the difficulty of getting the materials and experienced riveters. In addition many deck structures are made semi-portable so that tanks, engines and furniture are easily removed from the hull. Big ship practice is sometimes to weld each nut, or add locking nuts, or both. This suggests that the engine vibration is going to be altogether intolerable! Painting over the nuts, once they have been tightened properly, should be adequate. They must be close spaced, in accordance with normal riveting practice. (See table on page 63.)

The steel upstand should not be too low, otherwise there will not be space to get a ring spanner round the bolt heads. Worse, even a little water swilling along the deck will bridge the gap between the two metals. Although there is insulation, painting must be of a high order to avoid electrolytic action between the two metals. In each case the metal washers must be of the same material as the bolts.

Prefabrication

There are a dozen reasons for prefabricating deck structures. A cabin top made away from the ship can be inverted for welding and painting, so that all work is down-hand. The work can be raised to a convenient height for working, and there will be ample space all round, which is seldom true once on deck, since few small craft have wide side decks.

Prefabricating can be done near power supplies, which is always handier than relying on long lengths of power cables. It gives all trades a chance to work under good conditions. For instance there is no reason why much of the electric wiring, some of the joinery work, plumbing and so on should not be done prior to lifting the prefabricated section onto the deck.

In some building sheds there is limited head-room, so that the deckhouse can only be fitted after moving the hull outside. A more subtle reason for prefabricating is this: 'a ship should proceed from keel to completion without pausing.' This is not just a matter of economics, though that naturally comes into it. Anyone working on a ship which grows swiftly to completion feels a sense of achievement and morale stays high. So if components can be made off the ship and lifted aboard complete, progress is seen to be continuous and interesting.

Prefabricating allows extra men to work on a job, since there is a limit to the number who can crowd aboard at once. It makes it possible to start the cabin top before the deck is complete. This speeds up the time between signing the contract and receiving the final payment. In turn this raises the profit margin on the ship, because the overheads, or on-costs, are for the most part continuous daily burdens. Reduce the number of days spent building, and the overheads total is reduced.

Prefabrication also helps the stores and ordering departments in an unexpected way. If there are to be bought-in handrails on each side of a deckhouse, and a Kent Clear-View Screen, and similar equipment, these things can be put on either prior to lifting the deckhouse onto the ship, or after it has been secured. This gives two opportunities for work to be done in a logical sequence. If equipment has been forgotten, or has been delayed in delivery, or any of the thousand and one contingencies which do arise have occurred, then the matter is thrown up early. So often a shipyard finds itself with an otherwise complete ship, waiting for a very small number of quite minor items.

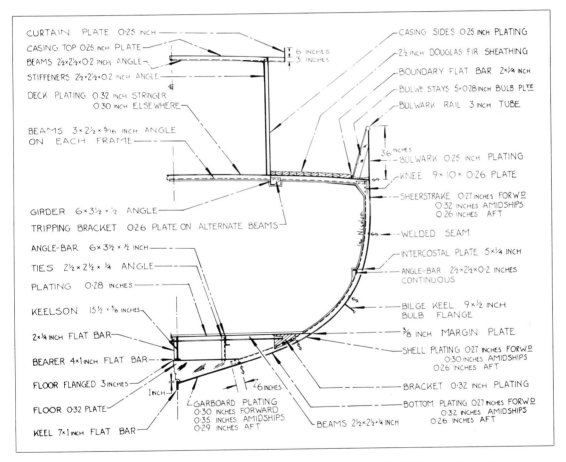

CURTAIN PLATE 0.25 INCH
CASING TOP 0.25 INCH PLATE
BEAMS 2½×2½×0.2 INCH ANGLE
STIFFENERS 2½×2½×0.2 INCH ANGLE
6 INCHES
3 INCHES
DECK PLATING 0.32 INCH STRINGER
0.30 INCH ELSEWHERE
BEAMS 3×2½×⁵⁄₁₆ INCH ANGLE
ON EACH FRAME
GIRDER 6×3½×½ ANGLE
TRIPPING BRACKET 0.26 PLATE ON ALTERNATE BEAMS
ANGLE-BAR 6×3½×½ INCH
TIES 2½×2½×¼ ANGLE
PLATING 0.28 INCHES
KEELSON 15½×³⁄₈ INCHES
2×¼ INCH FLAT BAR
BEARER 4×1 INCH FLAT BAR
FLOOR FLANGED 3 INCHES
1 INCH
FLOOR 0.32 PLATE
KEEL 7×1 INCH FLAT BAR
GARBOARD PLATING
0.30 INCHES FORWARD
0.35 INCHES AMIDSHIPS
0.29 INCHES AFT
6 INCHES
BEAMS 2½×2½×¼ INCH

CASING SIDES 0.25 INCH PLATING
2½ INCH DOUGLAS FIR SHEATHING
BOUNDARY FLAT BAR 2×¼ INCH
BULWᴷ STAYS 5×0.28 INCH BULB PLᵀᴱ
BULWARK RAIL 3 INCH TUBE
36 INCHES
BULWARK 0.25 INCH PLATING
KNEE 9×10×0.26 PLATE
SHEERSTRAKE 0.27 INCHES FORWᴰ
0.32 INCHES AMIDSHIPS
0.26 INCHES AFT
WELDED SEAM
INTERCOSTAL PLATE 5×¼ INCH
ANGLE-BAR 2½×2½×0.2 INCHES
CONTINUOUS
BILGE KEEL 9×½ INCH
BULB FLANGE
³⁄₈ INCH MARGIN PLATE
SHELL PLATING 0.27 INCHES FORWᴰ
0.30 INCHES AMIDSHIPS
0.26 INCHES AFT
BRACKET 0.32 INCH PLATING
BOTTOM PLATING 0.27 INCHES FORWᴰ
0.32 INCHES AMIDSHIPS
0.26 INCHES AFT

Fig. 36 An 85 foot fishing vessel. The details of this ship are based on Lloyd's rules. This particular craft is a Cummings design, and the whole emphasis is on substantial strength. Fishing vessels are sometimes tied up in harbour eight abreast, and occasionally at sea they have to go alongside other craft so that they need very strong hulls. In addition once they have secured a good catch they need to make harbour as quickly as possible to sell the fish at a good price even if sea conditions are atrocious. As a result reserve strength is paramount in the construction of a fishing vessel.

deck fittings and related matters

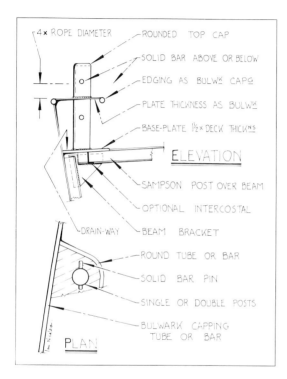

Fig. 37a On any heavy type of craft which is used for harsh work, really good mooring up and towing points are needed. Single or pairs of tubular samson posts mounted forward, amidships and aft are favoured since they are easy to make, easy to use, and can be very strong. Typical details are shown here though not all of them will be included in every case. For instance, it will not normally be necessary to have intercostal bars on the underneath, and extra thick deck plates are often omitted.

The samson post helps to stiffen the bulwark, and the bulwark gives extra support to the post. The bulwark itself will have stiffeners which are kept clear of the samson post to give good drainage and access for painting. One attraction of this type of samson post is that it does not need a fairlead since the top of the bulwark is well rounded, and a rope can be led to the post from any direction.

Hawse-pipes

A feature of the Dutch small ship scene is the high proportion of vessels which have anchors self-stowing in hawse-pipes. This reflects the ease with which a steel hull can be fitted with hawse-pipes. Compared with other materials, hawse-pipes on steel hulls cost half, largely because the pipes are easily welded in position.

Where hawse-pipes are fitted on tugs and other craft which work at close quarters, the anchor should recess into a casing in the ship's side at the bottom of the hawse-pipe. No part of the anchor should protrude, so that there is minimum risk of fouling when alongside other craft. A side bonus is the reduction in the amount of spray thrown up by the anchors when punching into a sea. In this connection anchors in hawse-pipes ought to be as high as possible. In the main it is bad practice to finish with the top of the shank above deck when the anchor is right home. Where this situation arises in spite of the designer's wishes, perhaps because the anchor is a long one and freeboard is limited, then it is essential to fit a roller for each anchor over the aft end of the hawse-pipe hole in the deck. Without this roller to guide the chain it is impossible to heave the anchor tight up—a thoroughly bad situation.

In every case some means of securing each anchor in the fully raised position must be provided, since the winch pawls and brake cannot be relied upon. Even where the winch is of the best, and thoroughly dependable, there is the risk that someone will accidentally let off a brake. The method of securing can be a sliding plate to shut the top of the pipe, and so exclude most of the water which tries to drive up in bad weather. But this type of plate, though desirable to keep water off the deck, is not satisfactory in that it seldom jams the anchor firmly. A better device is a steel wedge (with a keep-chain) which is hammered into the link which just protrudes. As the wedge is driven in the anchor is forced hard against the side plating. A second method of securing the chain is needed, and this may be the brake on the windlass.

On big ships sometimes the hawse-pipes are sealed at the top with cement before putting to sea, but this technique is not acceptable for the majority of small craft. The sliding plate has been mentioned, but it is usually a steel plate in steel slides, so that rust seizes the whole affair soon enough. A conscientious seaman on board will keep everything painted, in which case the paint causes the seizure. Better to fit hinged plates, with non-ferrous pins in the hinges, to avoid seizures.

In an ideal world the hawse-pipes would be exactly in line with the chain when it is streaming out to the anchor. Owing to the inconsiderate intervention of wind and tide the catenary of the chain is never the same from hour to hour, so the angle of the hawse-pipe has to be settled by other considerations. The pipe should never be so nearly horizontal that the chain comes in over an awkward angle where the chain meets the ship's side. Nor should the anchor even need a helping shove to get it going out. In practice the pipe must be nearly vertical and angled forward at the bottom. It will almost always need angling *outwards* at the bottom too.

Having settled the line of the pipe, it is then necessary to ensure that it tallies with the windlass. The chain must run exactly fore and aft onto the gipsy, and should rise up towards it, so that as much chain as possible is in contact with the drum before it drops off into the chain locker. Sets of rollers may be required to feed the chain exactly right, but this is a small matter compared with a chain which will not feed onto the gipsy, or one which slips once it is in place.

When designing the hawse-pipes it is worth remembering that this is a component which does not like short cuts. The drawing must be in plan, elevation and section, however much this may seem superfluous at first glance. The loft work too is a bit time-consuming for such a relatively small part of the structure. I mention this because on one occasion we found ourselves short of time. We decided, standing on the deck of the ship, exactly where the pipe was to pass through the deck, and had a hole cut. The pipe was made overlength and lowered down till it just touched the ship's plating. Here we had drilled a small hole to show the centre of the exit. Holding a wide parallel-sided board inside the ship's side we marked the angle on the bottom of the pipe, removed the pipe, and cut the bottom at the marked line. The pipe was put back in place and it fitted the side plating closely, though of course not exactly, owing to the bevel of the plating. We were now able to mark the ship's plating with the correct oval of the pipe to slip through at the bottom. This oval was cut out and after a little trimming the pipe now slid into place. It was still too long and the first job was to hold it so that it just protruded at the bottom end. The excess showing through the bottom was marked, and another line was drawn round the pipe at deck level. These two cuts were made, and the pipe was an exact fit. Later it was obvious that had the whole job been done in a conventional, big ship way, there would have been 50 per cent more man hours involved. The lofting and original draughting might have been fractionally adrift, so that trimming would have been needed. This is not a recommendation to cut out lofting, just a suggestion that the flexibility of a small shipyard should be used to the full. The designer in this case was prepared to get his hands and shoes dirty down on the job, and the bonus was worth more than just a new pair of shoes.

Where the hawse-pipe problem is a really tricky one it is worth making a model, even a crude one. Just occasionally the model will show up some off-beat answer. It may be that if the windlass maker can provide a wider axle, so that the gipsys are further outboard, the problem will be halved. Or it may be seen that the windlass should be ahead of the hawse-pipes, or one hawse-pipe can be aligned, and the other given rollers to take the chain to the gipsy. A model is a great tool for throwing up solutions when a drawing fails to give the needed inspiration. In this instance the model should be as big as convenient, and only extend over the relevant part of the ship.

Because the hawse-pipes are welded to the deck and to the ship's side they help to stiffen the structure just where it needs it — by the windlass. The pipes will be of a goodly diameter, to take the anchor, and so they form excellent pillars. As they are usually angled both fore and aft, as well as athwartships, they triangulate the whole structure and more than pay for their keep.

They have to be thick enough to deal with corrosion and chafe, though there should be cope at bottom and top to deal with this. A clever idea, not much seen, is the fitting of a water spray projecting into the hawse-pipe to clean the chain as it is pulled in. It can be made by welding a larger pipe outside the hawse-pipe, with sealing pieces top and bottom, so

that a water-jacketed effect is produced. Seawater is pumped into the water-jacket under pressure, and it squirts out through a row of holes right round the hawse-pipe. The holes should be near the bottom and angled downwards.

A critical factor in this whole matter is the selection of the anchor. A CQR can be used, but the recess in the hull is not a simple shape. It will pay to make the recess round the anchor, off the ship, and then fit it and weld it up. It is likely that the anchor may need coaxing into its recess, so that is a very good argument for having the anchor stowed fairly high — but not out of sight from deck — under a wildly sweeping flare. Also a very heavy anchor cannot be turned over to make it shunt into its housing neatly, so CQRs seem to be out for ships over about 50 feet in this special instance.

Any anchor which has its stock at the opposite end to the flukes, such as the common fisherman, is no use. The Stokes is popular because it is stockless, but the old Admiralty stockless has a poor grip, and will let go when wind or tide are strong. The new Admiralty anchors are the subject of much research and have much in common with the Stokes. It is no use exclaiming that the anchor is bound to be a success (regardless of its shape and proportions) simply because it is so heavy. Weight alone is no damn good, and it is a great shame that so few people, from designers to bosuns, seem unable to comprehend this fact. If only they would consider, they would see that a 40 foot boat can drag an anchor weighing a ton, if conditions are sufficiently adverse, since there is more than a ton of reserve buoyancy in the bow of a 40-footer. This is a department of science where medieval prejudice and lack of thought are resulting in a great many unnecessary insurance claims. What makes a ship secure is a good shape of anchor allied to a long, long length of chain.

An anchor which has rightly got a good reputation is the Danforth, and its various cousins such as the Meon. It can be made to stow fairly neatly in a hawse-hole, though there is almost always a part of the anchor projecting outboard of the plating.

If the hawse-pipe is through the stem it is very hard to recess the anchor, and inevitably a lot of spray is thrown upwards even in a moderate sea. A single hawse-pipe also poses the problem of the second anchor. How is this to be heaved aboard? If the ship is under 50 feet the problem is not too acute, it just needs muscle. But over that size a cat davit is required. As the whole point of a hawse-pipe is to avoid the miserable business of cat davits and tackles, it seems that a single hawse-pipe is seldom an intelligent economy except for craft under 45 feet.

Where the anchor comes up it has a bad habit of leaving a trail of destruction. If it stows in a well-flared bow, and if the sea is always calm when it comes in, then the paintwork on the bow may survive. But often the topsides are hammered and scraped as the anchor comes above water. To minimize this scarring some builders fit stainless steel plates below the hawse-pipes. These plates can be quite thin since they are backed by the ship's platings, but whatever the thickness the bottom edge should be bevelled so that no part of the anchor catches.

Where a stern anchor is fitted the hawse-pipe is not much of a problem provided the stern ends in a transom. Recessing the anchor fully is highly desirable, as it is for the bow anchor and with thought should present few problems for the designer and constructor.

Access hatches

Though at first sight access hatches seem perfectly simple, these items can cost quite a lot of money, bearing in mind that draughts-men's and loftsmen's time is involved very often. Hatches have deadlights in the top, clips to hold the top open, possible side screens, canopies and other complications. Then again a good hatch should not have a heavy cover, for safety. So careful design work and sometimes complicated fabrication is needed to keep down the weight.

All this adds up to a good case for buying in stock hatches. Among the firms that make them are Camper & Nicholson Ltd of Gosport, who supply aluminium framed hatches in three sizes. The smallest size is just a little skylight and indeed all three sizes can be used as skylights. The middle size is rather small for the main access below deck but is fine for secondary access. The biggest size is likely to be more expensive than a specially fabricated steel hatch although, of course, costs vary enormously from builder to builder. These hatches are strong, but would not normally be fitted on 'heavyweight' craft like fishing boats or small cargo craft where the chances of damage are very great. The top is of clear or smoked Perspex, according to choice. This Perspex is the most vulnerable part of the hatch.

Another disadvantage of stock hatches is that they are usually low sided. This makes them attractive to look at, light and easy to fit and fine where the weight of deck is critical. However on a great many commercial vessels the height of the hatch coamings is important and is governed by Ministry or other regulations.

If special coamings are necessary it's probably cheaper to make the entire hatch in the shipyard instead of buying in stock units.

Hatch coamings

The height of hatch coamings is very much governed by the ship's purpose in life. The futher offshore a small ship goes, and the longer she spends at sea, the higher her hatch coamings are likely to be. About 30 inches high is the maximum normally found, and this is too high to step over, so it is not a popular height with crews. Around 24 inches is not too high to climb over without an intermediate step, and so this height is found on fishing boats. It is also the height which some DTI inspectors insist be applied to small passenger craft plying offshore, though other inspectors seem content to accept about 18 inches.

On yachts a much lower height is favoured, in some cases the hatch coamings being actually recessed so that the hatch top is flush with the deck. This gives a smooth deck with plenty of space for sunbathing, stowing boats, or for working sails. It looks smarter, gives a cleaner appearance and often it reduces maintenance.

Where the hatch is not flush a good average on a yacht is about 3 inches high, since this will keep out a great deal of weather even if the hatch top seal is not perfect. It is also a good height for a hatch with side wings which is left open for ventilation in bad weather.

The height of the coamings is not related to the watertightness of the hatch top. There is a clear modern trend towards all hatches being of the clip-down type which, when new and properly made, can stand full submersion without letting a drop of water through. Low flush hatches used to be made on the principle that water about to get past them into the hull can be ducted away via small drains.

Practical builders and crews now realise that these small drains cannot cope just when they are most needed, and anyway they get blocked by dirt within weeks of being fitted. In short, there is nothing to equal the tight seal of a sharp metal edge well bedded on a new rubber gasket properly fitted and maintained.

Steel coamings should be set inside steel decks, and not on top. To be sure it is easier to set them on top, but it means that there is a ridge, maybe very small but very much there, which extends all round the hatch. This will catch crews' clothing and gear being passed through the hatch. The ridge looks bad, and starts corrosion as everything passed through the hatch chafes the paint off it.

Much the same can be said about hatch coaming stiffeners. It they are inside the coaming they are a thorough nuisance, and if they are outside they look poor, get chipped and then rusty. If they have to be fitted it is probably best to use something like RHS, but they can often be avoided.

Horizontal stiffeners on the coamings are in the same category, except at the top, where there should be no sharp edge of plate left upstanding. Such an edge looks bad and is always uncomfortable, sometimes dangerous. Where the hatch is mainly for the passage of crew or passengers a wood rim or doubling is attractive. If made of teak or the nearest equivalent hardwood, it is hard wearing, looks good and is practical.

Daylight through hatches

The ideal arrangement is to have the entire top

of all hatches of either transparent or translucent material on almost every craft. Vulnerability, however, precludes this on any ship which has to work hard for its living. An overall piece of Perspex can stand up to quite a bit of rough usage for weeks. Then a blow from something like a sharp-cornered box will crack Perspex even though the impact is quite modest. Perspex $\frac{3}{8}$ inch thick is usually used, but for racing boats it may be $\frac{1}{4}$ inch thick and on boats where conditions are tough $\frac{1}{2}$ inch thickness is advisable. In some respects fibreglass is a better material but it is not widely used in flat sheet form, partly because of its price and poor availability. It is reasonably strong, but only translucent — not transparent.

In practice quite a few designers put in common glass deadlights since these are in general use on other parts of a ship and seem able to stand up to rugged seagoing conditions. It often makes good sense to put deadlights in high hatch coamings as well as in the hatch top itself. Anyone who has lived in the confines of a small ship will know that comfort below decks is partly a measure of the amount of daylight in each compartment. Where privacy is needed, for instance over a toilet compartment, Perspex can be made translucent by rubbing it with emery cloth. The roughened surface should be inside because it tends to dirty more easily.

Ventilation

All ships need ventilation, but small craft need it triply, because they are small and of steel. The size of the compartments is limited and for crew comfort a constant change of air is essential. If there is no flow of air then moisture aboard will not be dried up, and rusting will follow. Water accumulates through condensation.

It comes through hatches and leaking portlights and into the cabins on the streaming oilskins the crew wear.

Ventilation is essentially a stream of air, flowing in from the outside, circulating round each compartment, then out and clear of the ship. The last condition is important, for a toilet extractor vent just ahead of a cabin inlet vent results in foul smells wafting in unwanted directions.

This whole subject may be summed up by saying that it is complex, big companies make millions doing nothing but ventilation, and above all, there is never enough of it on small craft. Attractive theoretical formulae are available but they seldom have successful application to small craft. However they do serve as a basis for planning, so here goes.

1 Every person on board needs 14 cubic feet of air per minute.

2 The air in each compartment should be changed about 8 times per hour.

3 Where a compartment is large for the number of people in it, the change of air per hour might be less than 8, but this seldom applies to small craft.

4 In toilet compartments constantly in use there should be 15 changes of air per hour.

5 In galleys the rate is 30 changes of air per hour.

6 In hot climates all these rates should be doubled. And doubled again if conditions are bad.

One conclusion immediately clear is that a ventilator of less than 4 inches diameter is doubly suspect, first because it is so small that it hardly allows a proper flow of air until a

gale is roaring down it, and secondly because
it cannot swallow adequate quantities of air at
normal wind speeds. A corollary is that though
two 3 inch diameter vents have a bigger cross-
sectional area than a single 4-incher, the latter
is liable to be more effective on its own until
the wind is piping up.

On the same line of thought, mechanical
ventilation is only partly effective on small
craft because it is not constantly in use. Mostly
mechanical ventilation will be by simple
electric fans inside small cowls or perforated
dishes or, less often, in apertures in bulkheads.
These fans will not be run much when the ship
is uninhabited, and may not be used often
when she is moored because of the drain on the
batteries. As a result, mechanical ventilation
must take a back seat in any planning and
discussions. It will be fitted in galleys for use
when actually cooking, and a similar condition
applies to toilet compartments. But for the most
part mechanical ventilation should be considered
a useful secondary line of attack.

On some craft, notably yachts built in North
America, mechanical ventilation is linked to the
main engines, so that when these are running
various electric ventilators also run. Also
engines are massive consumers of air, so that
they suck it in copiously through whatever
apertures are left in the engine compartment
casing. This can be used to advantage so that
air is drawn through the accommodation,
sweeping up moisture as it goes, before being
gulped into the air intakes of the machinery.

Before leaving mechanical ventilation it is
worth commenting that it is no more reliable
than any other electrical equipment afloat,
especially if drips of water fall on the sensitive
parts.

Fans may be used to pump air in or out. For
toilets and galleys they should extract, and the
closer they are to the source of smell and fumes
the better. In hot climates a fan wafting air onto
the crew is pleasant, especially if the fan is
silent and controllable as to speed and direction.
Like other electrical items afloat, fans have a
limited life and unreliability which is often
beyond the borders of morality. For this reason
ships intended for serious use in hot climates
should have all fans at least duplicated.

All ventilation is based on air-flow, and this
can only take place if there is both an entrance
and an exit. Just as important, each passage
must be big enough for easy flow with the
pressure differentials available. Many perforated
panels and metal ventilators do not work much
of the time, because the interstices are too
small. A 1 inch diameter hole is not much good,
and a row of them very little better.

Jalousies, or rows of parallel cowled slits in
doors, are effective. They can be used in both
locker and cabin doors. A cutaway slot at top
and bottom is usually better, and this is a
general principle: better a moderate size of slot
than a group of thin ones.

Each compartment must be given its inlet and
outlet, but they need not be of the same type.
For instance the galley can suck air in through
a slot in the door and eject through a fan. Or
it can draw air from outside via a cowl and
have an aperture into the engine compartment
to let the air out. However this is unusual, and
every effort is normally made to get air from
toilet compartments and galleys released
directly outboard.

On small craft a cowl ventilator is the basic
type. For a time it fell from popularity, perhaps
partly because it is prone to corrosion round the
base, also because it used to be expensive. Now
that plastic vents made of a pliable and there-

fore unbreakable material are available, cowls
are again much favoured. They can be swung
into the wind, or away from it in bad weather,
they gulp down a lot of air for their size, and
they work even in light breezes.

Just as popular is the mushroom vent, which
can be screwed down tight when conditions are
bad. The plastic version of this vent has not
proved a success even though advertising has
sold many. They are weak where the threaded
spindle joins the cover so that when they are
trodden on, as inevitably happens within the
first year, they break, leaving an uncovered
hole on the deck. Almost as inconvenient, when
the weather turns sour the crew are maybe too
ill or too busy to remember to screw down all
the mushrooms so that water comes aboard. In
addition the threads are prone to seize, the
sealing rings of rubber are not easy to renew
and in some versions the spindle projects too
far down into the cabin and scalps anyone
unwary. The mushroom vent would be better if
it attracted more attention from inventors and
engineers and less from advertising agents.

Swan-neck vents are rare, partly because
they are not very effective, partly because they
are unsightly in many forms. They are basically
pipes standing well up through the deck, with
the top turned through 180°. They act as
extractors and can be made relatively unobtrusive if they are worked in close to a
bulwark or cabin coaming. Another type of
extractor vent has a vertical stem and a
tapered horizontal pipe on top. This like other
types may be made part of a cabin side, with
the coaming forming one side of the vent.

There are various forms of flat ventilator,
some looking like upturned soup plates. They
suffer from an inability to keep out water when
conditions get rough, even though they may

have baffles inside. An inch of solid water on
the cabin top, which is not excessive, will
over-top the baffles with drenching ease. Masts
are sometimes used as ventilators, with a slot
or holes in front to take in air, or at the back
for extracting. As the holes are high, they tend
to be above spray level, but shields or skirts
are needed to keep out driving rain.

Bollard-vents are one of my favourite forms
of air intake. They are described in detail in
*Designers Notebook**. On a par are vents built
in as part of cabin tops or deck structures.
They have the virtue of unobtrusiveness, take
up hardly any deck space, can be made to look
sophisticated and they are sometimes an
economy.

All these different types of vents can be
integral with a water-box which excludes
spray and all but the heaviest waves. For
offshore work every vent should be baffled by
a water-box or some similar arrangement, unless
there are special circumstances. For instance if
the mast is substantial, and is used as an air
intake, it can be difficult to work in a water-box
at the bottom, assuming the mast is stepped on
deck.

Using part of the hull or superstructure as a
water-box has attractions. It keeps the appearance of the ship tidy, can be designed to take
in large quantities of air, is normally easily
sealed, is often relatively cheap and tends to
work continuously. The whole of the bow may
be bulkheaded off to be watertight, with an air
intake at each side near the deck. A row of
holes at the top of the bulkhead allows the air
to pass into the main part of the ship, while
spray and solid water drains out through holes
near the waterline. A watertight flat is built in

* Published by Adlard Coles Limited

Small steel craft

A teak deck is being laid on a steel one. The shipwrights have chalked the location of each beam on top of the deck and are planking from the outside towards the centre. They have already encased the steel bowsprit with teak. The steel lugs for the forestay and stemhead rollers have been welded on, like the rest of the steel fittings, before the wood work commences. The low bulwark there has a flange inwards which will support the teak rail capping and also the stanchions.

In this photo of the bow of a 30 ft sailing cruiser many of the advantages of steel are shown. The low bulwark has oval slots forward making a pair of closed fairleads, and the pulpit feet are welded to the bulwark, clear of the deck. This gives a little extra foot-room, makes deck cleaning easier and reduces the chance of corrosion of the pulpit feet. The plate holding the forestay is part of the stem and is welded to the deck which in turn forms the equivalent of a breasthook. A simple but very strong bollard is made from a short length of tube with a shaped capping plate.

just above the waterline, and there must be means of shutting the air inlets in the bulkhead.

Opening ports and windows form relatively poor means of ventilation except for craft used in sheltered conditions in the tropics. And even here they are not fully successful since they have to be shut during heavy rain, when a flow of air is still much in demand. Opening ports and windows cannot normally be left open for long periods, and they are expensive. It was one time unthinkable that a ship should be built with no opening ports. However lessons from craft properly equipped with other types of ventilators of ample size show that opening glass apertures are often just a nuisance. Plenty of fixed ports and windows, with perhaps one opening window in the galley, is often the most comfortable long-term answer.

Engine compartment ventilation has been left till last because it is a special case. In the tropics the amount of air driven or sucked into this space can scarcely be too great. In temperate climates and cold locations two intakes are needed, each having a cross-sectional area about 50 per cent greater than the combined intake areas of the engines. This is because the further 'upstream' the flow, the larger the air passages should be.

Since heat rises, and the source of heat is the machinery, it is best to locate air outlets above the hottest places. This may not be the main engines: in some ships the auxiliaries are air cooled and run more than the main machinery. However every vent is a potential source of rain, spray and sometimes solid water. So the precise location of each vent should be thoughtfully considered. Whatever happens keep them clear of electric equipment. Nor should they be put above unshrouded air

intakes in case water is fed into the cylinders. 'Above' in this context means 'anywhere near', since a heavily rolling ship may lie over to an angle of 45° just when water pours down the vent.

Stanchions

The cheapest, simplest type is a length of steel piping welded in place. They need drain holes at the bottom, a sealing cap on top, and horizontal holes for the lifelines. As a basic rule the diameter should be 1 inch bore standard piping, except just occasionally when a $\frac{3}{4}$ inch bore pipe will serve on non-commercial craft under 32 feet.

This type of pipe is vulnerable and suffers from corrosion round the base. A bent stanchion can be awkward to repair and this type of accident is common. A better, commoner method is to weld a socket on deck. This is made a suitable size for the standard stanchions which can be bought in galvanized or stainless steel or made up. A split pin holds the stanchion in place, so that replacement is easy.

When a ship is being built for service overseas, three or four spare stanchions put in with the spares for the engines and electrical gear will impress the owner.

When ordering stanchions the height must be specified, also the number of lifeline wires to be fitted. Stanchion sockets are normally put on deck, even when there is a low bulwark round the ship. However they may be set on top, especially where a little extra safety is needed, as on passenger ships. Putting them on top looks odd on most craft under 50 feet. Sometimes the stanchions are supported by a solid spigot welded to the deck and by the top horizontal flange of the bulwark.

Special stanchions are needed at the port and starboard gangways. On ever more craft, a gangway at the stern is needed for use when moored stern to the quay, as the crowding in harbours makes this type of berthing imperative. These gangway stanchions have diagonal legs to resist the pull of the lifelines.

Pulpits at bow and stern, available from chandlers in stock form, make good endings for the lifelines. They give security, especially when handling the anchor, and are compulsory for sailing yachts racing offshore. There is a growing tendency to fit floppy pulpits which feel insecure and have no reserve of strength, so that two people falling simultaneously will cause a fracture. It is not usual to triangulate the joins of pulpits, and more's the pity, because many need stiffening at the junctions of the pipes. Builders are learning to set pulpits inboard, where they are less vulnerable, but also at times much more restricting. On pilot boats all the stanchions are set right inboard, quite 3 feet from the outer edge of the ship. This makes it easy for the pilots to leap off the side deck onto the ladder of the ship, or *vice versa*. Other craft are now being fitted in this way, including work launches. However this location of the stanchions is only tolerable where everyone who ventures on deck is experienced, fit and aware of the dangers of going overboard.

Lifelines

On commercial craft the lifelines may be of piping because they are strong, last a long time, and provide real security. They are also heavy, can be ugly and are out of place on virtually any type of craft where speed, a 'delicate' appearance or top weight matter.

Wire lifelines stand up to collisions since they give to the load then return to position. They may be of stainless or galvanized wire, the former being about six times the cost of the galvanized wire. Plough steel wire—not the flexible type—is best used, and bushes in the stanchions will prevent damage to the galvanizing and eventually the wire, and in particular prevent chafe on plastic-coated wires. Wire specially for stanchions is available from Lee Ward Rigging, Chelmondiston, Ipswich IP9 1DR, UK. This wire is sheathed with plastic. A white covering shows up well in the dark and brightens dreary craft but the transparent sheathing is much more unobtrusive and suitable for quality vessels. Ward's also make end terminals which any intelligent person can fit, without having a rigger's skill. The terminals are expensive. However they are of stainless steel and will last longer than the ship, since they can be re-used with new replaceable inside cones over and over when the wire is worn out.

Each end of each wire needs a proper termination. There is a practice, aimed simply at saving a few pence, which consists of using various inappropriate wire ends. Wire clips look dreadful and crush the wire, seizings cannot be relied upon and do not look good, but splices are satisfactory.

For most craft two lifelines each side are adequate, but for passenger carrying three or even four are needed. Pelican hooks or similar fastenings such as small Stenhouse clips are used to release the wires at the gangway. Each gangway wire must be a short separate piece, otherwise when the gangway is opened the whole length of the wire will go slack, allowing people to fall overboard clear of the gangway.

Lifelines are tightened by rigging screws,

though sometimes lashings are mistakenly used. This again is intended to save pennies, but the people who do it should check the cost of a wreath. Each rigging screw needs locking with a length of wire through the barrel. Some have locking nuts at each end of the barrel but these nuts are traitors which let go without warning.

Masts

A ship may have masts of steel, light alloy, wood or fibreglass. Commercial craft will normally have steel spars because they are cheap, strong, easily made in a yard which builds steel hulls, and the disadvantages are insignificant. The trouble with steel is that it is a heavy material, and where top weight matters it is not to be considered for spars.

For fishing boats with steel hulls it is usual to fit steel spars though there is a new vogue for light alloy ones. Steel tugs and work boats have steel masts, though they are generally small, being nothing more than elevated supports for navigation lights. A few of the more rugged motor yachts may have steel spars, but this is rare.

One disadvantage of steel masts is that they are not normally tapered, as they are made from conventional steel tubing. This lack of taper used to be considered ugly, but it is becoming more accepted. In any case it is overcome without too much trouble. One technique is to slip the end of a slightly smaller diameter tube inside the bottom tube. A third and even a fourth tube, each with its outside diameter the size of the diameter of the lower one, may be added. The join is secured by a line of welding all round, the edge of the larger tube well ground away and the job is complete. It is not smart, and a better approach is to cut

from the top of the mast a long thin V. This V extends down the length of the mast. When the V-shaped plate has been removed the mast is squeezed closed, and a weld made to seal the mast together again. After grinding off, the mast has a neat taper, the extent of which is determined by the length and width of V removed.

Another method of getting taper is to use a steel tube with a wooden topmast. The tube is parallel in section, all the taper being out in the wooden part. Where strength is needed, combined with a good appearance, this approach has something to recommend it because it is cheap. On a big motor yacht, for instance, the mast might be required to support a derrick used for lifting inboard a heavy motorboat. The derrick will be of steel, and the mast too— up to the hounds, where the lifting blocks are secured. But the top of the mast, which is required to carry a load no heavier than a radio aerial, can be of wood, well tapered.

Steel spars will normally have their fittings welded to them. In this connection the fittings must be made up of plate, edge-welded and not joined in such a way that the tangs are face down on the tube. This requirement is in contrast to general practice on aluminium alloy masts (see sketch). The reason is that where a steel mast is fitted, windage aloft will not be important, as it is on vessels which are fitted with light alloy spars. If the tangs are put on face against the spar, the tang will vibrate with the rigging when the engine is running. This results in hair cracks across the tang and eventual failure.

The traditional type of rigging is made of plough steel wire rope, eye spliced at each end and shackled to tangs on the mast, as well as to chainplates at deck level. This approach is

Fig. 37b Side elevation. Metal tangs are welded to steel spars for shrouds, blocks and other fittings. The tangs should be welded on edge the whole way down both sides and round the ends. Tangs must not be fitted 'on the flat' and then a shroud shackled on. This is because shrouds vibrate in sympathy with the engine, so the tang will eventually fracture at the bend. The sketch on the left is the correct procedure.

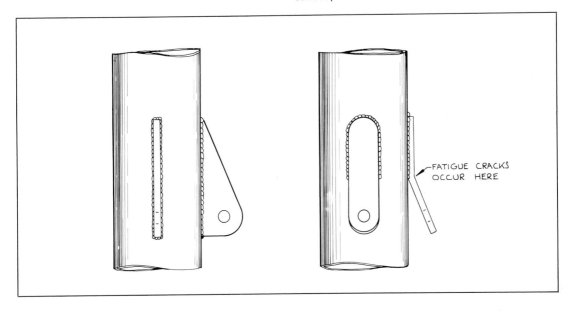

FATIGUE CRACKS OCCUR HERE

dying out because it is not particularly cheap in first cost and the wire does not last many years. Solid rod shrouds and forestays are now fitted on fishing boats and commercial craft. The next approach is to do away with rigging entirely and have a tripod, or even a four-legged mast. These may be welded direct to the deck (or deckhouse top) or hinged. Hinging is obviously necessary for craft which pass under low bridges, but it has other assets. For instance a yacht will normally be put in a shed to be painted, possibly for the whole of the winter, so her mast needs to be lowered to get under the roof. But even commercial craft need painting, and even if this is done in the open, it is convenient to be able to lower the mast to paint it. Lowering masts also mean that maintenance of the navigation lights and other paraphernalia aloft is much easier.

These tripod and quadruped masts will normally be made of round section, untapered tube. As the legs taper together towards the top, the absence of tube taper is not a worry. Horizontal tubes, between the legs to give them mutual support, are also useful. Set fairly close, they will act as rigid ratlines. Most yachtsmen appreciate an easy way to get aloft. Keen fishermen, especially those who fish for big game, consider it essential.

A conventional type of mast may be stepped on deck, or it can pierce the deck and have its foot down on the keel, or on a floor. Where the encastre effect is needed, as it may be for lifting aboard cargo, the mast is naturally stepped down by the keel, so that the deck helps to support the spar. Where derricks are worked from a mast the standing rigging wants to be a minimum, to keep the biggest possible swinging arc for the derricks. Under these conditions the rigging may not be able to contribute as much to the mast support as would be liked, and a buried mast is essential.

In all other cases it is usually better to step the mast on deck. Not only is the mast shorter and cheaper, it is easier to step, to remove and hence to maintain. But the main point is that a mast which goes through a deck nearly always has a leak round it. Mast coats are among the most inefficient of man's creations, and they last months rather than decades.

Boatyards used to building in wood or glassfibre buy goosenecks from chandlers. However, for steel spars it is best to make up the fitting specially. For a start the goosenecks supplied by chandlers are intended for linking booms to masts for sailing yachts. This type of gooseneck is not capable of allowing the boom to lift above about 45° and sometimes a good deal less, so that it is unsatisfactory for use on a derrick. Also it is designed to join to a light alloy or wood boom, and will not mate well with a steel one. Much the same sort of criticism applies to other standard mast and boom fittings.

Steel masts are sometimes used as vents or as exhaust outlets. In the latter form, some precaution is needed to prevent the mast causing burns to the crew. On one heavy 50 foot motor yacht, we designed what turned out to be an attractive mast. It had a steel inner tube to take up the exhaust, and an outer aluminium one. It looked good, and the outer casing did not get hot because we had holes drilled round the base. When the air in between the two tubes got hot it went upwards, drawing in cool air at the bottom.

On sailing yachts, whatever the hull is built of, the spars are likely to be of light alloy. This material is strong yet light, it needs little maintenance, and it is easy to work. In practice most yards buy their alloy spars in from the specialist firms which turn out vast numbers of masts and booms every year. Their addresses are available in the yachting magazines in advertisements.

Light alloy masts and spars make sense for all types of steel craft on grounds of minimum weight, availability and low maintenance. The only fly in the ointment is the cost. But for the little signal masts which many commercial small craft carry, the cost is not serious.

Wood spars have much to recommend them. They are easy to make, though a yard which concentrates on steel work may not have extensive wood facilities. In practice any competent wood-worker can make a wood mast, given a good plan. Alternatively the mast may be bought from one of the few yacht yards still specialising in this type of work.

Fibreglass is just coming into fashion for spars. It needs little maintenance, but it is not cheap, and the joining of fittings to the spars is probably best left to specialists.

Lifting eyes

Because of the surplus of strength found throughout small steel craft, fitting lifting eyes is easy. These eyes are for lifting the boat out of the water, or launching her by crane. Under some circumstances they may be used to move her. If she is quite small and light she may be shifted about in the building shed using two or three travelling beams working together.

A boat which has to take the ground at low tide may have legs, and these can sometimes be located at the lifting eyes. However it is usual to have only one leg each side, roughly amidships, whereas lifting eyes will be two in number each side, spread out towards the ends of the vessel.

The eyes must be at the ends of very stiff beams, or there must be notices by the eyes carrying a warning about the importance of using sling spreaders in conjunction with the eyes. It is hard to avoid having prominent lifting eyes, and this is unacceptable on yachts. They can be made portable, being bolted in position when required. Alternatively they can be located where they are covered by deck lockers, or fitted inside deck lockers or under life-rafts.

On sailing yachts, as the ballast is low down it is possible to have the lifting eyes down below the sole, on or part of the floors. The slings are led through the hatches, and it is usual to fit a skylight-cum-hatch in the cabin top for this purpose, the other leg of the two-part sling going down the main hatch.

This technique does not work on power boats because the eyes are so low they are beneath the centre of gravity, so that as the hull is lifted it tries to roll over. Side slings to prevent this can be used but it is poor practice, and much better to lift above the c.g. and have a stable load.

On the subject of stability, a friend of mine once spent two hours trying to lift a motorboat off a train with a crane. He rigged slings under the boat and gently lifted, but the slings were too far forward. He moved them aft and started to lift, but he had overdone the move. He shifted them a fraction aft and was astonished to find that the slings were definitely too far aft. This fiddling went on and on, with rising frustration for the crane driver, not to mention the luckless fellow hauling the heavy wire slings back and forth. At long last my friend

thought to look inside and found a great weight of rainwater. It was running from one end of the hull to the other, constantly shifting the c.g., so that the slings were always in the wrong place.

Lifting slings and their eyes and all paraphernalia connected with them must have a very useful factor of safety. One or two people always insist on getting a ride as a boat is lifted, not to mention the full fuel and water tanks, the bilgewater, the ton of extra ballast added since the boat was first launched, and so on. As a rough guide each eye should be able to support 6 times the weight of the boat before breaking, assuming there are four eyes each taking about a quarter of the load under ideal circumstances.

The eyes need careful aligning with the direction of pull, and the holes for the shackles or hooks must fit. Lifting hooks are very large, and not to be used except in special circumstances. Shackles and slings should be tested. A boat which is regularly lifted might with advantage carry her own slings stowed aboard permanently, when there would be no doubt that the spread of the sling legs was correct, and the shackles exactly fitted the eyes.

Small craft operating in ports which cater for big ships may find a shortage of small slipways. In such circumstances there will be plenty of powerful cranes, so that for bottom scrubbing or repairs the obvious and quick way to get the boat out of the water will be by crane. For this reason pilot boats, fire-floats, police launches and so on will often be fitted with lifting eyes.

One set of eyes may be at the transom corners, because this is a strong point, well clear of deckhouses. The forward pair may be clear ahead of the superstructure, perhaps by a heavy beam bounding a hold or hatchway. The eyes will be of thick plate, often with a massive washer welded round the hole to strengthen it. The eye-plates are commonly welded to the outside of the hull of commercial vessels, but the result is seldom tidy.

Lifesaving gear

A feature of steel construction is the ease and cheapness with which watertight compartments can be made. For sailing yachts a trough may be made in the deck, to take the life-raft. Normally the trough will have a semi-circular section to fit a standard raft casing, and be just slightly longer and wider than the packaged raft. A pipe leading overboard from the bottom of the trough is necessary to deal with accumulating rain and spray. Among the advantages of this idea: the raft is handy, yet cannot be swept overboard, as it could be if strapped down on deck. Its weight and windage are lowered. It is less of an eyesore, and less vulnerable.

The technique can be carried one stage further, especially on motor cruisers and other boats where deck space is short. The well is made so that the whole of the raft is below deck level. It must be covered by a loose-fitting grating flush with the deck and there must be facilities for lifting the raft out quickly.

Buoyant apparatus

This is the technical name for a variety of rigid life-rafts. The British Department of Trade and Industry regulations set out in the *Survey of Life-saving Appliances: Instructions to Surveyors* just how these life-rafts must be built to comply with the international life-saving regulations for seagoing ships. Though steel is not mentioned, it looks as if steel would theoretically be

permitted provided it was galvanized. The requirement is for a 'durable material' for the air cases, which are encapsulated in a wood framework and sparring.

These buoyant apparatus are not really 'life-rafts' as they are more like outsize lifebuoys for supporting people in the water. There is a Dutch version which is sometimes seen on craft in sheltered waters. It is nothing more than a steel box with lugs all round to hold the Courlene grab-rope. (Courlene is used because it is buoyant and has good resistance against chafe, as well as being rot-proof.) These mini-rafts are painted a red or bright orange and white chequer pattern, which is vastly better than the dull varnish colouring of the conventional, wood-sparred apparatus.

These Dutch mini-rafts are very simple and cheap, and have much to commend them. They are much more robust than a normal lifebuoy, and are vandal-proof. Most yards buy their buoyant apparatus from specialist builders who supply only stock sizes. As every experienced designer knows, a stock size is one that never fits anywhere! These simple steel substitutes can be made to fit an individual ship exactly. They can be tailored to fit on top of the wheelhouse, or between the funnel and the wheelhouse, or wherever there is deck space.

The mini-rafts are no substitute for inflatable life-rafts. For a start they have no life-saving equipment on them. In general they will support people in the water, but cannot carry more than one or two people clear of the water. They need two drains each, and should be tested annually, but that applies to all lifesaving gear. They need very little maintenance, and it is easy to think of instances when they would have saved lives. For inshore craft they have much to commend them. They also make sense

Fig. 37c To prevent large quantities of water being trapped on deck by high bulwarks it is usual to have freeing ports. These let out water fast whereas the small drains in the scuppers will only let it away fairly slowly. Sometimes the freeing ports are just long low slits in the bulwark, but of course these let water in as well as out. Doors prevent water getting in but they have to be hinged so that the pressure of water on the inside forces them out. To prevent anybody being washed through them guard-bars are fitted. The weight of the doors outboard of the hinge-pins keeps them shut. If the vessel rolls, the doors may clang as they swing open, even when there is no water inboard. This can be checked by fitting shock-cord round the guard bars and on to the hinge plates of the doors.

where there is either no statutory lifesaving equipment, or where additional inexpensive buoyant apparatus is desirable. With very little ingenuity they can be made with a watertight chamber for flares, daylight distress signals and so on. This stowage space needs access from top and bottom and here is another situation where a Henderson hatch would be ideal.

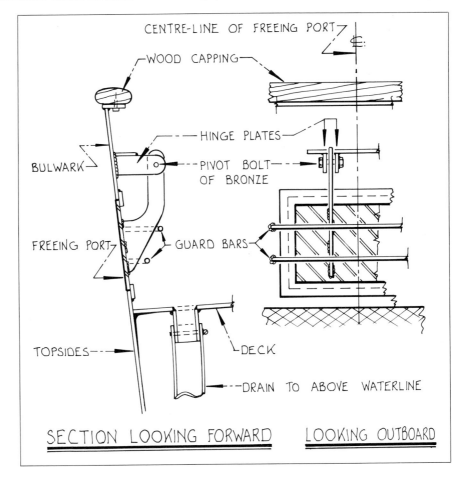

CENTRE-LINE OF FREEING PORT

WOOD CAPPING

HINGE PLATES

BULWARK

PIVOT BOLT OF BRONZE

FREEING PORT

GUARD BARS

TOPSIDES

DECK

DRAIN TO ABOVE WATERLINE

SECTION LOOKING FORWARD   LOOKING OUTBOARD

corrosion, protection, painting, polyurethane foam

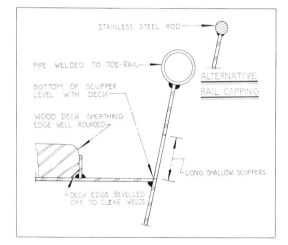

Fig. 37d A round tube welded on top is popular on fishing boats and work launches because ropes and nets slide over easily. On yachts a stainless steel rod is popular because there can be holes along the toe-rail to take sheet lead blocks and similar equipment. A toe-rail or bulwark needs scuppers and these look smarter if they are shallow but long. They should be considerably smaller then the size of a child's foot so that nobody can accidentally slip through them. The bottom must be level with the deck otherwise puddles will lie on the deck and cause rust.

Finish

An outstanding difference between a steel yacht and a commercial craft is in the finishing of the welds. On a commercial boat most welds will be left visible at such points as the cabin coamings, but the outside of the hull will normally be fully ground smooth.

On a yacht no visible weld will be left unground. As a result only an expert will be able to tell if a yacht is of steel or wood or fibreglass, without actually tapping the structure to see how it sounds. The grinding off takes time and practice, not to mention good welding initially. If the welding is not good, then grinding will leave a series of little craters, incidentally starting points for rust.

Grinding is best done with an electric portable tool with a right-angle drive at the head. This tool is heavy so all possible grinding should be done down-hand, and this suggests it should be done to components before they are built into the main hull. Grinding in some areas, notably interior angles and especially round the feet of small deck fittings like stanchion sockets, is slow and awkward. A better approach is to so design the structure and details that these welds are covered by deck sheathing or other wood or composition.

Grinding off throws out showers of sparks so that goggles simply must be worn. However welding goggles are not suitable, so a special pair must be available for each person grinding.

Some small items, such as bollards weighing less than say 10 lbs, are best ground by holding them up to a stationary grinding machine. If one is not available, then a stand might be made or bought for the portable grinder. More than one grinding stone will be needed and here, as in so many subsidiary branches of steel boatbuilding, consult the specialists who manufacture the equipment. The complementary technologies advance apace—for instance, there are occasions when it will be advisable to use flexible discs impregnated with a cutting grit, rather than the more conventional carborundum stones.

Shot-blasting

If a steel ship is to have any life expectancy it must be shot-blasted. Without this treatment far more maintenance will be needed, and as the cost of the blasting work is quite small, no intelligent builder or owner dispenses with it.

Shot-blasting consists of spraying every part of the steel structure with a jet of erosive sand which scours the metal. It removes the skin of mill scale, rust and every other deposit, exposing the metal. This is a gritty, unpleasant job, and so it needs meticulous supervision.

Painting must take place quickly after shot-blasting but exactly how soon after depends on conditions. If the boat is in a warm shed, and the weather remains dry, some builders feel that the hull may be left two days between shot-blasting and painting. Others strongly disagree, to the extent that some will not send their hulls to a shot-blaster on a Thursday, for fear that it may be cleaned off on the Friday but not painted till the Monday.

Paint manufacturers recommend that priming be applied within 30 minutes of the shot-blasting. Certainly in big shipyards, as each plate enters the fabrication ship via the shot-blasting plant, care is taken to get the priming paint on within 20 minutes. This speed cannot be equalled when a whole hull is being shot-blasted as the job is likely to take most of a day. It would be possible to blast an area, then paint it, then blast another stretch. But this would be expensive because the shot-blasting

plant would be idle half the time and the painters spending their time waiting for a chance to get back to work.

Blasting is normally done in a special shed, and so the hull has to be transported from the builders. This can be difficult, maybe impossible, so there are alternatives. A half-way stage is to take each sub-assembly to the shot-blasters prior to building it into the hull. A more satisfactory arrangement is to use portable shot-blasting plant in the building sheds because then the whole hull can be done after the last weld has been completed. But this is a mucky, dusty job and it makes a mess in the building shed.

Some builders buy their plates and section from the steel mill already shot-blasted and painted with what is called a 'welding primer'. This is a protective paint which can be welded through. The welding needs cleaning with a mechanical wire brush or a grinder and then careful painting, otherwise rust will soon appear at each join. If shot-blasted and primed plates are bought, then they have to be stored carefully in a warm, dry shed. And even then the steel is not immune, as a close inspection of a finished hull made from these plates will show: it is possible to see palm prints where sweaty hands have touched the steel, starting the first stages of rust. If pre-primed plates and sections are bought, it is necessary to go over the hull after completion, and before painting begins, to eradicate any sources of rust.

Buying in shot-blasted and primed plates adds less to the total cost of the ship than a full shot-blasting after the hull is complete. But if I was having a boat built for myself, for whatever purpose, I should insist on shot-blasting after completion. What is more I would personally inspect the shot-blasting before painting commenced, using a powerful torch to look into every corner, for this is where the rust is most likely to commence. I would be pleased to spend time and money on this stage of the building, because if it is skimped rust blisters will appear in 6 or 16 months. They will go on appearing no matter how much painting and scraping is done. For a yacht, provided she was not being built down to a very tight price, it would seem good sense to adopt a belt and braces attitude, namely: specify shot-blasted and primed plating and sections from the steel mill, and then re-shot-blast after completion. This may seem excessive, but it would have the effect of producing a hull with the minimum maintenance and a continuing good appearance. The grit for shot-blasting should be B.S. mesh size 30. If anything coarser than this is used the surface roughness will be excessive. As it is two coats of primer will be required to cover the surface effectively.

Painting

There are three separate approaches to painting. There is what might be called 'traditional style', using paints made up from formulae which are in many cases of some antiquity. Just a few painters actually mix their own. This type of painting is rare, expensive in labour and seems to have relatively little to recommend it. Then there is 'normal' painting, which was used up to about 10 years ago fairly generally. It is a middle-of-the-road course, not too expensive, not reliable, and not cheap, but often adequate and in some cases to be recommended for reasons such as a shortage of suitable knowledge, skill or material.

Most important of all, there are the 'new' paints, based on a few synthetic resins, mainly epoxy resins, and chlorinated rubber. These new materials may be called sophisticated, but they do enable ships to go far longer between painting. In some instances the indications are that provided enough trouble is taken it is possible that the paint may last as long, in some areas, as the economic life of the ship. This is certainly the paint-makers' current aim.

These new paints need a high standard of surface preparation. By the level a few years ago, the new requirements for surface condition are very special but the achievement of the required surfaces is not particularly difficult with modern equipment.

Chlorinated rubber resin paint is available from various manufacturers, including ICI, who call their make Alloprene. This material has resistance to both acid and alkaline attack, dries fast, is not easily permeated by water, and can be applied to give coats between 3 and 6 mil per application. This type of paint is recommended both for prefabricated components and full ship painting. What is called 'intercoat adhesion' is good, which is a help when building up the recommended thickness of about 12 mil final thickness.

In this connection a conscientious paint foreman or manager will find the instruments supplied by firms like Elcometer Instruments Ltd of Fairfield Road, Droylsden, Manchester for measuring paint thickness are a help, and are not expensive.

One of the main attractions of chlorinated rubber paints is that they are little affected by the ambient temperature, and can be put on when the air temperature is down to $-18°$ C. This is in marked contrast to epoxy resins which are much more critical of the conditions, and cannot be put on in typical frigid blizzard weather such as is so often found in shipyards.

Chlorinated rubber is used as a base for long-life antifouling paints. Their good intercoat adhesion is a special help here as the area round the waterline suffers a lot, and needs fairly frequent renewal. A paint which will not bond on well in poor conditions is not satisfactory for this location. For craft like yachts which are 'pampered' and hauled up, dried off and carefully prepared, the paint takes less punishment. However, shortage of labour and its high cost are tending to make yacht owners follow commercial ship practice.

Priming paint

This is obviously the most important coat, since it goes next to the steel. If it is not right then all subsequent painting is a waste of time. Though modern priming paint is tolerant, it will not adhere to a surface which has grease or oil on it. If there is dirt, then the paint will lie on top of the dirt, and peel off fairly soon. Nor are these paints effective over rust.

Hand wire brushing of new or weathered steel is not effective. Mechanical wire brushing or chipping — or both — are used successfully when repainting an old ship, but shot blasting is much to be preferred. It gets into the corners which is where most trouble starts.

For new ships, there is no other process worth considering except shot-blasting, as a preparation to priming.

Now that automatic shot-blasting of plates is common, special primers have been developed to go on immediately after the blasting. These paints dry in about 2 minutes, and give protection for about 12 months, provided that the paint is not scratched. They are fairly tough, and stand scuffing, but a sharp metal point will penetrate them easily.

Welding through these paints is easy, and the paint withstands high temperatures, so that the area of paint affected by the weld is local. These primers are not affected by the cathodic protection systems used in ships and are resistant to salt water. Naturally they should be coated over with under-coating and finishing coats as soon as the building programme allows.

Epoxy primers with a substantial inclusion of zinc are much favoured. They are put on about 10 or at most 15 microns thick, any thicker application affecting the weld quality. After welding up, prefabricated units are given another coat of paint to make a total thickness of the order of 25 microns.

Repainting under water

Where performance is important, on high speed craft for instance, the underwater part of the ship needs to be kept entirely free from weed, barnacles and slime. This may mean slipping the vessel every four months, possibly even more often to be absolutely certain of a clean surface. The rate of growth of fouling on the bottom of a ship depends on the water temperature, so the nearer the vessel is to the Equator the more often slipping is required. However it is also dependent on the composition of the water, and this varies from sea to sea, year to year. One irritating result of this is that a ship may remain clean for six months in a particular area, using a certain brand and colour of antifouling. The next year she may foul quite seriously even though the antifouling specification has not been changed, simply because the seawater contains different plankton, which in turn support different types and concentrations of marine fouling growth.

One obvious way to get round the problem would seem to be to use a white underbody paint, so that fouling can be quickly and easily seen. This is not a success because fouling also varies according to the amount of light available, and therefore the white paint encourages growth. In addition the white brands of antifouling seem to be less toxic than the more sombre colours. For racing craft it is occasionally the practice to paint the underwater body with a hard white enamel, and scrub off at frequent intervals when fouling occurs. The white enamel makes early fouling easy to detect.

The normal method of removing underwater growth is with a flat hoe such as is sold for use in the garden. This tool is fairly effective for knocking off the worst growth, but used alone it is far from adequate. Its steel blade takes most of the weed and shell off, but leaves behind a layer of slime in a great many places and also the base part of the barnacle shell. This shell is extremely hard and needs concentrated local chipping to get it off. In this respect a steel hull is much better than most others since it can stand enthusiastic hammering to get rid of the closely adhering crustacea.

Painting galvanized surfaces

It is fairly common to see paint being put straight onto galvanized steel. However, the paint will not adhere if degreasing is not carried out first. The traditional materials for degreasing are carbon tetrachloride and white spirit. After degreasing the procedure is to paint first with a self-etching primer and then with a light alloy primer. At first sight this appears to be a lot of trouble to cover what is already a protected surface. However galvanizing alone does not last indefinitely; particularly if it is exposed to any wear. If it is painted it will last a very long time provided the paint is kept up to reasonable standard.

Red lead

This was the traditional material for painting steel craft for a great many years. It is no longer used because far better priming paints are available. Its chief disadvantage is that a skin forms on the surface leaving the under part still soft so that the next layers of paint cannot remain stable. Just as serious, it softens when saturated with water. All this adds up to the fact that it is not economic at whatever price it may be available.

Painting guidance

Painting technology gallops ahead as fast as any other science. This makes it hard for any shipbuilder to keep pace because he is beset with so many arts and sciences all advancing rapidly. Recognising this, paint makers supply technical literature in a palatable and carefully classified form. There are several hundred manufacturers, but two who go to the trouble to help small craft builders are: Hadfields Marine Paints Ltd of Mitcham, Surrey, England with their associated companies all over the world, and International Paints Ltd of Grosvenor Gardens House, London SW1, which also has a world-wide organisation with offices at major ports.

Paint trim

The less wood trim a steel ship has, the more important and more subtle her paint scheme must be. A pretty boat can be made beautiful with careful painting, and one bordering on the ugly can be made attractive by clever planning of the colours and divisions of colour. Some basic, simple scheme is essential. The classic one is the single colour which service and police launches have. An attractive grey all over, with black decks, black name and numerals picked out in white, and perhaps white masts, can look superb. The flash of red or brilliant orange life-rings and floats sets the whole scheme off, from the black boot-top to the white whippy radio aerials. The secret here is not so much the choice of colour, as almost any grey or khaki or blue will serve, but paradoxically the lack of variety. It is almost always a mistake to use more than two basic colours on a ship, except for small items, the biggest being the funnel. Even here it is safer to paint the funnel the same colour as the rest of the upperworks. Big ships occasionally get away with contrasting funnel colours by virtue of the sheer size of the smoke stack. In practice, the funnel colour is often a crude advertisement of the ownership of the vessel. Like so much advertising, it stinks, not just literally.

A typically simple, successful colour scheme might be based on two shades of blue, or two of a stone colour. The hull will normally be the darker colour, with the boot-top and the deckhouses the same paler shade. Getting a boot-topping to match a paint for upperworks may be difficult, and the best approach will be to first buy the boot-top paint, then tint the paint for the upperworks to match. The deck may be the same colour as the deckhouses, or maybe a shade half way between the topsides and the superstructure.

When planning the paint scheme, two points of view must be considered. There is the way the ship will look from the water. Her deck will not be visible, but her boot-top will show. She will normally be distant, so that the contrasting small points of colour like the light boxes and life-saving gear will not be prominent. The second view is from a quay, whence the deck is likely to be visible and items like the white

capsules holding the life-rafts are much more prominent.

In the second view the colour of the deck is important, so when a composition deck is laid it must be of a colour which accords with the rest of the plan. Wood decks tone with everything, as does wood trim of every sort. From close up little details assume importance out of proportion to their size. It used to be fashionable to paint the insides of cowl vents red. This practice now looks dated and somehow vulgar. It is better to have the vents the same colour inside as out or maybe black or clinical white.

White is a good colour in almost every instance. If a boat has to be sold, paint her white, with stone decks and a dark red boot-top, and she will like good tinned food, not exciting but safe and sure to appeal to virtually all tastes. A white hull may be 'non-committal', but a white cabin top is. It is almost always a mistake to use a white super-structure over a white hull, even if there is a coloured cove line or deck edge line or coloured toe rail. A stone colour or a pale grey, especially blue-grey, on the upperworks over a white hull is usually successful.

Dark colours reduce apparent size, but they attract the sun, so that the inside of the ship will be startlingly hotter. If there is air-conditioning, then dark colours are tolerable in the tropics, but the cooling plant in the air-conditioning will have to work harder. And if it breaks down . . .

For special situations there are recommended colours. In the Arctic bright red, contrasting in colour with white ice, shows up well from the air. A bright orange is most suitable for lifeboats. Ferries operating across busy rivers should be painted startling contrasty colours so that in hazy conditions they show up early, as they ply across the grain of the traffic.

Minimizing corrosion and sacrificial plates

Two different metals in the presence of water set up corrosion. The water must not be pure, but then water in its natural state seldom is. Sea water is particularly efficient at encouraging this expensive erosion of ships and their components. It tends to be super-efficient in some of the more polluted rivers and harbours.

The first defence against corrosion is to use only one kind of metal. Failing that, use metals which occur close together in the galvanic series. If two metals which are far apart have to be used, then coat one of them with a metal which is located between the two opposing metals in the series (page 159).

The second defence against corrosion is to keep the metals dry. The best way to do this is to paint them all, very effectively, using modern paints of adequate thickness, regularly. If one metal cannot be painted, other metals in the area must be all the more effectively skinned with an impermeable paint. For instance it is rare to see propellers painted, so the hull round the props must be very carefully worked over with paint. This calls for extra supervision because it is just the area most difficult to work, what with the obstructions caused by the appendages, and the awkward angle presented by the hull bottom.

The third line of defence is the use of sacrificial plates. These are zinc or magnesium lozenges which are bolted to the shell, the rudder and other underwater parts of the ship. These sacrificial plates, being anodic to all other metals, get eaten away instead of the next most anodic metal in the area.

Specialists in this field are M. G. Duff and Partners of Chichester Yacht Basin, Birdham, Sussex, England. They will specify the location, number and size of sacrificial plates, together with instructions for fitting them. They also sell the plates. Though this is a field where experience is a vast help, it is noticeable that plenty of yards fit their own plates 'by rule of thumb'. The main concern is to have enough plates in the region where there is turbulence. This is round the propellers and rudders, near a log rotator of any size and at the aft end of bilge keels.

Naturally the sacrificial plates need thoughtful fixing. A bolt through a piece of zinc and through a shell plate invites trouble. The fastenings must be made through lugs welded to the shell, or the fastenings can be welded to the shell. A good place to fit plates is on a centreline rudder heel bar, behind the skeg. It is common practice to put the plates on the shell in such a way as to cause turbulence, which seems unwise. Locating plates where they can be effective without causing added drag and aereation calls for study. One approach is to fit sacrificial lozenges as extensions to the propeller shafts, aft of the locking nuts, in addition to those elsewhere.

Leading authorities disagree on this whole subject. Nevertheless broad principles are discernable in their discussions. Cathodic protection is not pure science yet, by any means. There is quite a bit of art to the solving of these problems. Provided everything is equal, then an arrangement of plates on one ship which is successful should work on another identical vessel, under the same circumstances. However everything, from the size of the propellers to the type of paint and the water in which the vessel floats, must be the same.

It seems that to achieve success in this field the naval architect should build up a case-book year by year, and depart from successful procedures only in a small way, carefully watching the results.

Stainless steel and oxygen differential

It is well known that if two different metals are adjacent in the presence of sea water (or indeed almost any water which has dissolved even a little salt), then an electric current is set up. This results in one metal wasting away and is the well-known 'electrolytic action'. The metals need not be different. Two similar pieces of metal with different impurities are just as eager to start generating a destructive current of electricity. Even, in some cases, the impurities or constituents in a metal alloy will set up electrolysis.

If a metal such as stainless steel has a crevice which is shielded from the air while other parts of the same piece of metal are exposed to the air, then an electric current is set up. This is called 'oxygen differential', since the critical fact is the difference in the amount of air available over the surface of the metal. The important thing is that *two* pieces of metal are not necessary to get crevice corrosion. The other very serious aspect of the matter is the shockingly fast rate at which this type of corrosion can work. As the corrosion tends to be very local, the results tend to be a quick concentrated weakening, often in a crevice where it cannot be detected. The trouble is prevalent where turbulence causes local aeration.

For these reasons certain institutions and companies forswear stainless steel entirely. Having proved to their own satisfaction that it can be thoroughly dangerous, they are prepared, indeed determined, to ignore its attractive appearance, its popularity on small craft, and its vogue generally.

The builder of small craft finds himself in a dilemma. If he ignores the material he will lose customers and his craft may look less attractive. If he uses it he runs serious risks.

The solution to this problem would seem to be that the builder should only use stainless steel where it is well above water. It can be used for unimportant components, although every precaution must be taken against crevice corrosion. Boats sold with stainless steel should be offered with a clear disclaimer to cover future trouble. The way to do this is to offer the complete craft with no stainless steel aboard, and submit an alternative boat with some stainless fittings on the clear written understanding that the buyer accepts responsibility in the matter of choice, and knows about the risk of crevice corrosion.

This type of corrosion will be minimized if all stainless steel fittings are located where they are normally dry, and are clear of hollows where puddles can lodge. In addition every fitting must be secured so that there is not even a tiny crack between base flanges of fittings and the deck, or between plastic handles and the metal handle. In short everything attached to a piece of stainless steel must be perfectly joined with no tiny hair gaps.

Galvanizing

A wise precaution, for long life and reduced maintenance, consists of galvanizing those parts which can be taken easily to the nearest company doing this work. Items like rudders and portable stanchions, hatch tops and water-tight doors are all easy to transport and will not cost much to dip. In fact compared with so many processes galvanizing tends to be inexpensive. It is normally priced on the weight of the article dipped. For this reason a tube may cost less to galvanize than the same length of bar, even though the tube has a greater surface area, and uses up more zinc. However, so modest is the cost of galvanizing that it does not pay to adjust the design of a component solely to reduce the cost of dipping.

For the best galvanizing it pays to shot-blast first. To be sure, the galvanizers first dip everything in a cleaning bath of acid. However over the passage of days the acid is used over and over again, till it becomes less effective. Worse, in some works there may be a rush to treat a lot of steel, so one particular fitting may not be left long enough in the acid.

The galvanizing process is very simple: each steel item is lowered into a bath of molten zinc, held there for a few minutes, then lifted out and allowed to cool, when the zinc hardens on the steel. In some specifications, notably those put out by the Admiralty, the designer calls for 'double dipping'. The idea is to gloss over the steel with a second coat, on top of the first, to give extra protection.

My favourite foreman galvanizer scorns double dipping, with language which, to my great regret is not suitable for publication. He points out that when anything already coated is dipped a second time, the first coat melts off, so that in total there is never more than one coating. He says that it is easy enough to achieve an extra thick skin by simply lowering the temperature of the bath. The corollary of this is that anyone wanting a special job should have the galvanizing done late on a Friday, because the molten metal is not kept up to its full normal temperature for the whole weekend.

When chain is galvanized it must afterwards be 'tumbled', otherwise it will not run freely. The links are fully or partly clogged with the zinc, so that they bind together, sometimes in short rods. Ungalvanized chain should never be used on small craft because it makes such a mess. From the point of view of working economy a chain should be regalvanized every time it shows signs of rusting, since this is far cheaper than renewing every few years. Renewing is a nuisance in any case because of the difficulty of getting chain which exactly matches the gipsys on the winches.

Good galvanizing lasts surprisingly well. Most items not subject to wear will last ten years, sometimes much more. Even chain will regularly last five years between galvanizing, and sometimes for longer.

Before anything is sent for galvanizing it should be inspected. Remove roughness of any sort by grinding or filing. Sharp edges should be rounded, concavities should be filled, sharp points should be avoided at the design stage where possible.

Sprayed polyurethane foam lining

With a portable nozzle a pale brown rigid foam plastic is layered on the inside of steel hulls. The nozzle has pipes at the handle which draw two chemicals from containers. These chemicals mix in the nozzle and are sprayed to a thickness which is generally over $\frac{3}{4}$ inch; and may be as deep as the frames or beams extend from the shell plating.

The mixture coming out of the nozzle is a liquid which is undergoing a chemical reaction. It swells as bubbles form and then hardens. Each bubble is a sealed cavity, and this is what gives polyurethane foam its quadruple qualities:
  corrosion inhibition

sound insulation
heat insulation
buoyancy.

Possessing these four attributes makes this
material one of the most important available
currently in shipbuilding. Its relatively limited
use is astonishing, and can only be put down
to the lack of advertising in a world saturated
with this mind-batterer.

Corrosion inhibition The foam sticks to dry
steel — or indeed anything else — with embarras-
sing tenacity. It can be scraped off, but the
job is tedious. If it is put on new steel which
has been shot-blasted then since neither air nor
water can get at the steel rust cannot commence.

In awkward corners the corrosion check is
most valuable, because there are places where a
paint brush can scarcely reach.

Many places are neglected by ships' painters
for lack of conscience, or because the panelling
is hard to remove, or maybe the owner is hard
up, or too ignorant to give proper attention to
the ship. Or the ship is continuously employed
without a break for maintenance.

It is worth remembering that when the
expense of foaming is assessed, the cost of
painting must be deducted. Taking a six-year
view, foaming-in may more than pay for itself
on this account alone. After all, repainting does
not consist only of slapping on expensive
chemical compounds. First there are panels to
be removed, and portable furniture, cushions
and other things. Then the surface should be
rubbed over thoroughly, at least when the yard
manager is about, even if this ritual stops the
moment he turns his back. While the painters
are about no-one else can work, and if they try
to they will get short shift, besides drips of
paint all over their tools. So the ship is out of

commission and tediously delayed, while
painters work twice or three times over its
whole surface. After that the panelling has to
be replaced and the mess cleared up.

The indications are that polyurethane foam
will prevent corrosion from inboard outwards,
so that wastage can only occur from outside.
Broadly speaking steel ships have in the past
'died' from inward, not from external corrosion.
So foaming should greatly increase the life of
the ship. As external painting is easier than
internal, and as the foaming should last as long
as the ship, it looks as if the expected life
should be much longer, so that the rate of
depreciation can be reduced.

Sound insulation The curse of so many modern
ships is not their wetness, which has been
largely cured by tight hulls and good windows,
improved hatches and features like Kent
Clearview Screens, nor is it handling, which has
been cured by single-lever controls and twin
engines. The curse stems from the engines,
those shrieking diesels which virtually every
ship now has. They are reliable, for which we
all thank God and our engineers, but they are
often loathed because there is no peace from
the moment they are started.

Diesel noise is the ruination of most yachts, it
makes executive and directors' launches
50 per cent ineffective because who can talk
seriously to a background of uproar? On
working boats the noise level reduces
efficiency, increases tiredness, enhances the
chances of mistakes.

Polyurethane foam acts as a sound insulator,
and is effective in proportion to its thickness.
A good case could be made for foaming both
sides of engine room bulkheads, if it was not
for the fire risk. For normal cabin insulation,

where heat insulation is the main consideration, the foam will be built up till it is level with the inner edges of frames, beams and stringers. But where sound is to be killed the foam must cover every part of the steel, because the steel transmits sound with great effectiveness.

Every effort must be made to keep the foaming continuous. That means that steel doors leading into the engine room, also hatches and trunking, should be insulated. With vents one way to absorb noise is to have a plate below and extending well beyond the vent inlet in every direction — with foam on both faces. Sound which gets past the baffle is taken up by the foam in the lower, wider part of the vent tubing.

The foam is not tough enough to walk on, so metal engine room tread-plating cannot be foamed on top, but may be covered on the under side.

Pipes which pass through the engine space are particularly annoying noise carriers. They are not easily blanketed, apart from foaming, and should be insulated all round and then covered with a fire-proof material. As polyurethane foam is not affected by fuels and oil the coating of pipes presents no problem. Flexible plastic and rubber pipes cannot be treated in this way. However noise is not transmitted by these materials.

Heat insulation This also means 'cold insulation' because polyurethane foam will either keep heat out or in, whichever is wanted. In cold climates it will make the heating plant about four times more effective, while in hot zones it will hold back the worse effects of the sun.

We designed a 41 foot ocean cruiser for a young couple to live aboard. It was foamed right through and they found that a single Tilley pressure lantern gave off enough heat to keep the boat snug in chilly autumn weather in Scotland. In fact it was so effective that they kept the main hatch open. This boat has an open plan layout, so that heating is not easy and there are also plenty of ventilators, which tend to let the heat escape.

Because heat rises the foaming is most important from the waterline up when the aim is to conserve heat. My personal view is that a thin layer of insulation around $\frac{3}{4}$ inch thick will give good heat insulation, whereas it is not all that wonderful defying sound. In practice the material is cheap and it makes a relatively small difference whether there is $\frac{3}{4}$ inch or $1\frac{1}{2}$ inches, so it would seem best to go for the maximum short of cutting down the available usable space in the ship.

Where costs are cut finely and heat insulation is the main consideration, the side decks and cabin top decks should be treated. This will be easiest when the boat is inverted. In fact for amateurs it will only be possible, normally, when the boat has been turned upside down.

Buoyancy Polyurethane foam makes good buoyancy because it sticks so well to any surfaces it is sprayed on. Other forms of buoyancy have an unpleasant habit of floating free from the ship they are supposed to support. This is a fault with buoyancy bags and chunks of buoyant material. Buoyancy provided by watertight compartments or containers suffers from leaks which lie undetected till they let water in. They tend to occur at inaccessible places where inspection is often impossible.

Foam may be attacked with a blunt or sharp instrument, but it still goes on providing support. It is not hard to remove, but this has to be done deliberately. A collision is not likely to cause much loss of buoyancy. The same collision, if it ruptures a watertight bulkhead even slightly, is likely to cause the loss of a small vessel since these can seldom survive flooding of two compartments.

A cubic foot of foam will support about 55 lbs weight in the water, although this figure varies a lot with foam density. Some allowance must be made for slight imperfections and big bubbles in the foaming. For this reason a safety factor must be inserted when calculating the number of cubic feet of buoyancy needed to support a given vessel. This is only common sense, in any case, as so often ships have weighty additions over the years. The safety factor depends on the class of vessel. For an ocean cruiser, if overwhelmed far out at sea, or struck (as plenty have been) by a large ship, it is unsatisfactory if the flooded waterline is only 2 inches below the deck. She will be nearly impossible to get home under such conditions. But a tug operating in an estuary which floats when flooded at this level is vastly better than one lying sunk across the main fairway holding up shipping. In this connection insurance companies should make a useful reduction in premiums where foaming in is sufficient to ensure that sinking is impossible.

Tugs which get caught by a tide or very strong cross wind when their tow line is tight athwartships have a nasty habit of turning over and sinking quickly. High-sided motor yachts also have standards of stability which are poor. Open steel boats, because of their weight, are less lively and therefore less likely to rise to seas breaking inboard. This inertia is an advantage in that it makes for a steadier platform for fishing and so on. But it is common sense to provide enough buoyancy to allow the crew to float home, even if they are up to their waists in cold water.

One very real disadvantage of buoyancy is that it takes up a lot of room. On some craft the space needed for flotation material is unacceptably large. On others such as lifeboats space simply must be found even if other features suffer. As a basic principle the foam should be put in at the ends of the ship, so that she does not float on end when flooded. The foam must be high up, to prevent the ship turning over, yet not all so high that she sinks deeply before the buoyancy comes into effect.

The sort of spaces which can be filled are:
the stem ahead of the chain locker;
the stern each side of the rudder gear;
under the sole, right up to the sole, but clear
   of the bilge sump;
between and under the tanks in the engine
   room provided there is good fire protection;
between the shell and the lining;
under the berths and settees clear of drawers;
inside small hollow spaces, ranging from two-
plate rudders to built-up skegs and deep
narrow forefoot bows.

Under certain circumstances over-seeing institutions like the Board of Trade accept foamed-in buoyancy instead of watertight bulkheads. Or where bulkheads are fitted, but they are too far apart to ensure flotation in the event of flooding, then foaming-in is acceptable to reduce the volume of over-size compartments. I came across this concession when designing a ferry. The Board's representative indicated that a special application would have to be made, but it was likely to be accepted.

A firm which does this work in the British Isles is Brown Sons Marine Ltd of Four Marks, Alton, Hampshire, England. This company will foam-in any ship anywhere in the world. Amateurs and companies who want to make up their own foam can buy it from their local chandler, who gets it from Simpson Lawrence Ltd of 218 Edmiston Drive Glasgow G 51 Scotland. In this form it has to be mixed by putting it in a five gallon drum, first carefully cleaned out, and whipped up with an electric drill fitted with a special paddle. The drill should be a $\frac{1}{2}$ inch or $\frac{3}{4}$ inch rather than a $\frac{1}{4}$ inch kind to allow for better stirring, and be rotated at about 1,400 r.p.m. If a small paddle is used, or one turning relatively slowly, the foam will be dense. It will be stronger but heavier than necessary and also more costly.

If the foam has to be cut away, perhaps for repairs or to put in or attend to a pipe or electric cable, repairs are easy enough provided spraying equipment is available. The foam will stick to itself with the tenacity it clings to virtually everything else, from hands and overalls to wood and plastics.

When applied it grows in a way which smacks of a conjuring trick. At first nothing much happens, so that it is easy to feel that something has gone wrong. Then the volume is seen to increase, slowly, and then faster and faster: it's like science-fiction. Next the growth slows, stops and finally there is a brown smooth skin over the top, like some newly devised brown bread. The skin should be kept intact if possible, since it is apparently thoroughly waterproof, whereas the 'meat' under the skin is not quite 100 per cent waterproof. However it does only soak up a very little. The skin is cleaner than foam which has been cut, and does not cling to whatever touches it.

If the foam has to be cut back to level it flush with frames prior to putting in panelling,

the work can be done with a knife having a serrated edge. This is a handier tool for this job than a saw, as relatively small slices will be taken off. The bluntest saw will cut through the foam when a big cut is needed.

The material will not hold fastenings; indeed it is hard to think of any way to attach anything to a block of foam. It would probably be best to ensure that lengths of wood are buried under the foam, then screw into the wood. Certainly where lining is to be fitted the wood cleating should be fitted to the frames before foaming. True the frames will lack the corrosion inhibiting effect of the foam where the cleating is located, but this is seldom an area where corrosion is serious especially as the frames tend to be one of the thicker scantlings.

It will take about two days for two men to do the preparing and foaming in of a 30-footer. The timing must fit in with other building work. It must be immediately after shot blasting, and before anything is built into the boat.

Galvanic series of metals and alloys

CORRODED END (Anodic or least noble)
Magnesium
Magnesium alloys
Zinc
Aluminium
Aluminium alloys
Cadmium
Carbon steel
Cast iron
Stainless steel Type 410 (active)
Stainless steel Type 430 (active)
Ni-Resist
Stainless steel Type 304 (active)
Stainless steel Type 316 (active)
Corronel 240 (active)
Lead
Nickel (active)
Inconel (active)
Corronel 220 (active)
Brasses
Copper
Bronzes
Monel
Nickel (passive)
Iconel (passive)
Stainless steel Type 410 (passive)
Stainless steel Type 430 (passive)
Stainless steel Type 304 (passive)
Stainless steel Type 316 (passive)
Ni-o-nel
Titanium
Corronel 220 (passive)
Corronel 240 (passive)
Graphite
PROTECTED END (Cathodic or most noble)

machinery and steering

Engine room size, layout and finish

Modern small craft are in one respect much worse than their forebears. Years ago, in the days of steam machinery and plentiful labour, the engine rooms of quite a large proportion of small ships were show places. They gleamed, a delightful array of cheerful, softly shining, polished brass and copper.

Today the tendency is to cram a pair of screaming diesels into an ill-lit cavern beneath an important part of the living accommodation. The result is that almost all modern engine spaces are hellish awkward, ugly, unkempt, so inaccessible that maintenance is moderate or poor or even non-existent. Few owners, masters or crew will show a visitor round the engine room of a typical small modern ship with much enthusiasm if they know anything of the past or the true potential.

My idea of an engine space is one where there is clear access all round everything. There is headroom in part of the area, even on a 40-footer, also reasonable sole area, so that moving about does not call for the agility of an animal crossbred from a mountain goat and a fly. There are handrails everywhere, but items which are dangerously hot or otherwise untouchable are protected. Both daylight and artificial light are as abundant as in any other part of the ship, being every bit as important here. There is no sign of rust, indeed every part of the structure and machinery which is not polished is painted, so that leaks show up instantly. Colour coding of the pipes, wires, tanks and so on add a splash of colour to the whole compartment. When special visitors are expected, a good quality carpet is laid down. And why not? There is nothing new about this, and a pride in the machinery is the best

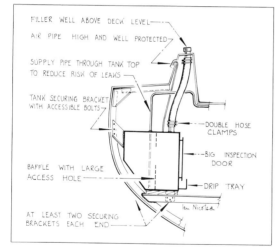

FILLER WELL ABOVE DECK LEVEL

AIR PIPE HIGH AND WELL PROTECTED

SUPPLY PIPE THROUGH TANK TOP TO REDUCE RISK OF LEAKS

TANK SECURING BRACKET WITH ACCESSIBLE BOLTS

DOUBLE HOSE CLAMPS

BIG INSPECTION DOOR

BAFFLE WITH LARGE ACCESS HOLE

DRIP TRAY

Ian Nicolson

AT LEAST TWO SECURING BRACKETS EACH END

Fig. 38a If securing lugs are welded on to a tank, they make the fitting of the tank a quick job, provided the lugs are thoughtfully located where they can be reached for bolting. There must be at least four lugs in all, even on a small tank. This tank has a supply pipe which reaches through the top of the tank and ideally it should suck from just above a small sump.

insurance as well as the only way to ensure reliability and economy.

Before anyone bleats that all this fine appearance is going to cost money, a few facts are worth considering. Initially it is possible that a good engine room may cost more than a cramped one. But the cost difference will be absorbed in less than three years' maintenance charges. It could be wiped out by a single failure in the machinery department. In practice the cost difference may be in favour of the spacious engine room, even if this means that the ship's overall length has to be increased to achieve the ideal. The reason for this is simply that a few feet of extra plating, an extra frame or two, cost little. But time is wasted in a costly way if engineers, fitters, plumbers, painters and electricians have to work literally upside down with their heads jammed between exhaust manifold and generator. Under such conditions they cannot follow plans, and incidentally the draughtsmen's time will be wasted if they spend hours contriving to fit quarts into pint pots.

Working in cramped engine spaces saps the enthusiasm of all the tradesmen on the job. It also makes inspection during the job hard or impossible since there is no room for the yard manager or foreman to get in to see what is going on. All sorts of incidental disadvantages creep in: special tools have to be made or collected from the store or borrowed or bought because conventional spanners will not fit; tightening awkward nuts results in bashed knuckles (time off to visit the first aid room) or breakages of adjacent fittings; standard equipment will not fit so special items have to be made or stock equipment modified to suit; installation time even for simple things like tanks goes up simply because lifting tackle

cannot conveniently be brought to bear, and so on.

It has to be admitted that there will be some craft in which the engine space has to be a troglodyte den. But a surprising number and variety of small ships can have convenient, safe, spacious engine rooms to everyone's advantage. The builder in steel should exploit the fact that he is almost always offering a special boat, designed to suit the owner exactly. He is working in competition with masses of stock boats, mostly fibreglass, mostly with the worst type of engine compartment. This is where the steel small craft has a trump card, since glassfibre is costly, so that a few feet of extra length is a consideration. More important, the g.r.p. builder is stuck with his mould. He cannot change size at the drawing board stage if he is working on a stock hull, as is often the case.

The builder in steel will often be making a ship for an owner who values prestige. Yacht owners are not the only people who have a strong pride of possession and a wish to impress visitors on board. For instance I was recently called in as a consultant naval architect by a river purification service. This government body was proud of its achievements and delighted that foreign scientists were calling from afar to view the research work. When it came to discussing their new research vessel, apart from seakindliness, reliability and all the obvious virtues, the director insisted that a major consideration was the prestige value of the new craft.

The same applies to police launches, directors' launches and company yachts, service craft, and even coastal lifeboats, since funds have to be raised from the public, who want to see where the money goes.

Engine bearers

There is diversity of opinion as to the best type
of engine bearers. This is because engines
themselves vary so much. Some can be dumped
down on the ground without any form of
holding-down bolt and left to run happily for
hours. Under the same circumstances less well-
balanced engines throw themselves about,
topple over, while others will quickly pound a
hole in the ground they are put on.

It is an old-established principle that engine
bearers should be long. Plenty of old-timers
insist that half the length of the ship is by no
means overdoing it. Anyone who has contended
with vibration problems will agree that
athwartships stiffening is essential all along the
length of the bearers.

It is obvious that engine bearers should
normally extend the full length of the engine
space. They can then be welded to the bulkheads at each end, with a bulkhead stiffener
extending up from the bearer. If the engine is
big, or if the bearer top is well up the bulkhead,
then there should be a bracket on the opposite
side of the bulkhead.

On craft up to about 45 feet the bearers are
often heavy L-bar or channel bar. Above this
size the tendency is to follow big ship practice
more. This basically consists of building up an
'egg-box' system of vertical plates under the
engine. The compartments will probably be
divided into fuel tanks, cooling water tank and
so on. If this multiplicity of vertical plates,
which are in fact deep floors and stringers, is
open-topped, then inspection and maintenance
is not too bad. But if tanks are made of the
spaces, at the planning stage care must be taken
that each compartment can be reached without
lifting the engine. This will mean cutting large

lightening holes, or having a fairly complex
arrangement of tank hatches, or both. For this
reason, and for general economy, simple deep
girders are useful for the engine bearers for
craft up to 60 feet or more.

One technique for assembling these girders is
as follows: an L-bar is laid on the frames, at
the correct distance outboard to take the
engine feet, and extending from bulkhead to
bulkhead. The L-bar is bracketed to the
bulkheads, and then a similar L-bar is welded
in vertically above the first. The second one
also extends from bulkhead to bulkhead, and it
is lined up to take the engine feet. Between the
upper and lower L-bars a series of diagonally
sloped L-bars are now welded. This will be
simple since precise fitting of the diagonals will
not be needed. The same applies to the athwartships diagonal stiffeners, which are also L-bar,
extending from the top of the bearers to the
frames.

This scheme can be used before putting in
the floors, which are then made part of the
bearers. Alternatively the floors can go in first,
with their tops aligned. In practice the outer
bearers of a twin or triple screw ship may be
outboard of the ends of the floors. When the
bottom L-bar is laid on the frames it will not
at first touch them all. It should be welded to
each one either with brackets or by bending it
in place.

Among the disadvantages of following big
ship practice are: the top foundation plate is
made of an extra heavy flat bar, which will
either have to be a special small order or be cut
out of a plate; the deep plate bearers will need
templates and will then have to be cut out of
plate; these vertical plate bearers will almost
certainly need lightening and access holes cut
in them, which will take more time.

It is good practice to design the bearers so that the engine can be moved fore and aft several inches on the bearer. This means that if the tops of the bearers are cranked, this should be done well away from the feet. Among the reasons for cranking the bearers will be a wish to keep the bearers deep, so that if they tend to taper off in depth at the aft end, it will be important to crank them upwards.

At the fore end the bearers may become unnecessarily deep, particularly if the shaft is steeply sloped. This will result in bearers which will be heavy and also make access in the engine room difficult.

Where the bearers do not end on a bulkhead they should taper out, and not end suddenly as this will result in a high stress point.

Even where there is a bulkhead or deep solid floor at each end of the engine space it is highly desirable to have a drip tray under each engine, including under auxiliaries. This is not only to keep oil and engine filth from spreading over the engine compartment as a whole, but also to minimize fire risk. The drip tray should extend under the gear box and any auxiliary components on the engine. In practice it will not normally be necessary to make up special drip trays. The structure under the engines is fully welded, lightening holes are avoided, and the resulting oil-tight well acts as a drip tray.

At the design stage the problem of holding-down bolts must be considered. There must be access for putting on and tightening both the nuts and the locking nuts. In some circumstances it may be hard or impossible to fit locking nuts, so that Nyloc or similar patent nuts should be used.

In a twin engine installation it is customary to mount the engines well apart, and run the shafts parallel to the centreline back to the

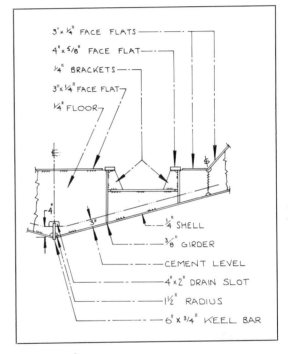

Fig. 38b Centreline and engine bed layout of the 53 ft NERC research ship. The absence of lightening holes and concentration on one size of plating, namely $\frac{1}{4}$ in, is noteworthy. Strength rather than weight-saving is the aim here.

propellers. This arrangement is simple; it ensures that there is space all round the engines within the limits of the total room inside the ship; it does not demand much design or engineering skill. It is not necessarily the best. For instance two engines need only three longitudinal bearers. Eliminating the customary fourth will reduce weight and work. It means that the inboard feet of both engines rest on one bearer so that it is probable that one engine will have to be slightly further forward than the other. It is likely that the shafts will have to be angled out at the aft end to locate the propellers in the best position. It is probable that the centreline bearer will have to have a wide top, to keep the engines as far apart as possible to improve access.

What makes this arrangement so attractive is that many ships anyhow have deep vertical plate keels. All that is needed is for this centre-line plate to be extended upwards to take a suitable extrusion or bearer plate, together with the same amount of athwartships bracketing as any other bearer.

Collision stops

These are metal chocks welded to the top faces of the engine bearers, close up and forward of the engine feet. Their job is to stop the engine moving forward if the ship collides or grounds or stops suddenly. In the nature of things small craft encounter this sort of trouble much more often than big ones. However small craft very seldom have collision stops because, on the whole, their holding-down bolts have adequate strength in shear. Also there are occasions when it is convenient to be able to move the engine forward or back an inch or two, during refitting and re-engining. Collision stops make this awkward.

Tanks which are not built in should have some provision for preventing them moving if the ship is suddenly stopped. The jolt on grounding is likely to be more severe than rolling even in the worst sea, so if the tanks have lugs welded on, which are bolted or welded to the ship, then the lugs should be designed to be most effective against forward movement.

Where the tank is held in place by straps, these usually extend athwartships, so there must be chocks or lugs or some such at the fore end of each tank.

Engine heat exchangers

One advantage of steel construction is that the ship's engine can be fresh water cooled conveniently. One method is to have a tank well down in the ship open to the sea at the fore and aft ends, with a scoop at the inlet and a reversed scoop at the outlet. Sea water will enter this tank as the ship steams forward and flow out the other end in a continuous stream. Immersed in the tank is a coiled pipe connected to the engine cooling water. A pump forces the water from the engine down, round the coil where it loses its heat to the passing seawater, and back to the engine. This system saves the expense of a normal heat exchanger and also eliminates the pump needed for circulating the sea water in a fresh water system.

A simpler lighter system eliminates the salt water tank entirely, and uses the shell of the ship as the heat exchanger. A flat tank is welded between two frames, well down in the ship, one side of the tank being formed by the ship's hull plating. The hot cooling water from the engine is pumped through this tank and back up to the engine to take on more heat. Probably the main snag with this system is the difficulty of getting an adequate area of plating to dissipate the heat into the sea.

In either system there must be the usual details such as an arrangement to top up the fresh water, and thermostatic control to regulate the heat exchange rate. One attraction of the first layout is that when operating on fresh water the open tank provides hot washing water when the engine is running. A possible disadvantage is that some forms of antifouling are believed to be adversely affected by very warm water. The internal sea water tank will need a good door for cleaning off the barnacles.

One type of heat exchanger which has always had a small but persistent degree of popularity is the external pipe version. This consists of three or four pipes for each engine, located outboard under the bottom plating. The fresh water from the engine circulates through these external pipes, which pass the heat to the sea.

The basic idea is simple, and fitting is not hard. It is easy to ensure there is ample heat exchange area simply by providing an excess length of exposed piping. A pump is needed to circulate the fresh water, but that is common to all systems. The resistance of the exposed piping has little effect on the speed of a normal moderate speed ship, but this system would not be found on a planing vessel.

The chief reason why this system is not universally adopted is the vulnerability of the exposed piping. If the ship grounds in an awkward way, or if she is hauled up by a yard which forgets to examine the docking plan carefully, or if the shipwrights blocking her off after hauling up are careless, then the pipes may get damaged.

In some ways the damage is not too disastrous, since cooling water will still flow round the machinery. However the water will become progressively more salty without anyone aboard being aware of this. As a result the engine could be damaged without the fact being apparent for months.

One small asset the system has: the main engines can sometimes be run for short periods when the ship is on the slipway, since there is a small amount of cooling and plenty of fresh water in the system even when ashore.

Propellers

The logical material for propellers is steel, if the hull is steel. This would, in theory, cut out any chance of electrochemical corrosion between the propeller and the hull. However the situation is complicated. For a start propellers are cast, so that the material used is almost certainly slightly different from the hull plating. This would not matter much, as the interaction would almost always be quite small, particularly as the hull is painted. More important, small ship propellers are produced in fairly large numbers, by repetition methods which border on mass production. They are normally made of a bronze, just which one depends on the manufacturer, each having his favourite blend, which will normally be an easily cast and machined aluminium or manganese bronze.

These manufacturers will make a steel propeller if asked, but it is likely to cost as much if not more than a bronze one, and take a long time to deliver. Bronze propellers are available quickly from the major manufacturers, who keep a stock up to a certain size, which is likely to be at least 24 inches diameter.

There was a time when iron propellers were made. Their virtue was that if they were damaged the blade snapped off fairly cleanly, so they were favoured for use in ice. Nowadays nylon-bladed propellers are used for ice conditions. These are made particularly by the Danish firm of Hundested, who also specialize in variable pitch propellers.

Another reason why bronze propellers are generally used is that many antifouling paints contain heavy inclusions of copper compounds. Bronze, with its large proportion of copper, will not react with a copper paint. Of course it could be argued that the material used for the propeller does not matter, since the blades and boss can all be carefully painted. This is a doubtful argument because paint is not likely to stay on the blades unless very carefully applied and never maltreated. Also, for the best efficiency the whole propeller should be kept smooth and burnished. It has to be admitted, however, that the loss in efficiency due to painted propeller blades is quite small, and probably not significant on most craft. It is on high speed craft that the loss is most noticed. A similar point occurs with nylon-bladed propellers. The material cannot be fined away too much at the edge due to the inherent lack of stiffness, so that the blades tend to have thick leading and trailing edges. This leads to a loss of efficiency.

Summarising, most steel craft have bronze propellers with adjacent sacrificial plates.

Propeller shafts

The steel-worker naturally tends to use steel for every purpose possible. He will assume that propeller shafts are of mild steel, but in many small craft this is not so. The position is comparable to that obtaining with propellers, namely the builder in steel tends to follow the builder in other materials, largely because the industry is geared to certain conditions. Thus we find that steel craft often have stainless steel or bronze propeller shafts. Bronze was much the most popular till fairly recently when its price rose so much that it about equalled stainless steel.

The position now is that many vessels have stainless shafts because they are fairly easily available, and wear better than many bronzes. There seem to have been few cases of corrosion by electrochemical action on stainless shafts, but one wonders how many have occurred and have been dismissed as 'a bad batch of stainless steel', or 'not up to specification', or some similar excuse. In practice propellers fit very well onto their shafts, so that there is probably little chance of crevice corrosion taking place.

Nevertheless recent research makes out a very good case against using stainless steel under water.

Stainless steel is expensive, and there are good reasons for using mild steel shafts. They are cheap, easy to obtain and to machine, they are strong, reliable provided corrosion can be checked, and they suit steel-working yards. The only real argument against them is corrosion, and this can be checked by various ploys. The Royal Navy encase their prop shafts in glassfibre, first painting the shafts with resin, then winding on fibreglass bandages. The glass is taken right up to the bearing surface, and the steel is carefully treated so that the g.r.p. adheres well.

Another approach is to epoxide paint the shaft, taking the paint right over the bearing areas. A technique which deserves to be better known is the building up of the bearing surfaces. This consists of spraying on a metal—often a stainless steel—along the shaft in the region where the stern gland and bearings occur. The sprayed metal forms a hard wearing, long lasting collar at the critical points. When it is worn, the shaft is removed and built up anew. In this way a new shaft is never needed, so that over a few years there is a very real saving here. This technique suits mild steel shafts which have been kept carefully painted. The bearings must be bigger than usual, to accommodate the swollen lengths of the shaft; and this in itself is a good thing, since there is a bigger bearing area.

One advantage of using mild steel shafts is that couplings can be welded on, this being quicker and cheaper than cutting a key-way.

Rudders

Only on small craft, under 28 feet, is it usual to

fit rudders made from a single plate. There are exceptions: the twin rudders on a fast 35 foot motor cruiser will be smaller than the single rudder on a medium speed 28-footer, so they might be made from a single plate. In practice they will need careful shaping however, in order to get efficiency, so they may well be cast. Then on cheap commercial and fishing craft where the initial cost is more important than efficiency under way, a single plate rudder may be selected.

Double plate rudders are made up in various ways. One method I favour is to use relatively thin plating, easily formed round a bar or tube stock. Where the rudder is large it will be necessary to have fore and aft stiffeners, suitably shaped to the correct profile. When this rudder is complete it will be relatively light but very strong. Its weakness will be that it will not have the plate thickness to withstand much corrosion, but this is combated by galvanizing and then painting with an epoxy, so the rudder should outlast the rest of the ship.

A simpler two-plate rudder is made by welding two flat plates onto a rod or tubular stock. The plates are pinched together at the aft end and welded there. Top and bottom sealing plates are needed, and the result is strong. It is not usual on small rudders to have any drain or plug into the hollow interior. Larger rudders are sometimes filled with rigid polyurethane foam.

If a spade rudder is welded to its stock, and the stock extends well into the ship, then shipping the rudder may be awkward. When renewal is needed, it may be necessary to either jack the ship well above the ground, or dig a hole to drop the rudder. This is annoying and expensive. In fact it can be hazardous to block a ship up high so some

means is needed of shipping and unshipping the rudder easily. This also applies to sailing yachts with counter sterns and deep rudders.

The usual arrangement is to have a bolted flanged coupling at the top of the blade. Many commercial craft and many motor yachts have rudders supported at the heel by a spigot into a bearing on the skeg. There may have to be flanges at top and bottom to release the rudder from both the stock and the spigot, but in some cases, especially on small craft, the stock can be lifted a little and the spigot is then lifted out of its bearing.

These external flanges are offensive, partly because the fastenings rust and seize. Almost as bad, the whole coupling is quite rightly made massive, since this is not a region where any risk can be accepted. As a result the interruption to smooth water flow offends any designer worth his salt. On some craft the flanges are made oval, which slightly reduces the burbling in their wake. A most unsatisfactory situation occurs when the top coupling shows above the waterline at rest. This is totally unacceptable on a yacht, and such craft as directors' launches and police launches should conform to the best yacht standards.

There are various alternatives based mainly on two ideas. One is to have a short stock, extending only a minimum distance inside the hull, so that the rudder and stock are dropped together. The other is to make the stock detachable in a more sophisticated way.

The short stock is strong, saves weight, and makes especial sense on power craft with dagger or spade rudders. This is a cheap way to tackle the problem, but none the worse for that. Where there is a rudder heel fitting, it must be possible, in fact it should be easy, to unbolt this. Countersunk bolts and recessed

The skeg and keel of this auxiliary yacht have been almost completely profiled before erection. Small joining bars across the gaps have been left to maintain the correct shape. The long aperture for the stern tube and the cut-out aft of it for the propeller are clearly seen. The propeller shaft tube will be fully welded all along the skeg and at the shell plating.

Machinery and steering

Twin rudders normally lose efficiency because water
floods over the tops of the blades. The blade upper
edge cannot be right up against the ship's bottom
when amidships because the rudder would foul
when turned inboard. On this ship fairing chocks in
the form of steel casings have been welded to the
shell over the rudders. This directs the water flow
and increases efficiency. The sacrificial plates are
seen on each rudder and duplicated above each
propeller.

nuts used here avoid the disadvantages of an obtrusive coupling.

A removable stock tends to need more planning, but is more likely to suit a bigger craft. One arrangement is to have a square stock which is turned at top and bottom. The bottom engages in a bearing under the rudder heel and the top has the usual quadrant or tiller, together with the rudder carrier. The blade is bolted to the square part of the stock. Another approach is to have a stock which extends into the top of the rudder and is keyed in. An aperture is made through the rudder to allow for putting the nut on the bottom of the stock, and this aperture can be filled with a semi-soft stopping like a non-hardening putty.

For bearings, at least on craft under 50 feet, it is often worth using Ferrobestos or Tufnol for the bearings. These materials are easy to work, relatively cheap, and renewal is simple. However machining should be done with due regard to the expansion which takes place after prolonged immersion in water. They are impervious to electrolytic action, which will be present if a bearing metal is chosen, and they should far outlast a crude steel-to-steel bearing.

Naturally rudders will be of high aspect ratio where possible, with a degree of balance which in practice should not exceed one-fifth. If a rudder is found to be insufficiently effective, at least because it is in steel any alterations should be easy. Lines to try are: increase the height of the blade till it only just clears the hull; add a little more to the balance, if need be above and below the propeller if there is insufficient room in way of the blades; add side rudders, parallel to the main blade, and far enough off to give a fair flow between the main blade and the wing blades; scrap the single central blade, and fit twin parallel

blades and so on.

In this connection, on twin ruddered craft it is essential to stop the tops of the rudders an inch or two down from the shell, otherwise when the blade is turned inboard it will come against the hull. A result of this is that there is a flow of water over the top of the blade, which results in a loss of efficiency. This may be partly overcome by welding to the hull a shaped fairing piece which has the same section as the rudder. When the rudder is amidships it appears to grow straight on up into the hull, and when it is turned the fairing piece prevents water flowing between the top of the blade and the hull.

Steering failure is serious on most craft, a possible exception being a twin screw small craft operating in unrestricted waters. There are two second lines of defence against a steering breakdown (apart from providing a radio to call for help or materials to rig a jury rudder). It is usual to have some arrangement for shipping a tiller on the head of the rudder stock if wheel steering fails. On larger ships this reserve may be more sophisticated, taking the form of a hand wheel right over the stock, to take the place of the hydraulic or remote steering with its wheel forward in the wheelhouse.

To make it easy to ship the emergency tiller the stock is often carried up through the deck, and is machined square. It is covered by a screw cap when not in use – and human nature being what it is – this cap is generally seized, never gets greased, needs a special tool to remove, which tool is lost, and so on. Anyone who has been faced with the emergency of a steering failure will appreciate this situation, and a conscientious designer will take some trouble to make the emergency tiller simply and quickly fitted. One arrangement is

Fig. 39a Rudder gland. One advantage of an all-welded hull is that the rudder gland may be fabricated of steel and welded in place. The details shown here are typical, but not all of them apply in every situation. The style of bearings are found in some small craft, up to about 50 or 60 ft, because they are so simple, cheap and easily made with limited facilities.

to have the rudder stock covered by a deck seat, so that no capping is needed. Another arrangement is to fit the aft hatch just ahead of the stock, so that the tiller is shipped through the hatch. This might be dangerous if a bad sea was running, because the open hatch would allow water below. Another approach consists of fitting a padded cover of proofed cloth, which is cut away to ship the tiller. Whatever scheme is used, the head of the stock should be heavily coated with a preservative grease like lanoline.

The tiller may need cranking either vertically or horizontally. If there is a deckhouse in front of the emergency steering position it may be impossible to see forward with a straight tiller. This calls for a tiller which extends out at about 45° so that the helmsman can look down the side deck.

If the stock breaks inside the hull the emergency tiller will be no use. Chains are fitted on some craft leading from the top aft corner of the rudder. Sometimes they are taken up on deck, on other craft they are shackled to eyes welded on the quarters. It will often be necessary to have blocks on the ends of these chains, to give a purchase to help steering, which will be done by ropes as if the boat was steered by a yoke.

On ocean cruising yachts a hole is made in the blade near the top, as far aft as possible. Some softish stopping is put in the hole. If the stock fractures, the stopping is pushed out, and a shackle inserted to take emergency steering lines.

Generally it will be impossible to withdraw a propeller shaft without first taking off the rudder. This applies to twin or single screw craft, and it has resulted in some builders drilling a special hole in each rudder, a little

It has in the past been usual to machine the top of the rudder to take the tiller or quadrant, but here again, welding on a rectangular section is cheaper, easier and usually more suitable for a small welding shipyard.

If the garboard is not thicker than the rest of the plating it is good practice to insert a local thick plate to take the gland.

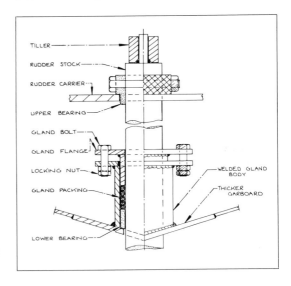

bigger than the shaft. To get the shaft out the rudder is turned right athwartships and the shaft slid aft through the hole. While this hole can be planned on the drawing board, it is probably better if it is burned out after both propeller and shaft have been fitted to the ship. This is not a cynical reflection on the accuracy of small shipbuilders, just an acknowledgement that there are very many factors involved. If the hole is pre-drilled and there is some small alteration subsequently, perhaps to the rudder bearing packing, the hole may not align with the shaft.

Fig. 39b Section through centreline of two-plate rudder. Rudders on craft up to about 50 ft are often of the simple two-plate type with few if any stiffeners. Relatively heavy plate instead of stiffeners makes sense, since all rudders are badly situated with regard to corrosion. They are moving parts and located in a region where corrosion can be expected to be high because there are other metals like bronze propellers close by.

The idea of cutting the stock short below the rudder bottom is to allow the bottom plate to be narrower than the top one. The chord width is reduced at the bottom, so that the rudder thickness should be reduced in proportion. Also, of course, the shorter stock is lighter and cheaper than one extending to the bottom of the rudder blade.

There are varying opinions as to the amount of blade area allowable ahead of the stock. Too much area results in a tendency for the helm to swing across, so that the ship becomes directionally unstable. This is extremely dangerous and disconcerting, so that it is worth sacrificing some advantage to ensure that it never occurs. By keeping

the stock well forward the amount of force needed to turn the wheel may be slightly up, but this is a minute price to pay for the self-centring effect of a rudder which is always slightly unbalanced with the centre of pressure definitely aft of the stock. (It must be appreciated that when the boat moves forward, as soon as the helm is put over a little, the centre of pressure moves ahead of the centre of gravity of the rudder area.)

In the cause of efficiency the gap at the top of the rudder should be kept small. However on twin rudders space must be left to allow the rudder aft end to swing in towards the centreline of the ship in spite of the slope down of the underside of the hull. Also for efficiency, the blade depth should be as big as possible relative to the chord width. (A rudder acts in a comparable way to a hydrofoil or an aerofoil. Knowledge of basic hydrodynamics and aerodynamics is an asset to any small craft designer. Even the most rule-of-thumb backwoodsman, whose only design criteria is 'The same as last time only with 3 inches more beam', should gain an inkling of flow patterns and behaviour.)

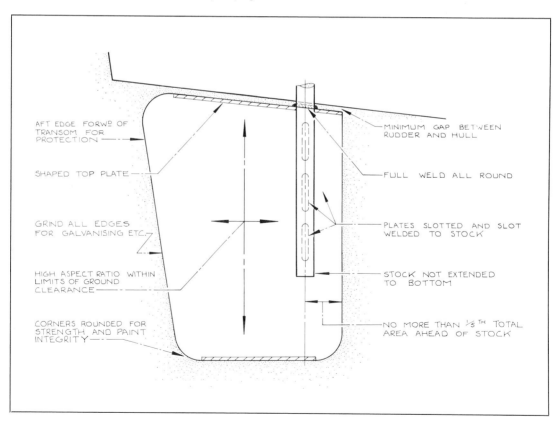

Electric wiring

Most of the rules and precepts for wiring a small steel ship will be the same as for other craft. Cable is fixed to cable trays, which can easily be welded to the structure. It will pay to fit these trays early on, possibly even before plating. They should not be low in the bilge where water may get at them, so it may be necessary for them to be on the beams. This would normally involve up-hand welding but if they are fitted before the deck plating, then they can be fastened from above.

Any vessel which is to be finished well must not have any electric cable showing, except for short lengths linking echosounders and so on. This calls for advanced planning, and a good case can be made for subcontracting the electric wiring. Firms which do this work will quote against a wiring diagram, and they tend to be adept at producing such plans. As plenty of small design offices (and big ones for that matter) are short of electrical specialists, this aspect of the matter by itself is a big inducement to contracting out the electric wiring. However subcontractors are not likely to use a variety of different coloured outer cable covers unless this intelligent practice is made part of the contract. The ship's crew will appreciate a colour code, since they will normally only handle electrical problems when there is a breakdown at sea.

Steel cable trays are too heavy to be used on every ship. Aluminium trays are better for fast boats, expecially those under 40 feet; even in the engine room there will not be many wires, so wood battens may be used instead. Wood is light and takes screws easily. Eliminating cable trays cuts down on the volume of material in the boatyard stores. Dexion, or one of the various forms of plastic cable casing, may be used instead of conventional cable tray. Yet another approach is to drill holes in the frames and beams, and secure the cables to these scantlings using nylon loops specially made for this sort of work. A typical manufacturer is Insuloid Manufacturing Co., Leestone Rd, Wythenshawe, Manchester.

Cables are encased in conduit on deck. However this is vulnerable, and where possible the cabling should be kept below deck or otherwise given full protection. There are various techniques for this. Some wires will be led up inside masts, to serve lights aloft. Navigation lights are conveniently located on the top or sides of deckhouses, so that all or nearly all the wiring is inside.

Electrical equipment on deck is downright unreliable. This is a widespread nuisance on small craft. The main trouble is that even the expensive sockets, switches and plugs cannot cope with bad weather. The difference between an expensive installation and a cheap one is that the latter fails sooner.

There is as yet no complete cure for this malignancy. Certain palliatives are suggested:

1 Where possible, there should be no component above deck. Switches should be inside the wheelhouse or other convenient covered part of the boat. For instance it may be best to have the switch for a foredeck floodlight just inside the forehatch.

2 Avoid deck sockets, above all. If cables cannot be continuous from power source to the unit using the electricity, then locate the junction below deck, and lead the wire through a gland. For such apparatus as Aldis lights used on deck, the sockets should be below, and the lead taken up through a hatch or port, or even a vent.

Stern deck arrangement. The transom has been swept up to give character to the yacht, as well as to form the aft toe rail. Though the side toe rails have wood cappings the aft one does not. Because the feet of the aft pulpit are in sockets welded to the toe rail, the deck paint can be easily renewed. Also, a likely source of rust, namely the toe rail socket where it meets the deck, is eliminated. Through the top of the transom there are enclosed type fairleads made by cutting an aperture and edging the hole with a steel moulding.

Fig. 40, 41 A 53 ft twin diesel research ship built for the Natural Environment Research Council by Tees Marine Services Ltd and designed by Keel Marine. Her operational area is South Georgia where she will carry personnel and equipment from the main base on the island to other parts of the island for exploration and scientific work.

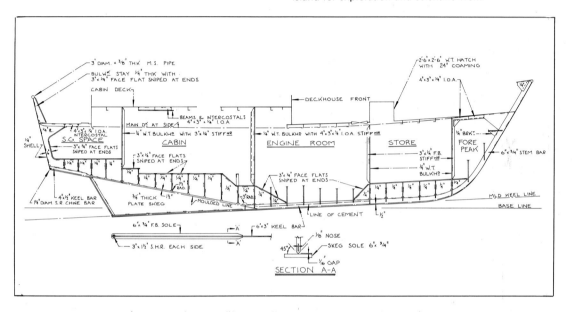

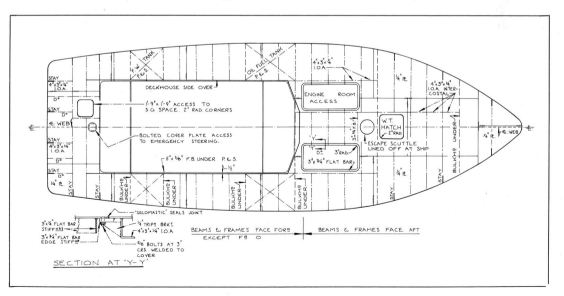

Built over 75 years ago, this magnificent little iron
ship has been given a new engine and special
propeller on a vertical pivoting shaft. A drive of this
type is particularly useful in such situations as
undocking with a strong onshore wind, since the
whole stern of the boat can be forced directly to
windward, with the propeller working across the
ship. This picture confirms the adage 'Steel ships
never die, they don't even fade away'.

3 On very small craft a number of fittings can be made portable. For instance a launch which seldom needs navigation lights might carry them on a board or stanchion, with a wandering lead attached. They are fixed in a deck bracket and the wandering lead plugged in below decks.

4 Where wires must be led through decks an efficient gland is important. The simple nylon type have much to recommend them, not least being their tiny cost and freedom from corrosion.

5 Electric wiring and components should be located high up, and certainly well clear of the main weather deck, with sockets and glands through a cabin top rather than through the main deck.

6 For working craft, especially those subject to harsh conditions, duplication is advisable. This must be carefully done, so that failure of one component will not affect others. Deck lights for fishing boats, for instance, should be in at least two groups, each completely independently wired, fused and located.

tanks, piping and plumbing

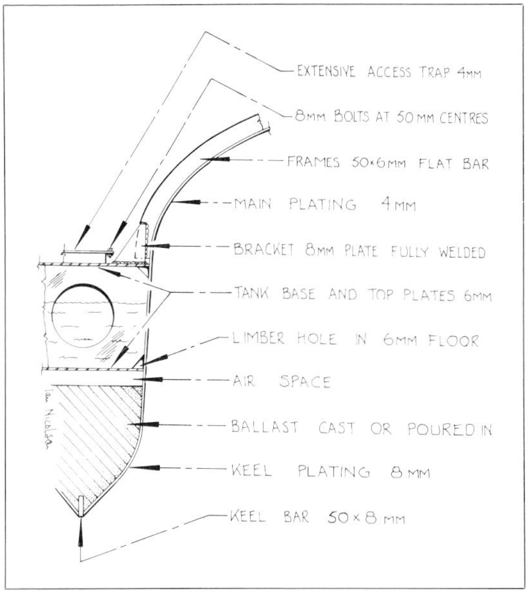

Fig. 42a Keel and tank construction. In a sailing yacht it is logical to get the weight of the tanks as low as possible, and therefore they are often built into the fin keel. It is sometimes difficult to weld down inside the fin keel so it may be necessary to plate up the bottom of the fin keel, next put in the ballast, then secure the lower tank plate, before continuing the plating up to the turn at the garboard. The access trap above a keel tank, or indeed any tank, should be made as large as possible so that anybody reaching through it can get to the extreme corners of the tank. This sketch is typical of a sailing yacht about 45 ft. (14) metres) overall length.

Tanks

One of the main advantages of steel craft is that tanks can be built in. As tanks are increasing in number in ships, this is an asset which is yearly more important. For instance there is a tendency, spurred on by actual or impending legislation, for small craft to have septic or sewage tanks instead of pumping toilets directly overboard. Then there is the spreading demand for greater tank capacity, as owners realise the advantages of bulk buying of fuel. In some regions refuelling is awkward and may involve a special journey, so that there is a tendency among yacht owners to carry what used to be considered massive loads of fuel, to reduce refilling to two or three times a season.

Built-in tanks are located so that their outer sides are formed by the ship's side, and their bottoms by the ship's bottom plating. One or both ends may be formed by full or partial bulkheads, and the top may be the ship's deck. Sometimes the transom, or a pair of floors, or the foc's'le sole, or engine bearers form some of the boundaries of the tanks. There are few limitations, except that fuel and fresh water tanks should not share a common division. At least two plates between them eliminates the risk of unsuspected contamination.

Though a double bottom in a small ship is unusual, it may make sense, in order to accommodate the tanks low down. An obvious and popular place for tanks is in the fin of a sailing vessel or motor-sailer. Here the weight is as low as possible and otherwise useless space earns its living.

Naturally tanks will not be carried right up to the deckhead if the designer is worried about stability. But on some ships, where there is a

Tanks, piping and plumbing

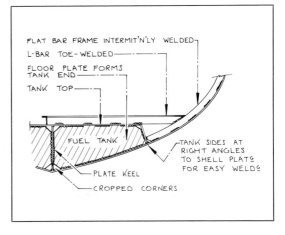

Fig. 42b Section view. Double bottoms are rare in small craft under 45 ft. However they are sometimes introduced to give capacious fuel and water tanks located down as low as possible. This naturally enhances the ship's stability. It also gives a measure of protection in the event of running aground on rock. The wells each side of the centreline tanks must have carefully designed bilge pumping facilities.

big load on deck — such as a winch — a strong well-stiffened tank end or side is conveniently carried up to the deckhead. Using this well supported plate to support the deck load is the kind of economy which can make the difference when contracting competitively or battling to reduce the total displacement.

As a basic rule the stiffeners should be put inside tanks on small craft to improve the available stowage, engine and accommodation space marginally. Tank stiffeners are needed in the same size and spacing as bulkheads, and here as elsewhere Lloyd's rules form a good guide. Baffles are needed whenever any tank dimension exceeds 24 inches. Properly spaced and fitted baffles take the place of stiffeners, and incidentally they need not be made quite the full depth of the tank. Baffles are particularly important in tanks located in passenger spaces, because the gluggle and splosh of liquids keeps people who are not used to the sea awake. One famous American designer used to have harsh things said about him in the small hours, because he would insist on putting water tanks below the settee berths. He had little choice because his boats were shallow draft with hardly any space in the bilge. But anyone trying to get to sleep on top of the gloopling water was in no mood to appreciate this most talented man's design problems.

Tanks for fuel must not be painted or galvanized inside but cleaned out thoroughly just before trials. As dirt will get inside the suction should not draw from the very bottom. A small well is sometimes incorporated in the bottom of the tank, with a draw-off cock. Water and dirt collect in the well, and in theory they are taken out every few days or weeks depending on how often the ship is used. In practice the cock is seldom accessible and is

used infrequently, so the usual two filters for each engine are essential and they must be located prominently.

A piece of metal gauze fixed over the end of the suction pipe prevents dirt being drawn in. Drip trays under the tank or at least under the draw-off cocks are stipulated by Lloyd's. If the drip tray does not extend under the whole tank, then some sort of trough may be needed under the tank door to catch the odd weep.

Water tanks are often galvanized, and need very careful washing out. It is possible, though very rare, to get zinc poisoning from a newly galvanized tank. Zinc, like lead poisoning, is accumulative. The body has difficulty in getting rid of the build-up of poison so that a subtle illness ensues, which is hard to diagnose because it is so rare and unlikely. The answer is to both wash the tanks well and treat them internally with one of the special paints made for tank interiors.

If a tank is to be galvanized it has to be portable, and this is both an added expense and inconvenience. For this reason water tanks are often simply built in and treated internally with paint. Whatever the internal coating the tanks need annual cleaning and inspection.

Fuel tank draw-off pipes are sometimes inserted through the top of the tank and extend down near to the bottom, or into the top of a small sump. The idea here is to eliminate any chance of a leak where the draw-off pipe enters the tank, and reduce the chance of a leak at the lower joins of the fuel supply pipe. The same technique can be used for the water tanks of long-range cruisers. A disadvantage of this idea is that if the suction pipe fails it can be difficult to get the contents out of the tank. However it is an undoubted safety precaution. It does avoid emptying the contents of the tank into the bilge when someone treads on the draw-off pipe and breaks it, while stepping through the bilge when the floorboards are up.

Tank doors

Except for small shallow tanks, the access panel must always be at least 2 feet × 2 feet to allow a man's head and shoulders to pass through for proper cleaning, painting and inspection. If one dimension is limited to less than 2 feet, the other should more than compensate. This is always true, but particularly so where the tank is against the ship's side or bottom, where inspection is doubly important and small local repairs may be needed.

Seldom seen, even though it can be an economical approach, is the tank with the whole of the top or one end removable. This idea saves making up a precisely fitting top (or end) since it overlaps onto the flange all round, and if it is $\frac{1}{8}$ inch too large or too small it will not matter. It also saves cutting the access hole in the top (or end) and welding

an angle-bar frame all round.

The bolts round the tank access door should be spaced about 2 inches apart, maybe $2\frac{1}{2}$ inches. Stainless steel nuts are easy to take off, but this material is about seven times the cost of mild steel, so few owners specify it. Galvanized bolts, with a good slobbering of lanoline on the threads, are a reasonable substitute. If the bolts are likely to be covered by bilge water they must be carefully painted over.

For a water tank a rubber seal is used between the flange on the tank and the tank door, but not for tanks containing fuel or lubricating oil, as they attack rubber. Neoprene will do for fuel tanks. Whatever is used, the whole gasket is cut from a solid sheet, and not made up from strips, because leaks will occur where the strips join at the corners.

Various composition gaskets are sold, and they must be treated with suspicion. One boat set forth with her fuel tanks sealed by a clever new gasket, made from asbestos and a binding compound. The fuel in the tank washed the gasket out of its lodging and after some hours the entire fuel system became bunged solid with asbestos flakes. This state of affairs did not occur at once, so the ship had passed trials and was well out to sea when the trouble was discovered.

Henderson hatches* make good inspection doors. They may also be used as fillers for water tanks on small craft, when they are fitted on top of the tank. These hatches are shut with a single lever, and seal onto rubber, which makes them reliable and convenient. However the only two sizes available give a clear opening of 5 inches × 2 inches, and

* Available from Henderson Equipment Ltd of Cowes, Isle of Wight, England

7 inches diameter, so that they are only of limited use for cleaning out and internal repainting.

Deck filler caps

The usual way to make provision for filling fuel and water tanks is to fit screwed caps flush with the deck, opening into pipes leading direct to the tanks. This arrangement is widely used and vastly unsatisfactory. Any rain or sea water swilling along the deck makes a bee-line for the filler cap and seeps below into the tank. Few caps have the standard of finish which keeps out sea water indefinitely, and plenty lack any form of flexible sealing washer. Most caps have poor facilities for tightening down. A common arrangement is a pair of small holes in the top of the cap to match a key with two quite small spigots to engage in the holes. Other keys have bars which 'fit' into a shallow slot in the top of the filler cap.

The first line of defence to keep the sea out of tanks should be a raised filler cap. It can be set on top of a hollow cockpit coaming, it might be set in the top of a bulwark, except that it would be vulnerable when going alongside, on a commercial ship where appearance is not paramount it could be on a pipe standing up clear above the deck. My company once designed a 60 foot motor cruiser and arranged well-protected seats across the aft end of the deckhouse. The tops of two seats lifted up to reveal shallow watertight wells. In one there were the fuel fillers, in the other the water tank inlets. Any fuel spilled was trapped in the well so that it could be mopped up before it fouled the svelte teak decks. For deep-water work we might have gone one further and made the folding seat tops to clamp down on a flexible

watertight Neoprene seal.

For a second line of defence the stock type of filler cap should be avoided. A cap which has a skirt all round, and a thread inside the skirt, acts to shed water. Also, the thread is inside so it is protected, whereas the deck filler cap normally has the thread on the outside. The type of cap recommended is easily fitted with a washer which can be renewed annually. No special washer need be bought, and it is simple to fit from sheet Neoprene.

This preoccupation with sea water exclusion is not a personal fad. Water in the fuel is hard to eradicate and if salt water gets into a tank it will hasten corrosion. Incidentally, tanks are often much more difficult to renew than other parts of the ship. My attention was focused on this problem when I took a new boat on prolonged sea trials up the Norfolk coast. The weather turned sour, with a fresh on-shore wind. So much water was coming aboard that the side decks were continuously flooded, and there was a constant trickle of sea water into the fuel tanks. One of the engine filters had a transparent bowl, so throughout the night I watched it. When the water level was half way up, the engine had to be stopped, the fuel shut off, the bowl emptied, replaced, fuel turned on, engine started—and off we went for another half hour or so. We forgot that sea water was getting into the fresh water tank by the same process and later we all became seasick drinking tea and coffee made from the mixture.

Occasionally a shipbuilder tries to get round the problem of leaking filler caps by having two caps. The first is large, and is flush in the deck, so that it is removed initially. Clear below the deck the filler pipe stands up, topped by a screw-on cap. Any water which leaks through the deck cap drips down into the bilge, to be sure. But so does any spilt fuel. For this reason this plan is unacceptable and it contravenes various safety regulations. In this connection the Ship and Boatbuilders' National Federation (of Great Britain)* have a useful booklet which covers such safety matters as this, and many other factors relating to small ship and boat construction.

For fresh water fillers, the inner and outer screw-on cap is acceptable, though not truly satisfactory. The whole point of having a steel ship is to avoid any traces of water inside the hull. Instead of fitting a leaking cap flush with the deck a better scheme is to have a cap which stands up from the deck just slightly, located in an unobtrusive corner, clear of walkways. Where appearance counts the cap should be made of stainless steel, or chromed; and like all fillers labelled with the tank's contents.

Bilge pump piping

On modern craft plastic piping is used for bilge suctions and discharges. It lasts indefinitely, is cheap to buy and work, and light in weight. However it is not fireproof. In fact some types are actually worked by softening in boiling water. When a boat is being built under government regulations or to Lloyd's rules, or the equivalent, it is likely that plastic piping will not be allowed, or only to a very limited extent. The suction must be of reinforced piping if the pump is powerful otherwise the pipe will collapse when the pressure inside is lowered.

Steel is one alternative, and it will be fairly cheap in a steel ship. A good yard will assemble

*Address: Vale Road, Weybridge, Surrey KT13 9NS, England

the whole piping, then dismantle it, have it galvanized, reassemble and test it. For many yards this is cheaper than piping in copper, but relative costs must depend on the complexity of the piping system and the current price of the materials.

Where there are watertight bulkheads a good scheme is to have one pump for each compartment. This is seen on some small service craft and makes for reliability and simplicity. However the practice is not permitted by some government bodies, which insist on two pumps centrally placed and piped to each compartment. The resulting pump layout, with valve chests, non-return valves and a multiplicity of pipes passing through watertight bulkheads is complex and expensive. I have heard serious complaints from British and Dutch small craft operators that this type of pumping system is much too complex for crews of small commercial and government ships. These systems are usually based on requirements originally laid down for big ships with trained engineers to operate them.

It can be argued that a simple system, based on one pump for each compartment, falls down if a pump fails. A good pump does not in fact fail often, and the risk is largely offset by having pairs of screwed plugs at the bottom of each watertight bulkhead; so that when required bilgewater is permitted to flow from one compartment to the next. Pairs of plugs, one facing each way, are needed in case one side of the bulkhead has a serious depth of bilgewater.

Individual pumps for each compartment regularly work out cheaper than a single or pair of pumps piped throughout the ship. Where power pumps are required the argument becomes more delicate. Small electric pumps are

Fig. 43 Section view. A technique used in some Dutch yards for salt water plumbing is shown here. A short length of steel pipe is welded carefully to the hull, the inboard end of the pipe having been first threaded. Thereafter normal threaded ships' fittings of brass, bronze and copper are easily attached. To cope with the electrolytic action a sacrificial plate is fitted near the outlet. It must be renewed at every refit.

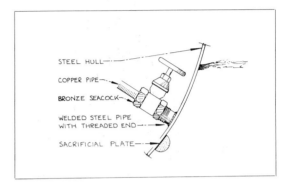

cheap, but if one is required for each compartment, then it may pay to lead pipes from a central pump to each compartment. If a ship is fully decked, or mostly decked so that rain water can only get into the bilge in one compartment, it will probably be more economical to have one power pump in the engine room and another in the open compartment, rather than lead pipes to a single pump.

The piping alone does not cost the money. The valves often need extended handles from the bilge to above deck. These extensions cannot always lead straight, so that universal joints and bearings for the extended spigots become necessary. Where diaphragm pumps are used for each compartment no strum boxes are needed. But if the suction passes through a valve before it gets to a diaphragm pump, then strum boxes are essential, which makes for a further expense.

Diaphragm pumps do need very efficient strum boxes on fishing boats used for shell fishing. The sharp edges of the broken shells are about the only hazards the rubbery diaphragm cannot withstand.

Plastic seacocks

The attraction of non-metallic seacocks is that they do not corrode. They have other assets, such as their light weight, pleasant appearance, reliability without maintenance, ease of fitting and so on.

A fairly typical range is made by British Steam Specialists Ltd. Available in a useful selection of sizes, they mate quickly and simply with fittings and tubes of the same plastic material. However they are not fireproof, so that they may not be acceptable at the ship's side in the engine compartment or galley. But

where truly effective fire-detection and fire-extinguishing systems are fitted, even in dangerous spaces it may be reasonable to fit this type of valve, at least on inshore craft.

Plastic seacocks are more expensive than their metal counterparts, but the extra cost is partly offset by easy fitting. If located in an awkward place, extending the handles presents no problem. They are bolted to the shell, which spotlights their main weakness, since bolts will corrode and must be examined at every survey.

In shallow, gritty water, the traditional type of seacock gets worn, and then leaks. One BSS type of valve has a diaphragm, so that gritty water does not affect it. Incidentally the diaphragms are renewable. In the smaller sizes, plastic cocks are not strong and must be located where no one will tread on them.

Basins

It is general practice in small craft to buy in stock washbasins from ship's chandlers such as Simpson Lawrence Ltd of 218 Edmiston Drive, Glasgow and South Western Marine Factors of

Pottery Road, Poole. There is such a wide
variety of sizes and types that most situations
can be covered. Where space is limited, there is
a strong temptation to put in a tiny basin, but
if the ship is to be used continuously this is a
mistake. The type of small steel craft used in
many fields, particularly rough commercial
work, are crewed by people who must
inevitably get dirty. They will not be excited
at the prospect of cleaning themselves in a
12 inch × 10 inch basin.

Where for any reason a stock basin cannot
be fitted a special one can be made up. On
commercial craft, it used to be common to see
stainless steel basins (and other furniture)
fabricated for a particular job on a 'one-off' basis
by specialist firms, but this is rare now because
of the high cost. A stainless steel basin is welded,
or more commonly bolted into place.

Basins may also be made up to fit special
locations from fibreglass but this involves
making a mould and the end product is likely
to be expensive unless the mould can be used
repeatedly.

Baths

On small craft under 60 feet fitting a full-sized
bath is seldom practical, unless luxurious
accommodation is specified. Sit-down baths are
made to fit into the confined spaces available
and also incidentally to save water. Where
there is less than 3 feet 6 inches for a sit-down
bath a shower is a good substitute.

In quite a few instances the designer will
find himself struggling to work in a bath in a
space which is infuriatingly undersized by
perhaps $1\frac{1}{2}$ inches. There are two or three
ways round this problem. A fibreglass bath can
be made up or alternatively a steel bath

designed and fabricated. Steel baths must be
properly finished with that special heavy
enamel made for just such a purpose. The
attraction of a steel bath is that it can be worked
in between two steel bulkheads. This means
that it will be as long as the compartment since
the steel bulkheads will form the ends of the
bath. Naturally the bath will not be made with
sharp interior angles but will be fabricated by
bending a single plate into a U shape. The top
inboard edge will need rolling round and a
decorative front will enhance the finish.

accommodation

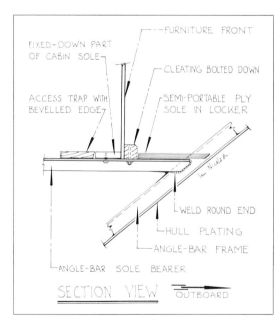

Fig. 44a Cabin sole and furniture. The cabin sole bearer in this sketch is a steel angle-bar welded to a frame to increase the hull strength. It also forms a strong base for the furniture which is screwed or bolted to a cleating piece, this in turn being bolted to each sole bearer. The ply sole in the locker is fitted before the furniture front as the job is easier at this stage. By keeping the ply away from the hull plating the fitting is easier and drainage as well as ventilation is improved. The access trap in the cabin does not extend up to the furniture front so that when the trap is lifted there is no risk that it will scratch the furniture.

General considerations

The internal layout of a ship is very little affected by the material of which she is built. Whether she is of wood, g.r.p., aluminium, concrete or steel, she needs amongst other things ventilation, furniture, upholstery and so on. There are a few special considerations which are treated here. Much of what is said relates to all types and kinds of small ships regardless of the constructional material. These aspects are included partly because of their general neglect in the designing and building of small craft, and partly because information about them is scarce or unpublished, or only available in forgotten back numbers of magazines.

Cockpits

This is an area where steel shows up to some advantages. A strong, fully watertight cockpit is easy to make, and may be a complex shape without incurring a big labour bill. I remember designing an ocean cruiser with a cockpit which ran right aft to the transom stern, where there were two drains. We worked in provision for the Calor cylinders at the aft end of the cockpit, under the aft side deck, accessible yet out of the way. If a cylinder leaked, the highly explosive gas just drained overboard instead of into the bilge. If the cylinders are stowed in the cabin, leaking gas lies in the bilge awaiting a spark to explode it.

This cockpit had curved seats, a tapering sloping sole, and a bridge deck which was lowered in the middle to make access into the cabin easier. The companionway into the cabin was offset, and the mizzen mast was set on a pedestal projecting from the aft edge of the

Fig. 44b Section view. If this technique is used for minor bulkheads large area panels can be quickly put in place with the minimum of fastenings. The channel acts as a deck stiffener. If the bottom of the wood is not carefully sealed rot will occur because water can lie in the channel. The best way to avoid this is to fill the channel completely with a sealer once the wood is in place.

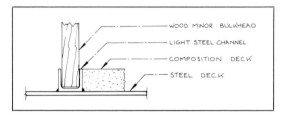

bridge deck. That big down thrust which is inevitable from any sailing yacht's mast when going to windward was easily carried by the aft vertical plate of the bridge deck. Working in all these changes of level, angle, slope and curvature in other materials would have been relatively tedious and costly, especially if watertightness and strength were to be maintained.

Where there is an engine below the cockpit a semi-portable well makes sense. This is lifted out, after unbolting all round, for removing the engine or doing main overhauls *in situ*. A similar but less radical technique is to have the whole of the bottom or a large part of it semi-portable, for the same reason.

When making the well it is a good idea to flange or bend the edges where this is possible. Both the top edges, where the sides meet the deck or seats, and the bottom edges, where the sides meet the bottom, look so much pleasanter if they are a smooth curve or a neat sharp bend. If welding has to be used here, then this is a good place for grinding or taking trouble to conceal the line of welding. So many visitors, as well as the crew, spend so much time in a cockpit that the standard of the ship is judged by this region.

Steel lends itself so well to self-draining cockpits that in the majority of cases the well is drained into the sea. Even on the littlest ships the self-draining cockpit sole must be at least 9 inches above sea level at the lowest point. There must be a firm slope towards the drains, this declivity being adequate to cope with all possible changes in trim. Traditionally the drains are at the forward end on sailing yachts, usually because this gives adequate room for the crossed drain pipes and means that the drain seacocks are accessible. However

there are good reasons for putting the drains aft. For instance most ships increase their trim by the stern, and aft drains are shorter.

Of course the ideal cockpit drain emerges above the static waterline. This can be done by draining through the transom, or on a power driven vessel by draining out both sides.

Side or stern drains above the waterline result in dirty driblets down the ship's side, admittedly near the waterline. This is circumvented either by fitting rubber lips, similar to those used by Yarrows at the deck edge of their frigates (see illustrations page 112) or by draining out at boot-top level. This means draining through pipes from the sole down to near the waterline. Whenever pipes are used to drain the cockpit, whether or not the outlet is above the waterline, seacocks are needed at the pipe outlets. This is one reason why transom draining is favoured. Also it is marginally cheaper.

It is one of the infuriating traditions of the industry that cockpit drains are made much too small. Expense lies behind the cheese-paring, since the price of seacocks goes up very rapidly as size increases. Builders work on the principle that self-draining cockpits will normally fill and stay full without endangering the ship. They also realise that it is a fairly rare thing for the drains to be asked to clear the well quickly and often. As a result only a few ocean cruising yachts specially built for experienced owners have adequate drains. As a working basis, two drains of at least 3 inches diameter are needed for every 15 cubic feet of well space. Drains need grids over them, and should be as near to the edge of the well bottom as possible to give total drainage.

Because steel is cold to the touch, and slippery to walk on, a grating over the bottom of the cockpit is usual. The traditional kind is best, with slats going both ways like a griddle. This is extremely attractive but expensive. A more common type has the battens going fore and aft.

Variations occur on these themes. For instance the simple type is improved by having a frame all round, and by making the battens narrow, but deep enough not to bend under load. Traditionally gratings are varnished all round the outer frame, but left scrubbed in the middle. If the cheaper variety follows this convention they look more 'tiddly'. What has been said about the gratings for the bottom of the well applies to the wood forming the seating. The traditional type of grating is rarely found on the seats, and somehow it never looks quite right unless done with exceptional skill and art. The frame surround needs to be wide, thick and well rounded inboard where it is under the knees. Probably the most effective seating is longitudinal battens which are fairly narrow and flat-S shaped in section, like a park seat, for maximum comfort. Alternatively, fitted cushions, each with a grab-line round and internal buoyant material, are both practical and smart. This finish finds special favour in American waters, and on inland craft.

Virtually all cockpits have coamings round. It is hard to get designers or owners to accept the fact that a self-draining cockpit does not need coamings. Few people will admit that a cockpit without coamings can be more comfortable. Having raced for a season on a boat which had no coamings, I am amazed that people tolerate these excrescences. They take up deck space, dig into the small of the back, fail to keep out bad seas and keep in water which should be draining back to where it belongs. They add weight and windage high up. They get in the way of sheet winch siting on sailing yachts, they take up deck space on power yachts, they pretend to keep people from falling overboard, yet fail miserably in this duty. I know I overstate the case, but in many instances a small ship will be better off without cockpit coamings. She will certainly be lighter and cheaper, and may look smarter without them. As for keeping the crew on board in bad weather, that is the job of personal safety lines.

If coamings are favoured, it may pay to make them quite small. Also if they are made as wide as they are high, they can be sat on, or walked over in comfort. Something perhaps 2 inches high and 3 inches wide, with well rounded edges, will keep out water draining down the deck, serving also as deck stiffeners, without being obtrusive.

Lockers round a cockpit are also traditional, and likewise suspect. Gear stowed here is continually wet if the lockers are open to the elements. In theory modern warps and fenders are weatherproof, but if they are stowed in open-fronted lockers they are not concealed from view, and so make the ship look untidy. Lockers with lids and doors which shut but do not hold out the water are often a snare, since they let in water, yet give the appearance of enclosing dry stowage. A compromise is cockpit lockers with sealed lids, or Henderson hatches to give access. The only trouble with this type of hatch is that it is rather small (7 inches diameter for the larger size), which prevents bulky gear being stowed through them.

Crew's accommodation

Many steel craft have accommodation for crew using the word 'crew' in a specific sense. It is used here in contradistinction to passengers, or owners, or directors, or anyone travelling in special comfort. The tendency in the past has been to make the quarters for the crew relatively less comfortable, more cramped, less well warmed and ventilated, in short, inferior.

This attitude has always been convenient in the past because it is an avenue for the ship-builder to save money. It is also a haven for the designer working under pressure, short of time and inspiration. He sketches in a few cot berths, whirls in a circle for the toilet, perhaps not even checking that the model chosen actually fits in the confines of the foc's'le, and passes the plan over for printing. Such was the past indeed.

Things are very different now. Crews no longer gratefully accept any job. Before agreeing to work on a ship they inspect their future living quarters. If the standard of comfort is found to be deficient, they haughtily stalk away, leaving the owner to find someone less demanding. Such people are not to be found so the inference is clear: crew's quarters must be as comfortable as the rest of the accommodation. As in practice the crew often live for long periods aboard, whereas passengers, or owners, or directors, or whoever is the human cargo are only aboard for a short time.

Also because there is a tradition that the

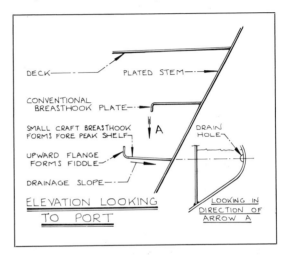

Fig. 45 Elevation looking to port. In small craft the available space has to be used intelligently. The small craft designer knows that stowage is always short, so he uses even the forepeak when he can.

crew's quarters are forward, the foc's'le needs special care during the design stage. It is almost always an awkward shape. What is worse, it is located right forward, where the motion at sea is worst. There are many strong reasons for putting the crew's quarters amidships or aft, not least being the desirability of having the galley where the motion is least, and the crew next to the galley.

Chain lockers

The location of the space where the anchor chains are kept is always a compromise which irritates the conscientious designer. For sea-worthiness the weight of the chain should be near amidships, and as low as possible. But the chain must be fed off the winch or windlass vertically into the chain locker, so in practice the locker is well forward, where the winch usually has to be.

On racing yachts, where weight must be kept away from bow and stern even if this is inconvenient, the chain locker is sometimes well into the middle of the ship. The path between the chain-pipe and the stemhead roller has to be surfaced with a rugged material which can withstand the chafe. Vertical rollers are at times needed to steer the chain correctly without fouling the fore hatch and other parts of the ship.

Chain is perverse, and needs every encouragement to go the right way. It has to be fed vertically into its locker, but in special circumstances will be angled about 20° off the vertical by a pipe or chute. If expected to slide down into a locker via a trough angled at 45° the chain will just pile up and jam.

A chain-pipe must have an internal diameter of at least three times the width of the links. Ignore theory which tells the slide-rule designer that a $\frac{1}{2}$ inch chain has a link width of $1\frac{1}{2}$ inches plus a little, to allow the links to swivel inside each other. The chain, never having used a slide-rule, does not follow the rules. It catches up a lump of mud or some pebbles, and enters the pipe with two links jammed at an angle, or the chain twists round and round as the boat swings to the tide. The resultant semi-rigid bar needs plenty of space as it enters the locker. Experienced owners prefer troughs rather than pipes to lead chain at an angle into the locker. A trough just overflows when the chain bunches.

A vertical pipe is annoying because the chain in it clinks when the boat rolls. On moorings this is infuriating, because it is hard to stop. A pair of holes through the pipe to take a light stick horizontally provides the only cure.

Where the chain passes through a wood deck a metal pipe extends down through the deck, completely protecting the wood from the chain. Some stock chain-pipes are not suitably spigotted, and others have futile little holes for the holding down bolts (not screws even though the deck is wood).

To make sure the chain stows and runs out freely the lockers have to be designed like padded cells, in that they must have the minimum number and size of projections. Bulkhead stiffeners should not end cut square at the bottom where a link can lodge under a flange. The best ploy is to put the stiffeners on the other side of the bulkhead. Lightening holes in floors cause snarl-ups, and so can the flanges across the tops of floors.

Chain lockers should be deep but not wide at the bottom, so that the chain cannot shift in a seaway. In practice the shape of the ship dictates the space available, as it is usually an inverted cone or wedge that suits the situation.

The centreline division is important, because the two chains must be kept apart most carefully. The division need not be carried right up to the deckhead, but it should be quite three times higher than the piles of chain. If the two chain-pipes through the deck are very close together then the centreline division must be taken up almost to deck level. The anchors are on occasions wanted in a great hurry, and any chance that they may not run out fast and free must be stamped out.

When the chain comes in it will be wet, often muddy, and sometimes have seaweed tangled in the links. This means:

1 The chain locker must be easily drained.
2 It must not have any pockets where water can lie.
3 It must be easy to wash out.
4 The limber holes need to be twice as big as the biggest elsewhere in the ship.
5 It should be easy to get a hose in for washing through.

6 Ventilation is needed to dry the moisture and exorcise the smells caused by rotting seaweed and primaeval mud.

Cementing in the bottom of the chain locker prevents water lying in puddles on steel. The cement will withstand the pounding of the chain as it pours in or thunders out, whereas most paints will not do so efficiently. The cement is cleaned easily, and raises the bottom of the lockers to a point where the hull width is ample for a large limber hole.

Ventilators, besides letting in air, so often permit spray, rain and at times solid seas to enter the ship, even when water-boxes are fitted. If water is going to come through a vent, it could not choose a better place than the chain locker, since no one sleeps there, nor prepares food or stows books. So it makes triple sense to locate a pair of ventilators over the chain locker space, perhaps with apertures in the bulkhead to circulate the air aft if the bulkhead is not watertight. In special circumstances even a watertight bulkhead has closable air holes, with screw-on caps hanging handy on safety chains, to put in place in the event of a serious accident. The holes have to be small enough for a man to be able to screw the caps on against a flood of water.

The bitter (inboard) end of the two cables must be secured, so that anchor and chain cannot be lost if run out too fast to be stopped in time. The means of securing must be down-right massive, since the jolt caused by a runaway anchor and all its chain will tear off a light eyebolt or eyeplate.

On some craft a hole is drilled in a frame flange, or even in a beam flange. The securing point is located above the top of the heaped chain, so that it can be released when needed. A big shackle is put through the securing hole,

and the chain passed through the shackle, then half-hitched round itself. The end is secured with a piece of Terylene so that no tools are needed to free the chain end, yet the Terylene takes no strain.

For some reason which no one has ever explained, even illogically, stern anchor lockers with stern anchors are seldom seen on small craft. Considering how useful they are, we can only assume that the aft anchor is another victim of the money-saver. For river and canal craft, for motor yachts short handed, for survey craft, dammit, for almost every type of craft, an anchor aft is a highly desirable convenience and safety factor.

As the aft locker must be well clear of the steering gear, it is worth setting it off well to one side.

Lining

As a basic rule all cabin accommodation and most working spaces such as wheelhouses are lined, or at least partly lined. Most engine spaces, cargo holds and 'commercial' compart-ments are left unlined. There are, as in so much small boatbuilding, a vast number of exceptions because there is such a diversity of types.

For instance it is axiomatic that the whole of the cabin space of a sailing yacht is lined. Go aboard a yacht ruthlessly designed to win races and it will be found that some areas are not lined to save weight. On some charter yachts lining is not continuous, partly to save money, partly to make maintenance easier. Look inside some engine rooms and it will be found that there is continuous lining sometimes to a superb standard. My father built a twin diesel yacht and lined the whole engine room with soundproofing, much of it overlaid with copper which was kept polished to match the burnished copper piping throughout the compartment. All this was set off by a red carpet on the gangway between the two diesels. This was in 1934 when labour was cheaper, to be sure. But it was a superb sight, it meant that the owner could always show his visitors round the boat and finish up with a climax. No owner ever had more pride of possession with better reason.

Most lining will be in the form of battening, or boards fastened to wood strips sometimes called cleats or cleating. Cleating is bolted or screwed to the athwartships flanges of the frames. Screws are usually adequate, and they should be round-headed ones. Some builders use galvanized steel which is satisfactory for cheap commercial craft, provided the galvanizing is hot dipped. (The electro-plating method of galvanizing is one of man's less successful inventions when applied to ships.) On high standard craft the screws may be stainless steel or brass with insulating washers.

The wood cleating should be painted before fitting. If it has to follow a sharply curving frame it can either be cut out of the solid, or a series of saw cuts make it easy to coax round the bend. If the cleating is fastened onto the fore and aft face of a toe-welded single-bar frame, then the cabin space is reduced by the thickness of the cleating on each side. This will amount to only an inch, but on small craft that makes a difference. Sometimes the inner face of the cleating will not follow the line of plating exactly. For instance a very sharp turn of the bilge may be too tight for some varieties of lining ply or faced board to match. In this instance the cleating will be less curved on its inner face, and here again it will be easier if the cleating is fastened to the athwartships flange.

In every case if it is fastened to this flange it will not matter if the cleating's outboard face is not an exact fit.

A lining of wood battens is easy to install and cheap. Slots between battens will be $\frac{1}{2}$ inch wide or less. They allow for air circulation and hence a dry condition behind the lining, but reduces the insulation effect which is dependent on stagnant air. The battens are painted or varnished before they are fitted, apart from the last one or two coats. It will be usual to use a hard wood such as one of the mahoganies. However if the battens are painted they may be of a soft wood. It is a good idea, before buying wood for battening or any other purpose, to get the advice of the seller. A well-established wood yard will have directors and managers with wide practical experience who will want to make a sale which will be followed up by many more. If their interest is aroused they can sometimes be persuaded to provide varnished samples of the various woods available. If in doubt the Forest Products Research Institution at Princes Risborough will advise on the properties of an individual timber. This is important these days when traditional timber supplies are drying up and previously unknown timbers are offered as panaceas.

Plywood makes a good lining. It is available in thicknesses from $\frac{3}{16}$ inch to 1 inch in marine grades. Sometimes a lower quality, called 'exterior grade', is used, but this seems to be a risk, especially on craft which are exposed to rugged conditions. The exterior quality may stand the moisture, the frost and other destructive forces for four to six years, but it is not a good long-term bet. Marine ply is sold in sheets 4 feet × 8 feet, and just occasionally 5 feet × 8 feet. The grain runs the length of the panels, which may matter where the material is to be used decoratively.

Where ply or any other board material is to be made to conform to the hull shape, it is best to get a sample and make sure that the thickness selected will manage the curve. It is not satisfactory to reduce the thickness of the panelling to achieve the required bend if it leaves the panelling so thin it flexes in between supports. Here again a simple test, with a pair of cleats mocked up the correct distance apart, is a good idea. For a racing boat it is acceptable to use panelling which does flex easily between supports, but not on hard used commercial craft.

The screws which hold up the ply cannot be dowelled, and in any case need removing every three or five years for painting, inspection, additions to the electric wiring and a half dozen other reasons. Some builders use decorative screws, like chromed ones, or the more attractive BMA finished brass screws which are a copper colour, either light or dark depending on specification. Other builders use raised counter-sunk head screws in this situation because of their 'finished' appearance. They look as if someone cared, especially when all the screw slots are aligned. Their disadvantage is that they stand out from the wood surface, so that glass paper applied prior to repainting or revarnishing takes the BMA finish off the screws, showing up a bright brass patch.

Various forms of hardboard have been tried for lining, but few can stand sea conditions. If in doubt a sample should be immersed totally for a month or two, and another left at half tide so that it covers every time the tide rises. If it stands up to these tests it will do for lining.

Various cloth materials are used for special applications. For instance racing boats or craft where weight must be saved are sometimes lined with a type of tapestry material with no backing, or with only a very thin supporting board. It needs no painting and when new looks attractive in the right circumstances, but it will not stand up to rough conditions. Modern synthetic leathercloths are available in a wide range of colours and finishes. Typical are Lionide and Lionella, which may be glued directly to bulkheads, or put on lining boards, or put over foam rubber padding on boards to give a deep upholstered effect.

Furnishing the cabins to a high standard may call for the services of a subcontractor. It is best to go to a company which has experience of this work, especially as they are used to doing a comprehensive job, including the cabin lining and ceiling. Interior decorating firms used to house work are not normally able to cope with this sort of job; they are incapable for the most part in raising and maintaining their standards to a 'sea-going' level. They cannot leave behind their steel tacks and screws so that rust weeps start before the last workman has stepped ashore. Specialist firms like Heals, of London, will quote from a drawing or after inspecting a bare hull. They will submit patterns and suggestions for decorations, as well as finished timber samples, door furniture and carpeting, all to tone. Such ship furnishing varies from the inexpensive, pleasant and serviceable to the frankly opulent, downright palatial or even extravagantly superb. Prices vary not by 10 per cent but by 2,000 per cent, from the cheap but adequate to the top extreme.

One of the simplest types of lining is simply a series of battens. These will probably be about 2 inches × $\frac{3}{8}$ inch with an air gap between of $\frac{1}{4}$ inch. For a good appearance the gaps between the battens must be absolutely parallel

Fig. 46 Fixing lining. It is usual to screw the lining to strips of wood fastened to the frames. The strips, called 'grounds', or sometimes 'cleatings', should be clear of the shell plating, also the lining should be away from the frames. This prevents moisture lodging. The screw has a washer under the head to insulate it from the frame. In theory the shank of the screw should have a tubular washer to keep it away from the frame too, but this is unusual, and something of a luxury. Occasionally, to properly insulate the screw, special flanged tubular washers are used which insulate both the shank and the head.

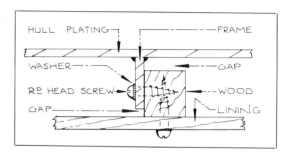

and constant. A variation on this battening which is attractive is a close spaced series of narrow battens, maybe only $\frac{3}{4}$ inch wide with a $\frac{1}{8}$ inch gap. This is naturally slow work, but the result in a fine wood matt polished is unusual, not difficult to do and a pleasant change.

It is bad practice to fasten lining direct to the ship's side or even straight onto the outer plating of a deckhouse. If any form of panelling is fixed to the plating then leaks will occur at the through fastenings. More important, lining is effective because of the air gap between it and the plating. This can be proved by measuring the temperature difference inside a cabin, between lining and plating, then outside the plating. At certain times and in some localities the results are surprising.

On a frameless hull it will often be necessary to weld on lugs to take the cleating for lining. The cleating must not be bolted or screwed through the hull, as this will start leaks. The same principle applies not only to the shell but to the deck and superstructure. In a few rather special cases a lining cloth is glued onto the exterior plating; but this idea is seldom a long-term success, or at all satisfactory in extremes of climate.

Lining grows in importance as the weather becomes unpleasant, be it too hot or too cold. Materials like glass wool are put behind lining to achieve an equable condition in the cabin, but in theory at least, stagnant air should be as affective as most insulation substances. However materials like industrial wools have a better sound-deadening effect than sealed air. And of course it is almost impossible to prevent air-flow behind lining without insulation, which explains why insulation material is relatively effective in practice.

Padding

Full headroom cannot be provided everywhere on all craft, especially in those below 45 feet in length. In practice it is not in the smallest boats that the lack of headroom is always the most acutely noticed. Aboard a small boat the crew are constantly aware of the lack of space so they take continuous subconscious precautions. Also small boats are seldom used for living aboard for long. On craft where there is headroom almost right throughout with perhaps two exceptions, it is all too probable that people will get hurt. They are off guard and forget that in the engine room there is that projecting header tank, or that awkward beam knee which obtrudes into the bosun's locker.

As a basic minimum, protruding structures should be painted a warning colour. Orange and white diagonal stripes, or red and white are best, never a single colour or a pattern which could be part of the background of the ship's structure. However colour warnings alone are only really adequate (and no more than that) in spaces like paint stores which are seldom visited.

The best way to deal with danger points is to pad them. This is true on all craft but especially so on steel ships since so many projections are sharp, unyielding and wickedly painful to meet. A rounded wood beam may be bad, its steel equivalent is doubly dangerous.

The usual form of padding is foam plastic rubber sheathed in a leathercloth. There are various suitable cloths available, but the most satisfactory for this job have a knitted backing cloth, as opposed to a woven one. A typical example is Lionella, available in a good selection of colours. Its woven equivalent, Lionide, is cheaper, and is offered in a variety of surface textures, some of which wonderfully imitate leather. But these woven cloths being more resilient do not fold, bend or generally 'handle' so successfully or conveniently.

The padding should be made all the same section and size, on a ship, to economise. Sailmakers in most ports make up lengths and areas of padding. As a general rule any firm which makes up the settee cushions will be able to tackle the job, and as the padding should match or tone with the upholstery, it makes sense if one firm does all the work.

Securing the padding is not easy since the fastenings should not show, or if they do they must not project. In no case should the fastenings pass through any structure which has an external face. This means that no holes should be made in the shell of a deckhouse, and of course never in the main hull plating.

The best all-round form of fastening is a row of bolts about 4 inches apart, through flanges of cloth at each side of the padding. The bolts may be brass or galvanized steel bolts are used — or stainless steel where money is an unconsidered material. If using galvanized bolts, be sure to put lanoline on the threads, since padding will only last a few years, so that renewal should be made easy.

Some padding is secured by Velcro, but it is not always satisfactory for this job. It will let the padding go if someone grabs hold, and is incidentally highly inflammable. Various patent fastenings like Prestadot, or metal turn-buttons are used for the purpose; but if they protrude, the fastenings are almost as much of a danger as the scantling they are trying to guard.

Padding is seldom used to full advantage. This must be attributed to the distressing habit of designers and draughtsmen staying ashore, instead of sampling their own wares. A good gash across the scalp would do more good in some design offices than an honours degree.

It is better to have 5 feet 9 inches headroom well padded than 5 feet 11 inches unprotected. Padding should be massive as often as possible, since foam plastic only $\frac{1}{2}$ inch thick scarcely does more than reduce the depth of inflicted wounds. Padding to be thorough should be of the order of 3 inches thick. It is needed not only overhead, but also on protruding vertical and horizontal stiffeners, angle-bars, handles, corners; in fact any hard component that is likely to cause damage to the crew.

On pilot boats and fishing boats padding is most important because these craft are out in all weathers, with people moving about on board. Tired men with cold hands and feet stumble about, very possibly in poor light. Lifeboats are more often used in bad weather than good, so they should have the most thorough protection possible. Yachts seldom have padding, which is a pity, because it can be blended in with the decoration, and makes a most practical finishing touch.

Safes

Vessels which cross frontiers need safes for

Fig. 47 10.35 metre racing cruiser Designed by Alan Buchanan of Gronville, Jersey. LOA 33 ft 8 in, LWL 24 ft 0 in, Beam 10 ft 0 in, Draft 5 ft 8½ in. Intended for Half Ton Cup racing, this fast auxiliary Bermudan sloop is a good example of carefully developed steel building. She has wood decks to save weight high up. The plating of the transom, the rudder and other parts is the same thickness as the hull plating, which simplifies ordering and enables plating offcuts to be used up. The backbone is a continuous bar the same size throughout, except on the stemhead where it is swollen to take the forestay fitting. Internal ballast is inside a hollow keel which is stiffened by floors carried up to form sole bearers. Some of these floors form the boundaries of the tanks and this yacht shows a good example of how complicated tanks are easy to work in steel. Good examples of simplicity are the engine bearers and the way the backstay plate is welded to the outside of the transom.

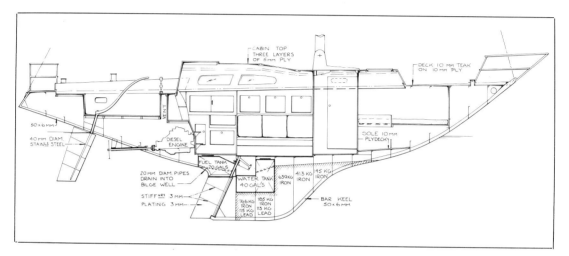

dutiable goods. Most others need safes to defy the growing plague of pilfering which sullies the world. A simple welded steel box is effective. It needs a recessed lock which is weatherproof or a strong hasp and massive padlock of hard steel. Both hasp and lock must be recessed or located so that a hacksaw cannot be used on them, nor a heavy hammer be plied to effect.

The safe must be situated high enough to avoid risk of flooding: it should also be large enough to hold cash, papers, bottles, passports, firearms and so on, according to the service of the ship.

Most safes will need lining and fiddles. If bottles or firearms are to be stowed inside, they must be prevented from banging about. Since papers are often stowed in safes, and since small fires afloat are only slightly less prevalent than burglaries, the position of the safe should be clear of the galley and engine compartment.

Above all, a safe must be hidden, since this increases its effectiveness a hundredfold. It should not be marked on the plans, but chalked on the ship by the designer. He will describe it as an extra locker, and since it will not be referred to as the safe till the ship is out of the builder's hands, the minimum number of people will learn the secret. The finest safecracker in the world cannot get to work until he knows where his quarry is.

Fig. 48 Details of 10.35 metre racing cruiser designed by Alan Buchanan. The section at frame 10 shows how the loading of the deck-stepped mast is carried. Bottom right are enlarged details of the beam, beam-arch and pillars which support the severe downward forces at the mast heel when beating to windward. Rectangular tube is made up into pillars and beam-arch by welding angle-bars toe to toe.

Bottom left shows the side deck and cabin top construction. Teak is used on the top surface for a good appearance and marine ply beneath for watertightness, strength and an easily maintained deckhead.

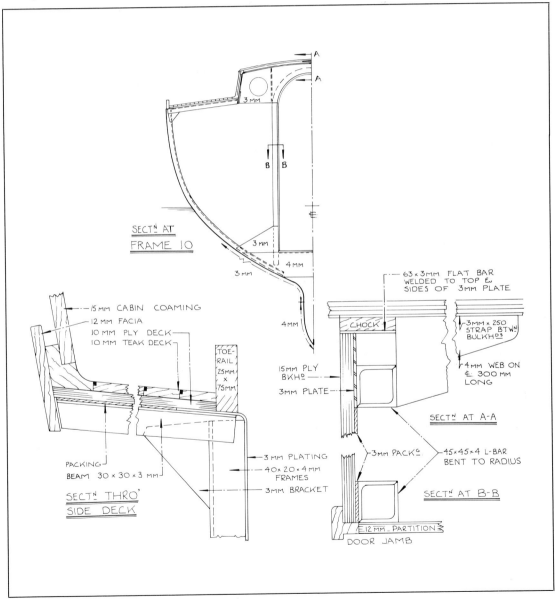

boatbuilding business

Lloyd's Register of Shipping

In some respects this section of the book is the most important. Lloyd's have in the past, and continue to have, a big influence on the design, construction and perhaps to a lesser extent the maintenance of small craft.

Even within the industry there is a good deal of misunderstanding as to what Lloyd's is and does. One reason for this is that until fairly recently Lloyd's did not actively pursue a policy of self-advertisement. One result has been that there is still confusion between Lloyd's, the Underwriting Corporation which deals with insurance, and Lloyd's, the Register of Shipping which is concerned with safety of life and property. Both are called 'Lloyd's' by the same people in different contexts, both are intimately integrated with all forms of sea-borne craft, they are interlinked in a dozen ways. The miracle is that the confusion is not greater.

We are concerned here with the Register of Shipping, which lays down standards to which craft are built and maintained. They have printed rules for the construction of yachts of the size which concern us, but their published rules for commercial craft and fishing boats cover bigger craft than we are discussing.

Some designers use the rules for yachts when working on commercial craft. They beef up the frames for fishing boats, reducing the frame spacing forward, and so on, since experience shows this is highly desirable. It is worth remembering that yachts are expected to live relatively sedentary lives, working only at weekends for seven months of the year. They are expected to be mollycoddled in harbours, with crews who take trouble to hang ample fenders out in good time. These considerations do not apply to commercial craft which are often operated by unfeeling men, paid by the hour, recruited from an uncritical labour exchange, semi-skilled if not downright inept. For this reason the yacht rules need to be used as minimum standards for many commercial craft.

To cut through the fog of confusion regarding Lloyd's rules, it is worth considering the four phrases which are bandied about, used unintelligently, and often applied to craft for sale:

These phrases are:

1 built to Lloyd's;
2 built in excess of Lloyd's;
3 built under Lloyd's supervision;
4 maintained to Lloyd's.

1 A craft can be built in accordance *to* Lloyd's rules, but she can still be a load of junk. The various components may be up to the size that Lloyd's require, and of the correct material, but if they are poorly assembled with ninth-rate welding then the ship will be a dud and maybe a drowner. Anyone can buy a copy of Lloyd's rules, and they are easy enough for a first year apprentice to apply. There are some ambiguities, but the rules are being revised. In the main the rules are relatively simple; except when it comes to building a boat which is highly specialised. So 'Built to Lloyd's' has very little meaning without further amplification.

2 Built *in excess* of Lloyd's sounds fine. It suggests a vessel of magnificent strength, robust enough to tackle Arctic ice or Pacific hurricane without taking a drop of water aboard. Alas, it is too often a broker's phrase, a deceiver either intentionally or unwittingly. If a designer draws up plans which in every respect conform to the scantlings which Lloyd's demand, and in one respect are marginally over the rules, then the boat may be advertised as 'in excess

of Lloyd's'. This claim is doubly misleading. If the boat described is a fishing craft, and the rules implied are for yachts, then the boat will be under strength for her job.

More important, if the scantlings are up to strength but the workmanship is poor, the ship is no good. The strength of any structure is the strength of its fastenings. This is the crux of so much in shipbuilding. Herein lies the main snare behind the glib phrase 'in excess of Lloyd's'. When it comes to the crunch, very few craft are both over Lloyd's scantlings and to a higher standard of workmanship than Lloyd's require. Such a ship would be costly to build and she is a rare find.

3 Any craft built *under Lloyd's supervision* in steel starts off with a good pedigree. Lloyd's will not agree to supervise a ship's construction unless the scantlings are up to their requirements. They are not interested in merely examining the level of welding without wanting to know what sort of plating is being used. A vessel which has this label starts off well in life. She may have been neglected for the subsequent 40 years and now be waiting to see how many people she can drown in one fell swoop.

4 Any ship which can boast of being *maintained to* Lloyd's should be sound and safe. Even here there are snags, because Lloyd's do not cover every possible aspect of ship safety. Their main concern is with the structure, the ground tackle, the machinery, and so on. A clean bill of health could be given to a vessel which lacked power to claw off a lee shore in a hurricane. Such boats are rarer now than they were 50 years ago, but they still exist. With a lot of windage above the water, not much 'grip' in the water, and little horsepower, it is entirely possible to be defeated by a

ferocious combination of wind and sea.

A ship which is maintained to Lloyd's will always conform to their rules. If a ship is built without regard to their rules and without their supervision, she may subsequently become 'classed'. She is examined by Lloyd's, who may insist on additions or alterations to bring her up to their standards.

A ship, to remain 'up to Lloyd's' is surveyed by them every two years. The surveys vary in intensity according to the age of the vessel. The gap between surveys and details of the extent of each survey are set out in the rules.

Here again there is a source of confusion as the machinery is not always covered by the survey. A ship may be 'maintained to Lloyd's' yet be so defective in the engine department as to be dangerous. To be sure, this is rare, but then so are disasters.

The Corporation of Lloyd's is the world's finest insurance body. It consists of individuals and groups operating as syndicates who insure all types of craft (and many other things from nuclear power plants to lives). One reason for the keen rates they quote is that they generally have a good knowledge of the ships they are insuring. They obtain this knowledge through Lloyd's Register of Shipping publications. One set of books covers merchant ships, another yachts in Britain and Europe, another American yachts, and so on. If a yacht comes up for insurance the underwriter just looks her up in Lloyd's Register of Yachts, to see if she is built and maintained to Lloyd's rules. If she is the underwriter knows she is of a good standard, and not likely to get into trouble. The underwriters will quote a keen price and expect to retain a profit.

Herein lie the seeds of so many controversies which plunge in and through and around Lloyd's Register. This body is concerned with safety, with insurability. Designers are much less interested in this. They seek mainly speed, or a low building price, or that impossible reconciliation between what the owner wants and what is practical at sea. The builder too is not vastly interested in insurability. He wants his ship to be well thought of, so that he will get subsequent orders. But if she sinks through no fault of his, he rubs his hands in glee . . . it means another ship to build.

This situation results in a conflict between Lloyd's on the one hand, and the designer, builder and owner on the other. Lloyd's demands are nearly always for thicker rudder stocks, heavier anchors, or more massive beams. Any alteration to the designer's original plans which Lloyd's requires will almost certainly put up the cost and weight, simultaneously reducing the speed and internal space. It is hardly surprising that Lloyd's are temporarily unloved by the 'other side'. I have heard things said about Lloyd's which would make a bargee blush. Yet the people who have said them will next week go to Lloyd's for help. Designers like to have Lloyd's massive, almost impregnable reputation behind them. It lifts a load of responsibility from the builder and designer and makes their job a little less of an unremitting worry.

Owners say harsh things about Lloyd's reluctance to gallop along with technical innovation. But these same owners know that it is bad policy to put a lot of money into a ship without giving her a pedigree to keep up her value. There are virtually no birthrights like a Lloyd's certificate, apart from the comparable certificates issued under similar circumstances by Bureau Veritas and the other supervisory bodies.

It is not entirely true that Lloyd's do not like innovation. What they dislike is untried ideas which might in practice prove dangerous. An example is the flexible stern tube, which swept to popularity because it was so simple and effective. It consists of a tube fixed in the bottom of the boat, through which the propeller shaft passes, with clearance all round. A stern gland is fitted on the shaft just ahead of the tube, and the two are linked by rubber hose. Pipe clips hold the hose to the tube and onto the gland. If the shaft wants to move, as it will when the engine is flexibly mounted, then it can, since the rubber hose is far from rigid. By making the tube large relative to the shaft the whole problem of engine alignment is eased. Not only is the flexible gland arrangement simple, it is cheap, light, as well as easy to make and install. This is everything that owner, builder and designer could want. Lloyd's will not accept this kind of stern gland because in practice there is a serious weakness: if the gland gets tight, without actually seizing, the rubber hose twists, wrenches, tears and an unstoppable leak results. Even if the engine is stopped, it is hard to stem the inrush of water round the shaft, so that the boat is almost certain to be lost. If the rubber perishes or the hose clips rust through, or any similar quite modest trouble occurs the ship is lost. With twin screws the risk is doubled, with high power it increases again. All in all, Lloyd's seem to be correct in taking a jaundiced view of this gadget especially when it is remembered that where there is an engine there is oil and grease. Both of these attack rubber.

When a ship is to be built to Lloyd's the designer first makes application to Lloyd's Register of Shipping at 71 Fenchurch Street, London, EC3 or at the regional office, whose address will be found in the local telephone book. Later the designer has to send three copies of the main structural plans, rudder and steering plans and so on. Lloyd's will probably want one or two minor alterations at least. If the boat departs much from well-established practice, then the changes asked for may be quite extensive. Lloyd's will on occasions negotiate with the designer, if he can put up a good case. But they are not interested in reducing weight even if it only means a $\frac{1}{2}$ per cent weakening of a secondary structural item. Their office files are packed with case histories of failures afloat. They have a vast backlog of information, so new ideas have to be good to gain acceptance.

Even if the plans follow well-accepted paths, Lloyd's have to examine them minutely. They may have a stack of other drawings to inspect, or they may be short-staffed. It is therefore important to allow extra design time, and possibly a little extra building time, when Lloyd's are involved.

Basically Lloyd's are a 'big ship' organisation, though they will probably deny this and point out how much their yacht side has expanded recently. However discussions with Lloyd's men throws up the fact that the big majority of them served their time and have spent much of their lives with craft over 100 feet. This means they are attuned to big ship methods and procedures. Perhaps more important, most of them have worked in shipyards, few in boatyards. There is a difference, a vast difference.

Lloyd's fees are an extra cost that has to be borne by the owner, so the question arises: are they always worth it? In general the answer must be: if in doubt, get Lloyd's, to be safe. If the ship is a big one the advisability of calling in Lloyd's is increased. Building a big yacht, for instance, should very seldom be undertaken without Lloyd's approval of the plans, even if they do not supervise the construction because the designer is doing so. Most yachts represent a heavy capital expenditure for the owner, so he would be foolish not to have Lloyd's in from the start. Just as important, most owners sell their yachts after 5 or 15 years, to buy a bigger or faster one. If she is to Lloyd's in every respect she is easier to sell. She will fetch a better price even if she is built to Lloyd's but not maintained to their standards.

However a commercial owner generally buys a ship to last a given number of years. He wants her to be as cheap as possible initially, cheap to maintain, and he writes her off over the planned number of years. He probably goes to the yard that built his last ship, he may order an identical one. He may have his own designer, or marine supervisor, or consulting engineer, who will supervise construction. These are all reasons for doing without Lloyd's.

If a fishing boat is built under the White Fish Authority in Britain, she must be to their standards. A charter fleet owner may be very experienced and know precisely what he needs, besides having the time in the off season to supervise work himself. Here are possible reasons for dispensing with Lloyd's services.

As a very rough dividing line I have noticed that relatively few steel craft under 55 feet are to Lloyd's. The greater the length, the higher the percentage built to Lloyd's.

The Ship and Boat Builders' National Federation

In Britain the Ship and Boat Builders' National Federation is the watchdog, the guide, the friend and the officially recognised body which looks after professional small craft builders. It is experienced, having been built up in the last 25 years to a powerful position, with the big majority of small ship and boatbuilding firms as constituent members. It might be argued that the ancillary manufacturers and component suppliers are beginning to have a dominant position within its ranks. This is because the actual builders are very much in the numerical minority. However they are well represented on the committees and the federation manages to look after small shipbuilders' interests efficiently.

The national federation has regional subsidiaries covering the whole of the British Isles. It also has specialist advisers in matters such as finance, business management, export marketing, and exhibiting – both in Britain and abroad. In special cases the national federation acts as arbitrator when a disagreement arises between builder and client. I also know of cases when the committee members have given advice to newcomers to small craft building, far beyond 'the call of duty'. This is a friendly industry, and is lucky to have a professional body run by competent full-time professionals.

The address of the Ship and Boat Builders' National Federation is Boating Industry House, Vale Road, Weybridge, Surrey, KT13 9NS.

Financing and related matters
Raising money

When building a small craft the method and techniques by which the tools, the materials and the boat are paid for are now so varied that a shelf of books could be written on the matter. An outline of some of the problems is given here, together with an indication of the answers. One reason why comprehensive details are not listed is that the situation changes from country to country. It changes annually as the chancellor of the exchequer, or his equivalent, shuffles the fiscal cards. To further confuse the issue, it even varies in different localities of a country, where regional specialised grants apply. It may, ultimate lunacy, vary in different parts of a city, as has been the case when Edinburgh was riven by a particularly stupid bit of bureaucratic planning.

Taking first the yard equipment, such as welding sets. These can be bought through a finance company. These in turn offer different schemes according to the category of purchaser (i.e. a private individual, a company, partnership, etc). The same finance houses will provide money to buy materials, rent land, and so on.

The owner can use similar companies to pay for the craft. There are now so many sources of finance it pays to shop around and compare interest rates. Shared ownership is also worth considering both for boats and for building equipment and even building premises. In the long and short run it will be found that a bank overdraft is often the cheapest source of money. A boat or building can be used as security.

A bank overdraft has the advantage that whatever money is paid into the account at once reduces the overdraft and hence the interest to be paid. From a builder's point of view a big initial outlay is needed to buy plate, welding rod etc. The owner usually makes a payment when the contract is signed, and another when the keel is laid. The oldest scheme in the shipbuilding world is to lay the keel within days of signing the contract, even if this means breaking the normal work sequence, or maybe leaving the laid keel without further work on it for weeks. The aim is to get the second instalment paid as soon as possible.

When obtaining money from a finance house the interest to be paid does not reduce, so that a temporarily fat bank balance has no special advantage. In addition, in the small craft world, the finance companies have lately been competing so strongly that all the disadvantages of price-cutting have arisen. Then again, finance companies pay commission for business introduced, and this is naturally added to the burden of interest.

One real advantage of financing through some form of industrial hire purchase is that it leaves other forms of credit, such as bank borrowing, untouched. Against this, if the commitment is begun when interest rates are high, then a drop in rates generally brings no advantage. For the wily, the way round this situation is to approach a rival finance company, and pay off the first with money borrowed at a lower rate from the second. However these money men tend to be clannish, so one has to be careful not to establish a reputation for excessive slickness.

Financial competition

Any individual or company planning the construction of one or more small craft on a commercial basis should take a hard look at the financial situation. Though this varies from country to country, most of the following remarks apply all over the world.

For a start, shipbuilding has been well established, since Noah built his ark 6,000 years ago. In the interval since then so many brains have been applied to the problems of shipbuilding through the years that it is unlikely that dramatic breakthroughs in knowledge can be expected. Continuing small improvements are likely, and without them no builder will stay

Fig. 49 A 15.4 m shrimp trawler designed by Keel Marine of Russia Row, London EC2 and built in Kuwait by local labour with no previous experience in shipbuilding. Supervision was by a British foreman plater and the construction was purposely kept uncomplicated.

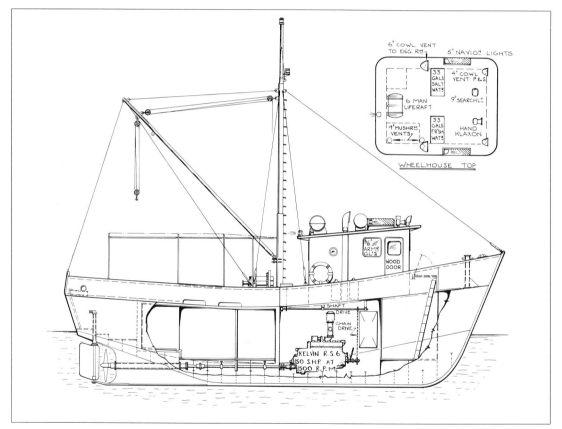

in business long. But big changes, certainly in steel building, should be viewed critically as well as with interest and enthusiasm.

Not only is shipbuilding long established, it is also universal. It is found, for instance, in Switzerland which has no coastline at all. This means that the competition is international. Small ships can all too easily be moved about the face of the earth, either under their own power, or under tow, or on larger ships, or in packages for assembly on arrival. The cheapest

builder is found wherever labour, materials and overheads are cheapest. There is always someone who is hard-working, possibly hungry, almost certainly with a lower standard of living, and often inconveniently close at hand. Competing with this kind of builder invites failure sooner or later. And in this case, 'the later, the deeper' is the rule for financial collapse.

To make matters more complex, the builder of small steel craft will often find himself in what can only be described as unfair competition.

Boatbuilding business

Fig. 50 Shrimp trawler for the Middle East. LOA
15.4 m, LWL 13.7 m, Breadth 5.18 m, Extreme
draft 1.775 m, Camber (straight line) 0.13 m,
Frame spacing 0.5 m. Loading figures : 4 tons of
oil fuel, 0.5 tons fresh water, 0.5
tons crew and effects, 15 tons fish and ice, 2 tons
nets and spare gear.

Fig. 51 Construction section at frame 15 of the
15.4 m shrimp trawler designed by Keel Marine (see
page 204 for other drawings). Fabrication is simple
to suit unskilled labour.
Fig. 52 The aft frame, seen looking forward, of the
15.4 m shrimp trawler. There are no flanged plates
and flat bar is used throughout instead of angle-bar.

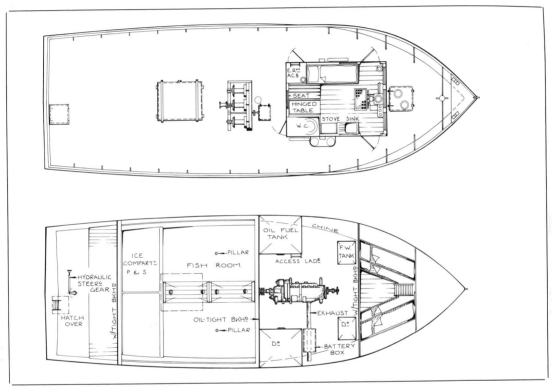

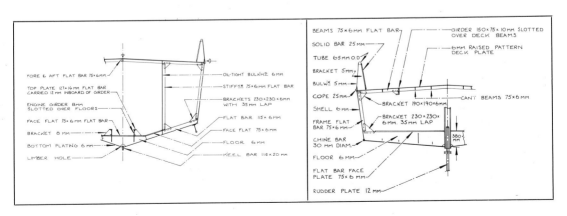

There are companies which are diversifying, perhaps because they are too dependent on some dying industry, or because they do not have the toughness and competence to survive in their own chief line of business. Such companies feel that small ships are easy to build, and so they enter the market, perhaps as a result of reading this book. If they have the backing of experienced estimators, naval architects and draughtsmen, accountants, loftsmen and such like, they may be successful. Otherwise they just depress the going market price for their chosen type of small ship. That and further redden their own bank balance.

Another kind of competition comes from the amateur, who feels that he can set up as a boatbuilder in his garage. While many successful boats have been built in unpromising situations, commercial building cannot be a lasting success in over-primitive conditions. That is not to say that massive new sheds are essential. Quite the contrary, any firm which spends a vast amount of money on new buildings and equipment tends to find it has priced itself out of the market. It almost seems to be the hallmark of a successful long-established small craft builder that the sheds look as if they were put up in a rush during the crises resulting in Napoleon's forays.

The following conclusions will almost certainly have the approval of the advisory accountants of such bodies as the Ship and Boat Builders' National Federation:

1 Competition in commercial small craft building is very sharp everywhere in the world.

2 To meet that competition it is almost always a mistake to aim at producing a boat cheaper than everyone else's.

3 Success is more likely to come if each craft built is very carefully planned for its own job, and built to a good, not just an adequate standard.

4 It is probably excusable to borrow money for a new building, or a new welding set, or a new slipway. But interest rates are too much of a burden for a successful financial year if money is borrowed for more than one or two major items in a small yard.

5 Since there is little difference between the cost of good and bad plans, only the best plans should be used.

6 Since no one man or one shipyard team can assimilate all the knowhow needed for every type of craft, financial success comes to those who develop one type of craft and stick more or less to that type.

7 Following this scheme establishes a more lasting reputation than massive advertising. It also costs far less.

8 While no one sells anything today without some form of advertising, small ships are not like beer, or cigarettes, or cars, or houses. They need relatively little advertising. Even with the most sophisticated modern production techniques, small craft in steel are seldom produced in adequate numbers to finance widespread advertising.

9 Because of the nature of the business, no one is likely to succeed as a builder of small craft unless he is dedicated to it. This means working longer hours than in other industries, and having the management skills to persuade other people in the firm to do the same.

10 As shipbuilding is basically an assembly industry, it is essential to have a very wide knowledge of component suppliers, ancillary industries and related subjects. It is no good making a profit on the hull and losing twice as much on the upholstery.

Index